The Life-Changing Power of Self-Love

An Essential Guide
by Tina Green

FEATURING: ALYSSA ANAYA, CANDRA ANAYA, DASHA ALLRED BOND,
KIM COLLINS, JAYNE JACOVA FELD, LYDIA GREENWOODS,
THAIS HARRIS, REV. STEPHANIE URBINA JONES, MADRONE KALIL,
BEVERLY LAZAR, REV. ANNIE MARK, CHARLEEN M. MICHEL,
NATALIE PETERSEN, HOLLY M. RAPPORT, SHARON SIEGLER,
DR. RUTH A. SOUTHER, LAURA SPINNER, LINDA JYOTI STUART,
LISA SWID, MICHELLE VESSER, HEATHER WESTLING

THE

Life-Changing
Power of
Self-Love

An Essential Guide
by Tina Green

Featuring: Alyssa Anaya, Candra Anaya, Dasha Allred Bond,
Kim Collins, Jayne Jacova Feld, Lydia Greenwoods,
Thais Harris, Rev. Stephanie Urbina Jones, Madrone Kalil,
Beverly LaZar, Rev. Annie Mark, Charleen M. Michel,
Natalie Petersen, Holly M. Rapport, Sharon Siegler,
Dr. Ruth A. Souther, Laura Spinner, Linda (Jyoti) Stuart,
Lisa Swid, Michelle Vesser, Heather Westling

The Life-Changing Power of Self-Love
An Essential Guide

Tina Green

Published by Brave Healer Productions

Paperback ISBN: 978-1-961493-13-1

eBook ISBN: 978-1-961493-12-4

ADVANCE PRAISE

"A beautiful, empowering book written by women for women. Let these stories of healing open your heart, release doubt and shame, and help you shed the heaviness of what was never yours to carry."

~ **HeatherAsh Amara,** *author of Warrior Goddess Training and The Seven Secrets of Happy and Healthy Relationships*

"In the complex dance of life, where both beauty and pain waltz hand in hand, our deepest wounds often originate from self-rejection and a lingering shadow of unworthiness—a timeless struggle. But what if there existed a pathway to the realm of genuine self-love, authentic compassion, and self-awareness? You'll find that path in Tina Green's extraordinary book, The Life-Changing Power of Self Love. This is not your everyday read; it's an illuminating expedition into the origins of shame and self-doubt, offering practical tools for soul-level healing in every chapter. I encourage you to travel this pilgrimage of self-discovery. The gift of transformation is waiting for you on every page!"

~ **Dr. Ahriana Platten,** *bestselling author of Rites and Rituals, Harnessing the Power of Sacred Ceremonies*

"This lovely book is filled with stories of hurt, trauma, and painful rejection. And these stories don't end with the pain. This group of empowered women has each experienced the life-empowering redemption that results from facing the pain and challenging the hurt, ultimately emerging as integrated human beings who fully love themselves and are, therefore, capable of loving others. Thank you to you all for sharing with such honesty and depth."

~ **Ruby Falconer,** *Teacher, Counselor, Writer, and co-author of Shamanic Egyptian Astrology, Your Planetary Guide to the Gods*

"Welcome to a new world where you are the most important person in your life!" declares Tina Green, lead author of *The Life-Changing Power of Self-Love*. For women, there may be no battle cry more radical or confronting—or liberating. Raised to please, to defer to the needs of others, to weigh our value in external approval, many women struggle to prioritize our own needs and give ourselves the regard we seek from others.

The Life-Changing Power of Self-Love changes the ground on which we stand—and the relationships in which we live. It invites us to embrace our sacred longing to come home to ourselves. And it shows us the way.

Twenty-two captivating stories from women leaders and healers make a mosaic of wisdom that awakens new possibilities for self-reclamation. As these fierce authors embrace vulnerability, power, gratitude, grief, inner guidance, and even cancer, our hearts and possibilities are expanded by the journeys they take and the stories they tell. Each offers a practice, strategy, or mindset for walking the transformational path of self-love that we can make our own. This book belongs on every woman's bookshelf. It will awaken you to your beauty, your bravery, and your capacity to give yourself the expansive love you've always yearned for.

~ **Sage Cohen,** *Author of Fierce on the Page,*
The Productive Writer, and Writing the Life Poetic.

"If you are seeking to love yourself fully, spa days and pedicures will only take you so far. The fierce honesty of the women's stories in these pages will help you cut the shackles of societal expectations that have bound you to a false self. It will guide you in navigating the underworld of your deepest pain and emerging triumphant with an inner voice that proclaims, I love you no matter what. Deep bows and high fives to Tina Green and her team of heroines for this vital and timely work leading the much-needed vanguard of the new self-love revolution."

~ **Marcella Friel,** *Founder of The Women,*
Food & Forgiveness Academy and Author of Tap, Taste, Heal:
Use Emotional Freedom Techniques (EFT) to Eat Joyfully and Love Your Body

"I am deeply honored by this inspiring collection of stories by women who have been courageous enough to take the journey of self-love and acceptance and write about it. In a society that mirrors a constant not good enough, especially for women, it couldn't come at a better time. In truth, I can't wait to give this book to my daughter as she steps into her life so that she may find her own self-love."

~ **Jeremy Pajer,** *best-selling author and Co-Founder of Freedom Folk and Soul, a transformational community of the healing arts*

"Extraordinary! In this new collaborative book by Tina Green, you'll find inspirational stories of finding self-love through rediscovering the power of our inner knowing. These compelling narratives read like a lighthouse and can guide us when we feel lost and adrift with life's challenges. Their narrative takes us through the carnage of devastating experiences to awakening moments of finding the way home to self-love by trusting the still voice within. The self-love practices shared in each chapter are additional gifts to support the journey to rediscover our essential selves through self-love."

~ *Carley Mattimore, Co-Author of Sacred Messengers of Shamanic Africa: Land of Zep Tepi and Co-Founder of Aahara Spiritual Community*

"*The Life-Changing Power of Self Love* by Tina Green speaks to the constant desire to be liked, to look perfect, to be all the things others find "beautiful." It helps readers redefine beauty and authentically tap into and love their own unique selves. I highly recommend it as a way to shift your thinking and create a more powerful self."

~ **Tabitha A. Scott CEM,** *CDSM, CHTP, Founder Global Institute of Growth*

TO CONTINUE YOUR JOURNEY ONLINE, VISIT:

https://www.LifeChangingPowerOfSelfLove.com

BEGIN YOUR SELF-LOVE PRACTICE:

- Meet and connect with the authors
- Join our community
- Attend events to cultivate your self-love
- Read our self-love blog
- Watch author interviews

DEDICATION

This book is dedicated to me.

In celebration of finally gaining self-love and acceptance in my fifties!

May my ongoing self-love practice heal the shame carried through my matriarchal lineage for seven generations of ancestors and seven generations of descendants.

Starting with:

My inspiring, creative, talented daughters, Grace and Sierra

My mother, Catherine Leahy,

My grandma, Anna Edith Leahy (1907-1984)

I also want to dedicate this book to my great-grandmother, whose identity we don't know. In 1907, in New York City, when women had few rights, she gave my grandmother up for adoption at birth, likely without choice in a shroud of shame. May the shame be lifted from her soul, and may she know how much I love and respect her.

DISCLAIMER

This book offers health and nutritional information and is designed for educational purposes only. You should not rely on this information as a substitute for, nor does it replace professional medical advice, diagnosis, or treatment. If you have any concerns or questions about your health, you should always consult a physician or other healthcare professional. Do not disregard, avoid, or delay obtaining medical or health-related advice from your healthcare professional because of something you may have read here. The use of any information provided in this book is solely at your own risk.

Developments in medical research may impact the health, fitness, and nutritional advice that appears here. No assurances can be given that the information contained in this book will always include the most relevant findings or developments with respect to the particular material.

Having said all that, know that the experts here have shared their tools, practices, and knowledge with you with a sincere and generous intent to assist you on your health and wellness journey. Please contact them with any questions you may have about the techniques or information they provided. They will be happy to assist you further!

TABLE OF CONTENTS

INTRODUCTION

Most women are trained from a very young age not to love themselves. We're conditioned to please others, look outside for acceptance and approval, try to be perfect, put ourselves last, and repeatedly abandon ourselves.

This conditioning is how our patriarchal system continues to thrive. Women not loving themselves is critical to the survival of this hunter-or-hunted system of oppression.

Do any of these sound familiar to you?

My body is ugly
I am ashamed of my body
I give my power to men
I have to be perfect
I am not enough
I always come last

Self-love alluded me until I entered my fifties. In the eyes of many, my life was thriving. I had multiple brilliant careers, earned plenty of money, owned a home, and was married with two incredible children. I checked the main things off the "Expectations of Tina" list.

Yet, I carried a lot of shame and was not authentic to myself or others. I put myself last in every way and did not love myself. I developed a deep resentment and lived with a low-grade depression that lasted for decades. I wasn't even aware I was depressed until I wasn't.

Many women don't understand the concept of self-love. It's often passed off as self-care, which makes it sound frivolous. It runs deeper than taking a walk, eating a salad, or having a spa day.

Self-love is a state of love and acceptance of one's body, mind, and spirit as is. Self-love means having a high regard for your own well-being and happiness.

Can you imagine loving and accepting yourself as is?

I remember very clearly when I declared that I wanted to love myself. I decided that eliminating my body shame was the key to the life I longed for, and I couldn't seem to find a solution to help me break through the shame, but I knew I had to get down to the underlying roots and expose them.

Inspired by witnessing my husband make profound changes in his life, I began working with his teachers. I signed up for a healing retreat in Teotihuacan, Mexico, an ancient city and a spiritual epicenter for thousands of years.

During our emotional opening circle, my teacher asked me to write down my intentions for the week. All I could think was, *I want to love myself. I want to love myself.* Even though I came intending to eliminate my body shame, it suddenly changed to, *I want to love myself.*

I wrote on my piece of paper, "To love myself."

We participated in a fire ceremony, where we each placed our intentions into the flames to bring them into being. The crackling fire was on the top of a temple, under the mystical, starry Teotihuacan sky. It was big, roaring, and hot. So hot that it was hard to stand close to it. There was a steady drum beat, and I felt the intense heat on my thighs and face as I leaned in and dropped my intention into the fire. I declared with conviction, "I want to love myself."

That intention, that ceremony, being witnessed and guided that week in Mexico, changed my life.

Throughout the many exercises that inspired a constant state of inquiry, I listened to myself share with others how I felt about myself and how I felt about my body.

"My body is ugly."

It was like an out-of-body experience where I heard myself talk about beliefs I had never spoken out loud.

"I'm ashamed of my body."

Wow, listen to how I feel about myself. It's ridiculous. I don't want to feel like this; I want to change this!

I also learned how codependent I was. My focal point was always on others. How can I please you? What do you need? How can I be so that you'll like or approve of me? I have to be perfect!

The most brutal truths I learned that week were how inauthentic and in denial I had been most of my adult life and how I abandoned myself repeatedly like a needle stuck on a scratch on a record. I experienced a lot of grief about this.

Throughout the week, I released my shame through breathwork and many powerful ceremonies, during which I cried, screamed, resisted, and gave myself grace and compassion. When I expressed my emotions and honored them, I could then release them from my body. I never really felt these emotions because I stuffed them down in my body for decades.

By the end of the week, I had released so much that I could finally love myself. I was in love with myself. I was committed to myself.

I felt so much lighter. I was in a state of euphoria for many months after that.

I don't ever remember feeling this good and this free! My heart feels happy!

I turned my focal point toward myself and was significantly less concerned with the approval, behavior, or acceptance of others. I sought only my approval and acceptance and became intent on cleaning my mirror.

I started dancing and moving my body in new ways.

Wow. It feels so good to dance with my arms up and away from my body! Woo hoo! I don't care who's watching!

I stopped judging myself and others. This one was hard to swallow. I truly felt how judgmental I had been.

I was more confident and willing to be seen and heard. I spoke my truth, especially to myself.

I started attracting people and opportunities into my life that I previously did not allow myself to think of as possible.

I was no longer willing to live that old life. I was reborn, I loved myself, and everything changed! Anything was possible!

What I've learned since then is self-love is an ongoing practice. It's foundational and remains strong with awareness, nourishment, and commitment.

Can you imagine loving yourself as is? It is possible for you!

The level of freedom is immense.

This book aims to help you discover ways to cultivate self-love and create a unique version of freedom in your life.

These pages are filled with inspiring, intimate stories of 22 women leaders, healers, and authors with the intention of inspiring you to step into your practice of cultivating self-love.

This book will energize you to bravely question your conditioning and shift your awareness of your relationship with your mind, body, and soul. I invite you to step into some of the self-love practices outlined in this book and build your foundation of self-love, acceptance, and freedom.

Welcome to a new world where you are the most important person in your life!

CHAPTER 1

LOOK AT ME!

OVERCOMING FEAR OF BEING SEEN

Tina Green

"There are two basic motivating forces: fear and love.
When we are afraid, we pull back from life.
When we are in love, we open to all that life has to offer with
passion, excitement, and acceptance."

~ John Lennon

MY STORY

How can I be worthy of respect if I'm fat?

The story I chose to believe was that people always saw my fat, ugly body first, which discredited everything else about me.

The powerful shame showed up whenever I was in a situation where I was required to be visible.

I walked up to the microphone and felt the heat rising. It's that old feeling of shame. I look at the musician about to perform. We make eye contact, and I quickly look away.

My body immediately heated up, and my legs began quivering.

"Welcome, everyone! This party, um, for my 50th, um, well, not really, I wanted it to be for much more. . ." I was awkwardly welcoming my closest

100 friends to my 50th birthday party—a huge celebration at my house for which I hired one of my favorite musicians, Eric Lindell, to perform.

I was so uncomfortable in my body and filled with shame, even speaking in front of a group of people who loved me and who I invited. I was fidgeting with my hair and doing awkward things with my arms, all because I was uncomfortable with visibility. It was all a blur; I don't even fully remember what I said.

I just want to get the hell out of here, let the band play, and get the attention off of me!

". . .Okay, well, that's all I have. Enjoy!" I put my head down and walked away from the microphone as everyone cheered for me.

"Hon, you forgot to introduce the band!" my husband yelled.

Of course, I did; how embarrassing.

I ran back up to the microphone and said, "Eric Lindell and the Grand Nationals," and they launched into their first song as I hurried away from the microphone.

Thank God that is over.

I started to dance with my friends, and my dancing was a clear representation of my body shame. It was a simple sway back and forth and slightly bobbing to the beat of the music with my arms always by my side. The same movement repeated over and over. It would only change if I had a few drinks; then, maybe I'd loosen up and vary it a bit.

At some point in my life, I understood the cultural message that fat women were less than. They weren't respectable and were less capable. I managed to get through my various careers, receiving a lot of respect but staying primarily behind the scenes and hidden. I found roles where I excelled with little visibility. I longed for positions where I could help my organization grow and reach more people, and I had plenty of opportunities to step into them. Still, I hid in a supporting role instead of seizing the opportunity. I was very good at avoiding what I longed for if it meant I had to be seen beyond my comfort zone.

This dynamic played out when I was a holistic chef for a non-profit meal delivery service. Once a month, I had to make dinner for the Board of Directors. It was primarily leftovers from our current menu, with a few added side dishes or artisan bread to make it a bit fancier.

I was proud of the food I prepared; it was healthy, delicious, and designed to help cancer patients recover from treatment or surgery.

I set up a buffet for them, and when it was time to introduce myself and the food, I would simply go down the line, "Hi, I'm Tina Green. The buffet includes Indian-spiced lentil soup, sourdough bread, falafel and tahini sauce, sautéed vegetables, and quinoa tabbouleh. Enjoy!"

I can't wait to get out of here; I feel hot.

There it was again, the shame. It prevented me from proudly presenting myself and my creation as the delicious, nutritious, and beautiful food it was.

If I had a do-over now, I'd present that meal and showcase my mastery:

"Hello, everyone, and welcome. I'm Tina Green, the Chef and Site Manager. The teens and I have prepared a beautiful meal with a Middle Eastern theme. We are excited for you to sample the delicious and nutritious food our clients will enjoy this week. Our menu tonight is vegan and includes my personal favorite soup: our Indian-spiced lentil soup, along with crusty sourdough bread if you wish. As an entree, we prepared baked falafel with tahini dipping sauce. On the side, a quinoa tabbouleh salad and a medley of summer veggies harvested from our garden. I hope you enjoy it, and thank you for all you do for us!"

Doesn't that sound so much better? Do you know what the difference is? I love myself now, and I'm no longer ashamed or afraid to be seen.

In any organization, especially non-profit, networking is essential, and I resisted it. I was happy to chat with someone and leave it at that. I avoided taking it to the next level, exchanging information, suggesting a follow-up, or extending an invitation.

Even after I broke through, learned to love myself, and released my body shame, as described in the introduction to this book, I had years of ingrained habits and fears I needed to shift. I habitually hid myself because of my fear of being seen. Even though I knew I had all the tools to achieve anything I wanted, the fear was there, and it held me back. The voices lived in my head and even in the heads of people close to me because we were all used to me taking on a supporting role, even when I had the authority and skills.

I knew that awareness was the first step towards making a change, so I was actively taking note of the situations where that feeling came up in my body and thoughts.

I no longer felt the hotness that represented shame, but I did feel nervousness or tightness in my diaphragm, which turned out to be my signal to hide, avoid, or back off. I was surprised at how much it came up for me.

Gosh, this feeling comes up more than I thought. It's so exhausting and disappointing.

I wanted to eliminate the habit, the tendency to go right to that signal in my body. I knew from my experience in releasing my body shame that I needed to participate in a powerful ceremony with the intention to step through fear in a way that would move the energy, give me confidence, and interrupt that tendency.

Since I experienced so much freedom from shame, I continued to stay active on my healing path. I decided to take on fear. I brought forward my fear of anger, conflict, and being seen.

Over and over again, my old operating system spoke out, "Avoid anger and conflict; you still have to hide, and you're not ready to step out."

The critical voices, who were also attached to my old operating system, were still expressing,

"You need to slow down and integrate."

"You don't know enough."

"I don't see you doing this."

"You're approaching it incorrectly; this is how I do it."

"This other person has been at it for decades; how could you be ready?"

I recall a critical moment during a ceremony on an author's journey that included all the authors of a collaborative book, *Shaman Heart: Turning Pain Into Passion and Purpose,* by Stephanie Urbina Jones (also a co-author of this book). There were 28 of us, and we learned we were about to do a firewalk.

What?!? Oh my god, this is going to be fantastic! I trust them, but I'm scared!

We gathered around neatly stacked, criss-crossed pine logs four levels high, created by Jeremy Pajer, a master firewalk facilitator and trainer. It's impressive.

Dang! He knows how to build a fire! I'm so excited!

Jeremy started, "Okay, everyone, take a deep breath, and let's connect with the fire."

"We are going to light the fire together as a community, and those fears you want to release will fuel the fire. I will light the first few papers; then, you can light each other's paper. You can speak your fears if you feel called."

When it was my turn, I shared my intent, "I am releasing my fear of anger. Anger from myself and others. I avoid anger, and it keeps me from speaking my truth and following my heart."

The raging fire was so hot. The circle widened further and further, and we all sang the sacred fire song to a steady drum beat over and over.

"Fire, sacred fire
Burning through the night
Come to me in the dreamtime
Bring me visions of light
Circle round, spiral down
To this heart open wide
Healing light burning bright
Dry these tears I cry."

It takes a little while for the fire to be ready, so we head back inside to prepare.

"Are you ready to walk on 1,500-degree coals?" Jeremy asks, with a big smile on his face.

I hear some gasps from the group.

The coals are ready. We drum, chant, yell, dance, and the energy rises and rises!

I stand at the edge of the coals, watching with excitement and fear as each person pulls up their energy, bravery, and conviction and walks across the coals.

Okay, I'm ready!

I step to the edge of the red, flickering, burning-hot coals; my heart is racing. The tribal beat of the music and my cheering friends are encouraging me.

I step onto the coals with conviction and walk to the center of the coals. I stop, close my fists, thrust them straight up to the sky, and scream with all my might, "I am allowed to be angry!" Everyone repeated to me, with the same conviction, "I am allowed to be angry!" I walked the rest of the way across the coals.

I ran into the arms of a few friends who were waiting to celebrate with me! We hugged and jumped up and down.

Oh my god, I did it! That was incredible! My feet are not burned. I want to do it again!

I felt ecstatic and empowered! I walked on the coals about ten more times.

My energy stayed high for days after that, and I noticed something significant shifted inside me.

I feel different; the firewalk shifted my relationship with anger. The energy has moved! I feel bolder and empowered.

From that point on, I allowed myself to feel my anger instead of stuffing it down, and I wasn't afraid of confrontation or facing someone else's anger. It was huge for me, allowing me to speak my truth instead of avoiding it.

Speaking my truth is a big part of being seen. Not speaking my truth, avoiding anger, and avoiding having hard conversations was a way that I hid.

After having this firewalk experience, it became apparent. In order to move energy that is an ingrained part of my operating system, I have to, in front of witnesses, step out of my comfort zone, set a clear intention, open my heart, be vulnerable, and have a powerful embodied experience. I can't talk or think myself out of it or will myself through it.

Exactly one year later, I participated in my second author's journey for the book, *Shaman Heart - Sacred Rebel*. On this journey, we each had a wooden arrow to keep on the altar for the week. Whenever we discovered something stopping us or holding us back, we used a Sharpie to write it on the arrow. Throughout the week, I wrote,

"Giving crumbs in relationships."
"Fear of being seen."

"I'm not ready."
"Sovereignty."

At the end of the week, we had a closing ceremony that involved the arrow. It was called an "Arrow Break."

I was excited about this new challenge because I knew that every time I participated in a ceremony with intention, I moved energy out of my body, such as shame or fear, that was holding me back, and I reclaimed my freedom and self-love.

I had a track record at this point. Through these experiential ceremonies, I had lifted my body shame, gained self-love, lifted my fear and avoidance of anger, and now I was going to take on my fear of being seen and thinking that I was never ready to take on my dreams. That dream happened to be writing this book.

Jeremy was also the facilitator for this ceremony, and Glenn, one of the participants, assisted him.

"Close your eyes, and take a deep breath. Take a moment to think about your intention for this ceremony. What do you want everyone to chant while you attempt to break the arrow?"

My intention will be, "You are ready!"

This time, I am so scared. More scared than I was for the firewalk.

Jeremy demonstrated by placing a wooden archery arrow in the soft part of his throat and the other end against a board that Glenn was holding. As the group loudly and enthusiastically chanted his intention, he stepped forward and broke the arrow with his neck.

Clearly, he didn't get hurt, so it's possible. I can still feel the fear rising up in me!

I watched almost every person go up and do their arrow break. It's so fun and exhilarating to witness and be a part of each person stepping through their intention. It was powerful for every single person.

I still feel so much fear. I think the fear is more about being seen than the arrow break. It is being the center of focus while being vulnerable.

Finally, It was my turn. I shared, "I want everyone to know that I am filled with fear right now, and it's more about being up here and being seen than it is about breaking the arrow."

I want you to chant, "You are ready!"

I rested the arrow's point in the notch of my collarbone and the other end against the board. I could feel it poking into the soft skin of my neck.

Can I really do this?

The group chants loud and enthusiastically, "You are ready! You are ready! You are ready!"

I instinctively shut my eyes tight, raised my arms, let out a primal scream, and stepped towards Glenn, and it broke. I leaned into his arms as he gave me a big, long hug.

Wearing a huge smile, I felt the adrenaline rushing through my body. I looked around, and everyone was smiling and cheering.

I am ready.

And so it is.

My intention was bigger than my fear!

After going through these experiences, I now live with a lot more authenticity and dance with my arms up and away from my body! I don't default to hiding and am much more comfortable being seen, standing in my truth, using my voice, and following my heart.

If the tendency to hide arises, I can recognize and shift it quickly. My confidence and empowerment grow with every step out of my comfort zone, and the edges of my comfort zone are actively growing. It's an ongoing practice.

THE SELF-LOVE PRACTICE

I recommend starting with baby steps toward being seen by stepping out of your comfort zone. You'll learn that being seen doesn't have to be scary, and you'll soon realize that the fear comes from a "story" you are telling yourself. You can rewrite any story.

What you will need: A journal and pen.

Step 1: Raise Awareness
Start to become aware of how you're hiding and why. What is the story you tell yourself?

Some common examples of how we hide are how we dress, whether we share or speak our truth, if we avoid hard conversations, how we navigate conflict, how we participate in our community, and how we engage in relationships. The list could go on, and it will be unique to you.

When you become aware of something, you can note it in your journal along with the "story" that you have around it.

Example:
Awareness: I feel shame when I dance in front of people, so I avoid dancing.

My Story: People will laugh at me when I dance.

Step 2: Set an intention
Setting a clear intention is very important.

Example: I want to dance for the joy of dancing and not care what people think.

Step 3: Create or identify an opportunity and seize it
There may be daily opportunities, or you may have to create an opportunity.

Take the hard step out of your comfort zone.

Give yourself grace and compassion.

If you're struggling, don't beat yourself up; try again, picking another opportunity. Remember, you're taking baby steps.

Step 4: Journal
Write about your experience. How did you feel? Was it more challenging or more straightforward than you expected? Would you do it again? How can you expand your comfort zone more?

Step 5: Celebrate and rewrite your story
Celebrate by writing about it in your journal or by sharing it with a trusted friend.

Write your new story. Speak it out loud.

Example:
I can dance in front of others, experience joy, and not care what others think.

When you step out of your comfort zone, that is where the learning, growth, and magic happen.

I invite you to join my free 30-day Expand Your Comfort Zone Challenge at http://www.ExposingTheRoots.com/ComfortZone. You will receive daily prompts guiding you through different ways to step out of your comfort zone and cultivate your self-love simultaneously, and you can share your experience with others in the community.

Read more about Tina Green at the end of Chapter 2.

LEARNING TO RECEIVE LOVE

LETTING GO OF RESISTANCE

Tina Green

MY STORY

Where's Daisy?

"Daisy! Daisy! Come on, girl!"

Oh no, where is she? I have a bad feeling about this.

I was 15 years old, and it was summer break. I woke up to an empty house and couldn't find my dog, Daisy, who usually woke up with me. She was our family dog, but really, she was my dog. She was most attached to me.

I threw on shorts and a t-shirt and started walking around our two-acre property, calling, "Daisy! Daisy!"

She always comes when I call her, where is she?

The dread was starting to build in my stomach. I decided to walk along the road. I had a sinking feeling; maybe she was hit by a car.

Oh my god, oh my god, Daisy.

There she was, lying on the side of the road. She looked like she was sleeping, but she was dead. I sat beside her, lifted her lifeless head onto my lap, stroked her soft ears, and sobbed.

My baby girl, I love you so much. What am I going to do without you?

I sat with her for a long while, then I wondered,

I can't carry her to the house. What am I going to do? I don't want to leave her. My dad will know what to do. I'll use that emergency number he gave me.

I gently laid her head on the ground, kissed her, and ran to the house with tears streaming down my face.

Where is that number?

I found it on a ripped piece of paper tacked onto our family bulletin board next to the telephone on the wall. It said, "Dad, emergency." I dialed the number.

I thought the "emergency" number he gave me was his work phone number. It was not. It was his new home. A girl I didn't know answered the phone and said, "He's not home right now." This was the moment of utter confusion when I discovered he had moved out and was living with another family.

I had no one to talk to, cry to, or comfort me. I sobbed into my pillow alone in my bedroom. My closest companion, Daisy, was gone, and my dad left. He chose a new family I didn't even know existed.

It was more challenging than your average heart-breaking family divorce. He left without talking to my brother or me. He told our mom not to tell us, and she complied, just as she was trained to do.

From an early age, I learned men were in charge and given respect and authority. Women were submissive and did as they were told. As a young girl, I remember thinking,

I wish I could be a boy. Everything is so much easier for them. Being a girl is hard.

I loved my dad so much. I admired his patience, intelligence, and success, and while I spent much more time with my mom and loved her, I wanted to be like my dad. I longed for his attention, approval, and respect. He graduated from college, had a successful engineering career, made good money, and was respected. I valued what he had.

Now, I know my dad was doing his best, and I love him dearly. My mom, too. Looking at my family more closely, this is symptomatic of a long history of lack of emotional intimacy and communication skills on both sides that continues to this day. It didn't start with Mom and Dad. It passed through many generations.

There's no doubt this event in my life shaped many beliefs about myself and what to do when a relationship didn't work: Leave with little to no communication. I also learned to abandon myself repeatedly, and I believed I was not important.

There wasn't a single adult in my life who checked in on how I was doing when all this went down. It was confirmation: I was not important. How the demise of our family and the loss of my father and my beloved Daisy impacted me didn't matter.

Now, I'm in my fifties, and I've released the pain from many wounds and shifted my beliefs about myself from shame to self-love. Still, the awareness and growth continues.

In recent years, I found myself thinking about my relationships and my community,

I long to have close, intimate friendships. I want to build a local community. Why can't I seem to make that happen? I'm so frustrated.

I have many friends who I love and love me in my community. What I don't have is intimacy.

There it was: I was still figuring out how to be in a healthy relationship, particularly with women. As a child, I had no examples of women in intimate, close relationships. I was geared towards finding a man and having an intimate relationship with a man, but in my mind, that was more physical intimacy.

What I longed for was emotional intimacy. I have this with several friends who live across the country. I also wanted more face-to-face time with local friends with whom I could have honest, vulnerable conversations. Friends who consistently make time for connection and support and cheer each other on when we're reaching for our dreams. Friends who understand the importance of these relationships and see the value in setting aside time to nurture them.

My perception was I had friends who didn't have time for me because their lives were so busy, directing their energy toward their jobs and children. I also wondered if it was turning some people off that I made positive changes in my life, and I spoke and wrote openly and honestly about the changes. Either way, they didn't seem available for friendships with emotional intimacy. Even scheduling a weekly walk seemed impossible.

I found this very frustrating. I entertained the idea of leaving my community and moving back East.

Starting over again. Ugh. In my fifties, I don't want to be starting over again. I'm just gonna have to figure this out.

I decided to set an intention and pray to my higher power.

Divine Mother,

I am so grateful for your unconditional love and guidance, especially these last few years. I'm thankful you have come into my heart. I know you are always with me. I want to share that I long for intimate friendships in my community and intend to create them. I ask for your love and guidance as I seek the answer to this sacred longing for intimacy.

Thank you, thank you, thank you.

I also brought this intention to a week-long healing retreat. The retreat was built around a specific program called The Toltec Medicine Wheel of Transformation (see resources to learn more). In this program, I've had many transformative experiences. I lifted body shame, gained self-love, and overcame big fears. This time, I wanted to figure out why I couldn't seem to have intimate friendships.

I had my intention set, and while I didn't realize it then, it was already working on me.

Over the week, I found myself feeling irritated with two women. One was a teacher, and one was a participant.

Why am I feeling this way? They aren't doing anything to me except giving me love and support. Come on, let it go.

I couldn't seem to let it go. I felt tightness in my chest and a familiar nervous irritability growing. We had a full day digging into our family of origin and ancestors. It filled me with emotions and awareness about how dynamics from my childhood and lineage shaped my lifelong beliefs about myself.

No wonder. Growing up, I didn't have examples of true emotional intimacy, so I now have to figure it out.

LEARNING TO RECEIVE LOVE | 15

I've had a pattern throughout my life of walking away from relationships that weren't working. I recognized they weren't working, but I had no idea how to be in a healthy relationship, have hard conversations, and be vulnerable. I often felt shame, and avoiding it and walking away was easier. As I walked away, I stuffed down my sadness and grief and convinced myself I was better off without them. I didn't need them in my life.

The pattern of walking away from or avoiding relationships when there is a challenge, putting myself last, and attracting people who aren't emotionally available kept replaying in my life like a broken record.

Why would I dredge up things like this from the past? Because wearing a cloak of shame that doesn't belong to me and feeling like I'm not worthy of receiving love is unacceptable. I want to be my true self, free to pursue my dreams and passions, and this means looking at my "shadow" side, my parts that are denied, suppressed, or hidden from view. Addressing these hidden parts allows me to unleash my true potential. I also want to stop the cycle and model healthier behavior for my daughters.

When I was at the retreat, I was feeling a growing irritation with two relationships where I did have emotional intimacy; I kept asking myself,

Why? Why am I feeling this way? Am I jealous? Am I competitive? Am I feeling self-conscious? What is it?

That evening, we had several powerful activities planned to work through ancestral trauma and let go of aspects of our lineage passed on to us that weren't ours to own or carry. To begin, my teachers invited me to sit on a cushion in front of a mirror and look into my eyes. The room was dark; the flame of a candle illuminated my face, and mystical music played in the background.

I was still feeling irritated.

Why am I so upset? What is this?

Staring into my bitter eyes, I continued to ask myself these questions over and over for about 15 minutes. My irritation continued to grow, and I was now angry. I wanted honesty; this is a form of self-love, being honest with myself and not being in denial.

Then, it came to me like a lightning bolt.

Tina, you are resistant to receiving love, especially from women.

Oh my God, that's it. Of course, these two women gave me more love than I was willing to let in. My protection was challenged.

I started crying.

A tsunami of grief immediately overcame me. It didn't take me long to realize my resistance to receiving love impacted every relationship throughout my life. This resistance was at the root of my longing for intimacy.

It's how I'm showing up in the world. My struggle to find intimate relationships was only as strong as my resistance to receiving love. It was me. Again.

I sobbed and sobbed and sobbed. For one and a half days, I couldn't stop crying. I was in a river of grief over all the relationships that could've been, the ones I walked away from, and my relationship with my husband. I was coming to a place of acceptance that my tendency to protect my heart and my lack of healthy relationship skills kept me from having close, intimate friendships.

I now had to own my part in this dynamic. Yes, others were constantly busy, and that's a real issue. But I, too, needed to acknowledge the fact that I was emotionally unavailable. A relationship takes two, and to be successful, both have to be giving and receiving. I was always giving but allowing very little receiving.

Being honest with myself feels brutal sometimes, but I have to do it to change this.

I participated in Toltec Sacred Journey Breathwork at the retreat, and during the breathwork session, I experienced the most profound grief I've ever felt. This specific type of breathwork is a tool that has been very effective for me in pulling out of my subconscious precisely what I need to see and what needs attention. In this case, it was the suppressed grief from lost friendships, losing Daisy, my dad's departure, and the many years I resisted receiving love.

Luckily, I was in a place where I could let it flow. The 15-year-old Tina needed to cry; she was asking for attention and wanted someone to ask her if she was okay and what she needed. Tina wanted someone to consider her well-being. She needed to be held, to feel loved, and to feel like she mattered.

After that breathwork, I was able to re-assemble and feel human again.

I'm feeling so tender and vulnerable, and I also feel lighter, a lot lighter.

During those one-and-a-half days of free-flowing grief, it felt like it would never end, and I'd never come out of it. The grief was so painful and all-consuming that I wanted to die to escape the intense darkness. No wonder our culture has trained us to avoid sadness, anger, and grief. It's hard, and feeling these emotions is critical to move forward without carrying the baggage.

After the retreat, when I was back home, I continued to experience waves of grief. They'd come upon me in the most unexpected moments. Sometimes, the tears gently fell when I saw something that touched a memory; other times, it was full-on sobbing. My heart was open and raw.

Sigh. I thought this was over, and I had moved through it. Clearly, there is more.

There were days when I woke up crying in the middle of the night. I was surprised by this, and it helped me understand that I had found a core wound, something buried so deep, and it had permeated my entire way of being.

I am so grateful. It feels like I'm grieving the death of a loved one, except it's me. I'm mourning the end of the old Tina so I can be reborn without carrying this wound in my body, mind, and spirit.

Once I understood that I was in resistance, it made sense. I thought about all the people I attracted. Because of my resistance, they each had to work very hard for me to open my heart. I'm grateful for the ones who tried and didn't give up on me.

That intention was still working me. After all the grief, it was time to lay my raw, open heart and intention on my altar once again. I prayed.

Divine Mother,

I am so grateful for your unconditional love and guidance. I know you were holding me through all the grief. Thank you for being in my heart. I'm ready to receive love. Please guide and help me feel safe as I shed my layers of protection and allow others to give me love.

Thank you.

Now, in my day-to-day life, I'm walking the path of least resistance. I now know how resistance feels in my body, and I can identify it quickly when it comes up. I ask myself, "Why am I being resistant to _____?" Many times, my answer is, "No, I don't want to resist this."

I'm actively working on creating the intimacy I desire. It takes time. I feel positive about the future because I'm no longer resistant to receiving love. I'm clear about who is available and with whom I'd like to deepen my relationship. I have started that process by having honest and vulnerable conversations with friends.

I did just this at the retreat, and it shifted my relationship with both women. I now have a deeper, emotionally intimate relationship with both of them because I was willing to be vulnerable and share my feelings, and I could receive their love.

I also shared my process with a close friend when I returned home. She also reciprocated by sharing an intimate and profound experience she had on a recent healing journey. I feel a new depth in our relationship because we both trusted each other. Ironically, as I wrote this paragraph, she left me a voicemail telling me how much she loved and appreciated me. I let it in. I cried.

I've taken the needle off the record for myself and my daughters.

If this pain remained stuffed in my body, it would only grow and continue to rule me and my relationships. Even though it was hard, and I wanted to die in the middle of it, I'm so grateful I allowed myself to feel that pain and shed the emotional burden. Now, I'm feeling free and open-hearted instead of frustrated and resistant.

This is self-love.

THE SELF-LOVE PRACTICE

A powerful way to raise self-awareness is to spend time with your reflection in the mirror. Awareness is the first step to transformation. Setting an intention is the second step. Once you've set your intention, it will always be at work.

You will need: A mirror, candle, matches/lighter, a dark space with privacy, a journal, and a pen.

1. Find a dark space where you can have quiet and privacy.

2. It's helpful if it already has a mirror; if not, bring a portable mirror into the space.

3. Light the candle, turn out the lights, sit or stand in front of the mirror, and allow only the candle to illuminate your face.

4. Stare into your eyes and say, "I love you" as often as you want (at least once).

5. Continue to stare into your eyes for at least five minutes or as long as you want.

6. Allow your emotions to bubble to the surface. Notice your thoughts and feelings.

7. When you're ready to end your time with the mirror, write about your experience in your journal for a few minutes. How did it feel? What emotions came up? Did you feel resistance? If so, what are you feeling resistant to? Was it hard to say, "I love you?" What surprised you?

8. Repeat every day for a week.

9. At the end of the week, consider your experience and what came up for you. It may be helpful to review what you journaled each day.

10. Write down your intentions. What do you want to change?

11. Share your intention(s) with a trusted person in your life. Being witnessed is a powerful way to set your intention in motion.

I'd love to hear what you discovered with the mirror exercise. Please feel free to share your experience by emailing me.

Tina Green is the "Self-Love Queen," the Founder and Transformational Coach at Exposing The Roots. She is also a best-selling author, an ordained minister, and a certified celebrant.

Tina brings her grounded and vital mother energy and lived experience to everyone she serves. Through coaching and embodied experiences such as breathwork, ceremony, and ritual, Tina partners with women to create a foundation of self-love. She empowers women to rewrite their stories and honor and release old stories or beliefs that no longer serve.

Tina believes that when a woman learns to love herself, everything changes, and anything is possible.

Her transformational offerings for women include private coaching, breathwork, women's circles, workshops, retreats, ceremonies, and initiations.

Join Tina's free "Women's Self-Love Community" for inspiration and access to free self-love events:
https://www.facebook.com/groups/theselflovecommunity

Tina wants us to celebrate more! She wants to honor you with more than cake and presents. Tina creates personalized experiences such as coming-of-age ceremonies for teens, rites of passage ceremonies for all stages of life, initiations, weddings, baby blessings, home blessings, milestone birthdays, anniversaries, and celebrations of life.

Tina is also an integral team member and collaborator with the non-profit, Freedom Folk and Soul. She is the Director of Operations and Communications and has Master-Apprenticed with Jeremy Pajer and Stephanie Urbina Jones for several years in Teotihuacan, Mexico. She and Jeremy will co-facilitate the Toltec Medicine Wheel of Transformation, a powerful map of transformation based on ancient Toltec wisdom and Native American Traditions, over four long weekends in Northern California starting in 2024.

Tina also has 20 years of experience as an executive in non-profit and financial services.

She lives with her husband, two teenage daughters, two dogs, a cat, and a bunny in Northern California. She is a lifelong student, foodie, outdoor adventurer, music and theatre lover, and traveler.

Join Tina's Private Women's Self-Love Community on Facebook for inspiration and access to free events:
https://www.facebook.com/groups/theselflovecommunity

Connect with Tina:

Website for Self-Love offerings: https://www.ExposingTheRoots.com

Website for Celebrant offerings:
https://www.morethancakeandpresents.com

Inspiring blog: https://exposingtheroots.medium.com/

Facebook: https://www.facebook.com/ExposingTheRoots

Instagram: https://www.Instagram.com/ExposingTheRoots

Freedom Folk and Soul: FreedomFolkandSoul.org

Email: Tina@ExposingTheRoots.com

CHAPTER 3

PURPLE REIGN

HOW I RECLAIMED MY POWER

Dr. Ruth A. Souther, Author/Editor

MY STORY

"One of us is going to die tonight." Hot tears ran down my cheeks and dripped from my chin as I crouched behind our detached garage. Over and over, I stabbed the ground with a large butcher knife, feeling the crunch of earth and rock each time.

"Either I cut my wrists and bleed out, or I go into the house and bury this knife in his heart."

That was my choice.

My husband was 'recovering' from a heart attack that happened on our son's 18th birthday. While I sat beside him in the cardiac intensive care unit, I felt a surge of love for a man who alienated me through alcoholism, choosing a lifestyle of bands, bars, and other women rather than me.

There were good times, lots of laughter, two great kids, and pieces that fell back into place while I wondered if he would die or come back to me as a changed man dedicated to our family.

Although he was unconscious and didn't know my thoughts, I believed this was a sign from the universe that we could kick-start our twenty-year marriage and finally create a good life together.

But no.

He resumed drinking, smoking, and partying immediately after his release from the hospital. He needed one of his idiot friends to drive him because he wasn't allowed behind the wheel per doctor's orders.

"Why? Why are you doing this? You survived a massive heart attack—it's a chance to reset, to start over. Please, don't keep drinking and smoking, I beg you."

He said, "If I'm going to die, I'm going to live the way I want."

Which did not include me.

My heart broke, and confusion set in. Now what? He was our primary financial support, and although I had a job, it was much lower pay.

As he lay drunk and passed out on the couch, just a couple of months from his heart attack, I fumed and cried, both furious and wounded—his complete disregard for me, our family, and any possibility of stability evaporated.

At that moment, I felt nothing but hatred.

I wanted to die.

I wanted him to die.

I spent hours stabbing the earth, imagining it going through muscle and bone.

"If I kill him, I'll go to jail," I sobbed. "If I kill myself, I'll never see my family again."

My teenage children returned home before I dared to choose. Their laughter echoed down the driveway and prompted me to creep back into the house, clean the dirt off the knife, slip it back in the holder, and hug my kids as they came inside.

For the moment, the crisis was past.

I repeatedly asked myself, "Why don't you file for a divorce? What is wrong with you, keeping up this co-dependent, fake marriage? You're not happy, why stay?"

I didn't see any way to accomplish it, that's why. Finances, to a stupid stubborn streak of "I don't want it to be my fault" drove my refusal, even after the near-miss of violence. He wanted it to be my fault to absolve him of his destructive behavior.

However, within six months, he did leave. He found an apartment and moved out while I was at work. There was nothing adult about it, more passive-aggressive, blaming behavior; somehow, my rage overshadowed my relief. And grief.

He twisted the separation dialogue into, "I had to leave her. She's crazy. My health was suffering."

In the meantime, I accepted a job transfer to Springfield, Illinois. I needed a change, and I was ready to start a new life. My adult son stayed in Danville while my fourteen-year-old daughter moved with me. For the first time in years, I felt at peace, and yet, I still didn't know who I was beyond a dysfunctional marriage.

The first day on the job, I was asked, "Where did you get that red hair?"

Other comments continued, "Your red hair is gorgeous."

"Did your mom have red hair?"

"Your red hair is so curly and cute as a button."

I didn't have red hair. It was strawberry blonde, which was as close to my natural color as possible. The lights in the office in 1990 were the sort that even changed skin tone and shouldn't have surprised me by the shift in color.

"Red. Yeah, welcome to the third floor, Red." My co-worker laughed, and I was 'Red' from that moment on.

Staring into the mirror at home, I thought, It's funny how others keep asking where red came from because I've always wanted to be a redhead but never dared to do it.

Although I'm a rather bold creature, marrying someone who did his best to embarrass and denigrate my choices wore me down. I carefully chose my battlefields to survive with a modicum of personal pride.

But now, almost single, the suggestion of being a redhead made me smile. I couldn't afford a salon style, so I went to the nearest Walmart and bought a box of hair color. I became 'Red' in reality. I loved it. My co-workers didn't notice the change—my close-to-ex-husband did, and he hated it.

"Why would you do that? Makes you look ridiculous. Do you think that will attract another man? You know you'll never have it as good as you do with me."

"Eh, suck it." My bold reply. That made me even happier.

My ex wanted my hair grown out as he preferred long hair. I admit to passive-aggressive behavior, too, as I kept it as short as possible out of spite. But with this reinvention of self, long, curly, red hair became my badge of honor, my re-discovered external truth.

During the sixties and early seventies, I wore 'hippie' clothes, bright colors, bell bottoms, miniskirts, and all the trappings. It was a grand time and truly reflected my personality. Having kids at a young age and being in a dysfunctional marriage stole my creativity.

Twenty years later, I regained my balance and emerged from the shadow into light. It was a world of wonder I forgot existed. My mystical journey began when I walked into a little new-age crystal shop called Earthmagic. That place and those people started my evolution into a spiritual awakening that filled me with angst, but a different kind—the uncomfortable truth of soul evolution.

I took a Tarot class, which ended up being a lifelong passion, and spawned a book, *The Heart of Tarot*. Through this medium, I took the opportunity to look deep within myself. Each week, each card turned over was a message to strengthen my understanding of myself. I faced my fears and did my best to sort the messiness of my life.

Throughout the fifteen weeks of class, one card continued to surface.

"The Queen of Swords, again? I don't get it. Why does she keep coming up? Is this deck stacked, or what?"

"It's your deck, darlin'," the teacher responded.

I groaned, complained, whined, and got mad, and yet no one would explain it to me. By the end of the session, the entire class knew what the Queen meant for me and my circumstances. I still didn't.

The picture on the card is vibrant and brutal. In one hand, the Queen of Swords held a bloody head, which took me back to the moment I was willing to kill or be killed for a chance at freedom. In the other, she held a massive sword with the tip pointed down. The Queen is part of the Royalty, and is the challenge to change, but I either didn't know how or refused to look at what I would have to sacrifice.

Turns out, she held a mask. Her mask. She would no longer be a pawn in anyone's game and would not submit to outside pressures. The sword represented her truth. She didn't have to threaten anyone with it; she knew who she was and would take no prisoners if it came to a battle.

The Queen clearly stated to cut loose those old beliefs. She said: *Unmask yourself, let people see the real you. Hold your truth within your heart—no one can take it from you.*

Ahhh. Of course.

Through the Queen's direction, I forgave my ex-husband, and I forgave myself. He and I even forged something of a friendship before he passed away at 51. I'm grateful for that intervention and resolution.

Over the intervening years, my hair color often changed. At first, it was different shades of red. I had a lot of fun with the ranges, from crimson to deep auburn, to orangish-red to fire-engine red. Eventually, my skin tone changed as I grew older, and I returned to blonde hair.

My spirituality grew along with my confidence. I married a remarkable man, who is my soulmate of 32 years. I started teaching Tarot and Astrology and expanded my knowledge on various subjects at every opportunity.

I began to write after a long hiatus, and the *Immortal Journey Fantasy* series was born.

I ventured onto the stage in a play I've always wanted to do: The Vagina Monologues. There is nothing more empowering than that production in the company with a group of strong women. For the first performance, I had bright pink streaks added, appropriate, I felt, when doing a triple orgasm on stage during *The Woman Who Loved To Make Vaginas' Happy* and screaming 'Cunt!" while performing *Reclaiming Cunt.*

Mmm hmm, I thought, looking in the mirror at the pink. *I'm loving this.*

I performed in The Vagina Monologues ten times, with my hair getting brighter each production. I even wrote my own Monologue and read it on stage during a preshow performance. It was about menopause and the struggle to stay sane, but that's another story.

Then Covid hit. My beautiful blonde and pink hair grew out to—gasp—white. I decided to go bolder when I went to my hair 'artist.'

I went purple.

The transformation was astonishing. My hair reflects the wholeness of my identity and all the work I put in to be authentic. A great deal of healing happened with the color purple, and on occasion, I tried others like green, blue, turquoise, and back to pink. I adored each change, but purple is my soul's truth.

I reign with great joy as the Purple Queen.

Working with Tarot taught me to believe in myself and trust my intuition. Through the study of card images, symbols, colors, and elements, I found my true calling. I have dozens of decks, but my favorite, the one I learned on and the one I offer as a tool, is from the Thoth deck, where Queen is high. There are no Kings. Feminine awareness, sensitivity, and insights become the call to action.

The following is an excerpt from The Heart of Tarot. You don't need a deck to follow or do the exercise. Simply answer the questions in journal format.

The Queen of Swords is the Observing Mind. She brings a balanced process, exposes your true identity, and offers intellectual clarity. Once you can communicate through objectivity and discernment, the personal analysis begins.

The challenge is establishing a profoundly objective and balanced process of thought based on an observing mind. The Queen of Swords is the ability to logically calculate and remove obstacles that block the path to success.

You become the master of your true identity when you cut away the resistance that masks your intellectual clarity. When you use your gift as the analytical communicator, you become the defender of logic who uses words to heal wounds and create harmony.

You can examine your faults from a detached state of mind and achieve far beyond the pressures of the past. You see the patterns established with an objective discernment that allows you to deepen your awareness, grow, and evolve into a higher consciousness. You seek truth, clarity, and authenticity from this place within your thoughts and words.

There are other things to consider when working with the Queen. It is possible to develop an unsympathetic and somewhat harsh manner of communication simply because you believe you know best. Your ideas become the single most crucial driving force behind your actions, which could manifest in an inflated sense of self-worth.

Impatience and cutting words become habits despite the hurt you inflict on others. At this point, it is easy to become unreasonable as you justify your behavior. You lose sight of the power behind the spoken word and lash out if you feel your control slipping away.

The Queen of Swords offers the opportunity to recognize and act upon a defense of logic, to cut away unnecessary ideas, and to focus on mental clarity. Trust when the truth is revealed, you are empowered and capable of changing the world. A focused mind can cause a revolution.

THE SELF-LOVE PRACTICE

Answer the following questions honestly. Read over your responses and write another entry after considering your words. Walk with an authentic presence and then come back and answer the questions again. How have they changed? How have you changed? Note your progress on the road to self-love.

1. When have you acted on emotions rather than logic?

2. How many times have you lied to yourself?

3. What mask hides you from the truth?

4. How do you feel when you stare at your reflection?

5. Do you trust your intuition to guide you?

6. When has your behavior been unreasonable?

7. What was the root cause of your actions?

8. What gives you the strength to communicate objectively?

9. Are you able to listen with an impartial mind?

10. Can you accept the power of your own identity?

Ruth Souther is a metaphysical and natural arts practitioner in Springfield, IL. She is a Master Shamanic Breathwork Facilitator, Master Reiki Practitioner, Hypnotherapist, Ritualist, Priestess, and Minister. She holds a Master's in Shamanic Intuitional Practices and a Doctorate of Shamanic Psychospiritual Studies and is an Initiated Priestess.

She facilitates Vega's Path Elemental Priestess, Universal Priestess, and Elemental Mystery School, a new addition as of 2024, which takes her Priestess Path program to Nashville and Teotihuacan, Mexico.

She authored *The Heart of Tarot (an intuitive guide to the cards), Vega's Path: The Elemental Priestess,* and three novels: *Death of Innocence, Surrender of Ego, Rise of Rebellion,* and many more stories are percolating in her mind.

She is a facilitating member of The Edge of Perception (NFP spiritual organization) and, along with other members, creates a safe space to offer rituals and ceremonies.

In the summer months, you'll find her in Michigan at a family-owned cottage on Lake Gilead, surrounded by kids, grand and great-grandkids, and many cousins. It's her happy place where creativity flows just as the water ripples.

At home, another lake beckons her to boat, kayak, and enjoy all the wildlife that wanders, flies, or creeps into the yard and waterways. A cold beer on a hot day, floating on the pontoon with family and friends aboard the boat, is the most delicious way to spend a day.

Reach Ruth at:

ruthsouther52@gmail.com

www.vegaspath.com or www.Facebook/vegaspath

Edge of Perception | Springfield IL | Facebook

Ruth Souther | Facebook

Ruth is a contributing author and board member/Chief Editor of Crystal Heart Imprints—an independent cooperative press supporting and guiding authors and artists in their creative projects.

Visit www.crystalheartimprints or Book Cooperative Association | Crystal Heart Imprints | United States for more information.

CHAPTER 4

WELCOMING HOME THE QUEEN WITHIN

HOW BREAST CANCER BECAME MY GREATEST TEACHER

Kim Collins, C.C.H.

MY STORY

"It is not good, it is not good." The doctor tactlessly delivered the news of my biopsy results with a good dusting of fear tangled in his voice. My husband turned ghost-white and seemingly fainted for a moment. I simply went numb.

There's no way this could be happening to me.

I asked the doctor to look at the chart to make sure they had the correct patient.

How can I have breast cancer? Maybe the charts got mixed up?

The doctor double-checked the results, undoubtedly to appease my bewildered gaze and dispirited plea.

Alas, sure enough, it was me.

Kim Collins, age 41 (at that time), no breast cancer in family history, vegetarian, yogi, energy healer, meditator, herbalist, never put anything on my skin if I couldn't eat it, healthy supplements and herbs daily, living my dream as a musician, herbal tea drinker (okay, maybe this rock star did drink her fair share of wine too), practitioner of Ayurveda, positive and happy disposition (most days). The list of a robust and pure lifestyle goes on. Surely, when Aretha Franklin sang "Natural Woman," she was talking to me! (Insert chuckle here).

How exactly does breast cancer come to the mystic village herbalist? After all, when my friends were sick or heartbroken, they came to *me* for natural remedies, advice, and care. I was the one that was supposed to help others to heal. I was the healthiest person I knew. Or at least I thought.

So, no, *this can't be happening to me.*

It was my big wake-up call, indeed. Cancer does not discriminate. My healthy and spirit-driven lifestyle did not make me immune. So what could it be? What was causing my body to attack itself?

This was going to be my quest for the next decade to unravel. I didn't realize it at the time, but I was meeting my greatest teacher. My Guru.

This diagnosis marked the BC/AC portal on my life's timeline: "Before Cancer and After Cancer."

It was my time to harness the powerful Queen archetype into my life and draw upon her confidence, her worthiness, and, most importantly, a whole lot of self-love.

Maybe you've been there too, ready for the big shift in your life. Ready to get unstuck, but you just don't know how until something traumatic occurs to snap you awake. Like a thief in the night, we steal love from ourselves unwittingly. The con man of our mind cheats us of self-worth. True, perhaps our negative self-talk has been forged by comments of others, abuses tolerated, but somewhere along the way, our subconscious imprints it in our body on a cellular level. And this is where disease can manifest in the physical.

After much exploration through plant medicine and growth (there's a lot of backstory here), I had revelations about a childhood wound in regard to receiving and being seen or heard. My wounds were not given to me by my loving parents but rather via elementary school bullies and three teachers when I was in second, third, and fifth grade. I overlooked these seemingly small events my whole life, but they formed a belief system in me that, over time, kept being buried, which, as we know, creates an even stronger wound. And it buries our light. It feeds our subconscious belief that we aren't worthy or lovable enough. Then, we end up overcompensating love to others while leaving our cup empty.

The fear of being seen is an inner child wound that forms when we are shamed in childhood from being our authentic self. We can start to heal from this wound by giving ourselves what we want to receive from others: Validation, acceptance, healthy boundaries, and, yes, self-love. The irony is that we don't always fear being seen, but rather, we fear being rejected if we are seen. For us to step into our soul's highest purpose and make a true impact with our lives, being seen is not optional. It is required.

You have to remind yourself that what you think of yourself is far more important than what others think of you.

As an empath, intuitive, and claircognizant, I'm highly sensitive. I feel so much—too much. I used to care so damn much about what other people were feeling and thinking that I didn't stop to check on myself because I was more focused on taking care of others. Fear and grief fed from the well of my childhood wounds, the underlying cause of most emotional turmoil in us all.

I was grieving inside for a long time and didn't even realize it. This grief and fear created a perfect storm in my body that contributed to the cancer.

Until you go through a life-changing experience, you tend to think your body, state of mind, and health will always be there for you. According to the Yoga Sutra, mistaking the impermanent for the permanent is the leading cause of suffering (avidya, or spiritual ignorance, illusion). One of the many things my breast cancer diagnosis taught me is that no matter what we do, things change. The universe reached out to remind me what a delicate, pliable, shifting, and, yes, changing existence life really is.

Almost all of you reading this have either had some sort of relationship with cancer or at least realize that at some point in your life, you will. Needless to say, it's not an easy day when you or a loved one are told they have the dis-ease.

I decided I could choose to take one of two routes: I could pity myself, choose fear, and only listen to the mainstream doctors for treatment. Or I could follow my heart, find strength, and study alternative cancer treatments to heal myself and, thus, hopefully those around me. After all, when we heal, they heal.

I wanted to beat this cancer, but I didn't want to make myself sick in the process, nor risk the trade of this cancer for another one down the road because of chemotherapy, radiation, and hormone treatments. My whole adult life has set me up for this moment. I have always led a natural healing lifestyle, so why would I stop now when my life depended on it?

This was my self-love moment.

And everything shifted.

It was like a homecoming.

She flew in like a tornado.

Dorothy and her red shoes proclaiming, "There's no place like home. There's no place like home." Only to find that she was never hunted by a wicked witch and instead was cozy at home in her own bed.

She had not gone anywhere.

This was the homecoming.

I was here all along, finding myself right where I needed to be: Comfortable at home in the soft bed of my body.

Kim, you aren't in Kansas anymore.

A whole lot of life happened between my cancer diagnosis and now. I cured myself of the aggressive breast cancer holistically within six months without toxic protocols or pharmaceuticals through a raw food diet, herbal medicines, and other natural modalities. When the word got out about the young woman in Nashville who beat cancer naturally, people from all over were curious to hear my story. I was asked to do interviews for newspapers and magazines, speak at events, raw food talks, and holistic health workshops, and even received book publishing offers.

I gifted free holistic health consults to those diagnosed with cancer. I even started a non-profit to offer grants to those seeking to heal their cancer holistically. My health business, Own Your Ohm Health (named so because I want to encourage us all that we are our own most powerful health advocate), took off effortlessly.

As an energy healer and herbalist of 25 years, I created an online apothecary of herbal medicine, teas, and natural body products that garnered fans across the country. I became a licensed hypnotherapist to be able to go deeper with my clients. I opened my own healing retreat center and facilitated countless sacred ceremonies including Kambo medicine, women's circles, and retreats. I toured the world traveling with my band, The Smoking Flowers (in which I play drums and sing with my husband). Life was incredible and started to flow for me as soon as I healed from cancer and learned to let go, trust, and love myself. I was shining— unapologetically and authentically me. I had found my deeper purpose as a medicine woman, healed myself, and committed my life to helping others in the process. I saw all of this before it happened in visions when I was in my twenties. But the most important vision I had thirty years ago was yet to be realized. Here I was at age 51, going to the Amazon jungle, invited by an indigenous Shipibo Conibo Shaman for five weeks to train as his Shaman Apprentice and complete a Master Plant Dieta. This is the current house I dwell in, a path deep in the shamanic arts. The master plant dieta, along with Grandmother Ayahuasca, changed my life forever. I was beyond grateful to finally find my medicine in life that offered me a chance to live and love from the highest version of myself.

My dreams came true once I started advocating for myself and made self-love a priority. Every single goal I set out to do, I accomplished. Yet I had to hit rock bottom to arrive here.

So I went to the jungle.

I went to the jungle to find self-love again.

I went to the jungle to learn how to let go.

I went to the jungle to dive deep into the mystery of Pachamama, to have her hold me and teach me how to lovingly hold myself again.

I went to the jungle and had a rebirth at age 51. It's never too late in our lives. I commit to my practice and now have the tools to work with on a daily basis so that I can help others more deeply.

What happened in the jungle is a whole other book. But what I want to offer you, dear reader, is the courage and the support that you, too, can heal, no matter what age. You hold the Queen (or King) archetype within, and it's your birthright to find the flow of self-love and free yourself.

Isn't self-love the most beautiful love affair we could ever have? Loving all your parts, no matter how messy: your body, your mind, your shadows. Making the commitment to build your life into something you don't want to escape from.

Because ultimately, how you love yourself is how you invite others to treat you and to love you.

THE SELF-LOVE PRACTICE

Love is a choice. Love isn't something you go out and seek; it is simply who you are. It's our choice to honor this in ourselves daily.

So, if it's who we are, how do we dig through all the deep layers of our wounds, heartbreaks, shadows, bad habits, and old thought patterns to reveal this love?

When you think of being a queen in your own life, what comes up for you? Are you embodying queen energy in everything you do?

It takes daily commitment through self-discipline to step into higher levels of our queen-ness. Love is the highest frequency. When we step into this vibration on a consistent level, we exist as pure love light and can thrive in all ways.

THE FREQUENCY DETOX

As we grow higher in our frequency and consciousness, we can find ourselves no longer attracted to things we used to surround ourselves with or behaviors that used to consume us. Instead, we gravitate more to other things/thoughts/people that fit our new energies and our hearts.

Here are a few prompts and affirmations to think about as you begin your frequency detox regimen to rise to the higher vibration of self-love. A diet of letting go of the things that no longer serve you. First, you must be able to create the space for self-love in your life by saying goodbye to what you're no longer interested in. My suggestion is to write these down, list the things you're no longer interested in for each prompt, and speak the affirmations out loud daily for three months:

1. I am no longer interested in investing my heart and time in friendships that are one-sided.
   (List the relationships you would like to nurture instead.)

2. I am no longer interested in watching shows on TV that do not nurture my brain in the same way that healthy food nurtures my body.
   (List the type of healthy entertainment you can shift to instead of mindless or violent entertainment.)

3. I am no longer interested in suppressing my shadows. Instead, I seek them, accept them, and learn from them.
   (Name at least three shadow parts of yourself you would like to transmute or acknowledge without shame or guilt.)

4. I am no longer interested in holding myself back to make others feel comfortable. I speak my mind and express my thoughts clearly with truth, empathy, and love.
   (What are you holding back due to fear or ridicule? How are you keeping yourself small?)

5. I am no longer interested in allowing my failures to destroy me. They do not define me. They are, instead, great teachers in my life.
   (List a couple of these teachers in your life and how these setbacks helped you to grow.)

6. I am no longer interested in putting anything in my body that is not nutritious and healthy. I am no longer interested in remaining sedentary; instead, I honor and move my body on a daily basis.
   (List a few ways you can clean up your diet and make a commitment to start exercising or dancing more.)

7. I no longer choose fear. I choose courage.

8. I no longer allow my emotions to consume or control me. Rather, I let them flow through me and understand they are but a road map that can lead me in the right direction for my life.

THE MEDICINE WOMAN PATH

We can also invite self-love into our lives by prioritizing our spiritual wellness every day. Here is a simple plan and an intro to the Medicine Woman Path. This path is a calling to step into the ways of the spirit orchestrated by the living and loving intelligence of Pachamama herself. Allowing simple, nourishing moments, gratitude, and self-compassion. We all have a Medicine Woman inside of us. She is the wild woman, the divine queen holding court in our hearts. When you honor her, you can unravel and discover your unique medicine to cultivate more self-love in your life. Connect the ethereal with the earthly by adding mindfulness, meditation, and inner peace in every step you take.

Sacred Everyday: Infuse ritual into your daily life. Make each action an offering. For example, as you sip your morning herbal tea, get to know the plants you are drinking. See them as a friend you are meeting for the first time. Learn about the spirit of that plant. Feel the warmth of the tea spirit caress your soul.

Body as Temple: Your body is a vessel of love. Listen to her speak to you: Her whispers, her tensions, her joys, and her pleasures. Eat nourishing, whole, plant-based foods that reflect the divine in you. Care about every single thing you put in your mouth. Food is the best way to set up our auric fields to a higher vibration. Respecting our body as sacred is the ultimate act of self-love.

Mindful Movements: Your body is an instrument. Feel its every breath, the stillness, the stretch, and the softness. Daily yoga, pranayama, and meditation help to ground our bodies into the present moment. Create a daily movement regimen and make it as routine as you would brushing and flossing your teeth.

Savoring Moments: Savor every moment as a divine connection where you can transform the ordinary into the extraordinary. Try earthing or grounding. This technique restores the connection between the body and the electrical currents of the Earth and can create harmony and balance. Sit outside daily for ten to twenty minutes, barefoot in the soil or grass, close your eyes, and face your third eye towards the sun. Allow the sun's energy to feed your pineal gland while the frequency of the Earth penetrates your body below. The research on this practice is amazing. Earthing can help to reduce pain, inflammation, stress, and an improvement of overall mental well-being. When our bodies are in tune with Mother Earth, we invite peace, harmony, and love.

It's our inherent right as women to be queens in our bodies. It's our right to feel the power of our own sensual, soft, flowy energy. It's our duty to witness it and honor it in others.

It's time to call on your queen within.

Feel her.
Deeply.
In your bones.

It's been your season of shedding old traumas, old belief systems, and old skin. The serpentine dance.

Medicine woman, priestess, queen, you knew you were always there.

You've been waiting on yourself, sometimes so powerful you were actually afraid of yourself.

Message received: Get out of your own way.

Stay guided by intuition, listen to yourself better, open yourself more fully, and receive and embrace all the magic that resides within you.

Do not dim your light. Do not be afraid of outshining others. Stop trying to fit into a shoe that just doesn't fit when you were born to be barefoot.

I share my story, my life, and my vulnerability with you so you know you aren't alone.
I see you.
Don't dim your light to fit in any longer.
Wear your crown proudly and barefooted. Move into the long-forgotten power of being a wild woman.
Unafraid.
Unchained.
Loving yourself unabashedly.

Get out of your own way, sister. Aho.

Kim Collins is a trained Curandera Medicine Woman, kambo practitioner, board-certified hypnotherapist, herbalist, health and life coach, holistic cancer coach, Reiki Master, intuitive energy healer, sound healer, plant medicine integration specialist, retreat facilitator, public speaker, High Priestess and Shamanic apprentice in the Shipibo-Conibo lineage. Her given Shipibo name is Bidi Neraté, which means "Goddess who walks among the space and stars."

Kim has studied natural health and nutrition for 30 years, including Ayurveda, herbalism, yoga + mysticism, and the Native American and Amazonian shamanic arts.

She specializes in the use of herbs, plants, vitamins, lifestyle, natural substances, and techniques for supporting good health. Her small batch herbal Apothecary includes natural body products, herbal medicine, and spiritual accessories that focus on ancient herbalism and techniques, infusing energy vibration into every batch. Kim focuses on the mind-body connection, where one's emotional and mental state is just as important as physical health. She is a retreat facilitator and ceremonialist and offers a wide variety of options at her retreat center, Ajna Wellness Retreat (East Nashville, TN), for personal curated ritual, overnight stays, ceremony, and other community events.

Kim is also a public speaker, independent researcher, creative raw/vegan cook, juicing expert, Feng Shui interior designer (she can create a healing space for your home), and is an accomplished musician of 30 years touring the world with her husband and her band The Smoking Flowers. She believes that her Native American roots gave the foundation to her belief in the body's innate ability to maintain itself in good health when given an appropriate healthy environment provided by our Mother Earth.

Connect with Kim:

Website: https://www.ownyourohmhealth.com

Instagram: https://www.instagram.com/ownyourohmhealth

Shop the Apothecary:
https://www.ownyourohmhealth.com/apothecary-products.html

Visit Ajna Wellness Retreat:
https://www.instagram.com/ajna_wellness_retreat

To make an appointment (long distance Zoom or in person) email:
info@ownyourohmhealth.com

Music: https://www.thesmokingflowers.com

CHAPTER 5

SURVIVING IN THE CORPORATE WORLD

HOW TO LISTEN AND TRUST YOUR INNER GUIDANCE

Charleen M. Michel, Ph.D.

MY STORY

Can I do anything I want if I put my heart and mind to it?
How can I be myself and let my light shine bright?
How can I let my protective shields fall? How can I show self-love
and kindness to others? Am I in the right place?
How high a price am I willing to pay?

"At the center of your being, you have the answer.
You know who you are, and you know what you want."

~ Lao Tzu

"You're a girl. Girls get married, have a family, and take care of the house."

I want to be more than just a wife and mother.

I loved working with fabrics and studied textile technology at the University of Massachusetts. I lived with my parents and realized self-love and happiness can only come from within. I wanted to be independent, but I had to be patient.

After graduating with a B.S. in 1979, I received a full teaching assistantship for graduate school. I could now be independent of my parents. I prepared to move to North Carolina.

"What will we do without you?"

Should I feel guilty?

No, it's time for me to go.

Two-and-a-half years later, I received an M.S. in textile chemistry from North Carolina State University and a research assistantship funded by NASA to further my graduate studies. I was honored to learn from female and male scientists as I developed a water-resistant epoxy resin for the space shuttle shields.

I am going to outer space. I am proud to be a scientist.

The year 1985 was significant in my life.

I received my Ph.D. in Fiber and Polymer Science and started corporate life as a Research Scientist in Polyester Fibers Research with a global chemical company in Kingsport, Tennessee. The job was fantastic, but the location was not.

I feel stuck between my heart and my mind.

In September, I traveled with my boyfriend to Switzerland, whom I met during my studies. I was about to realize a dream I had when I was 20 years old to visit the Swiss Alps.

My choice is to move to Switzerland and marry a Swiss.

My boss was shocked!

"What? Don't you like your job?"

My parents were also shocked.

"You're moving to Switzerland? It's so far away."

Should I feel guilty again?

No, I am following my heart and living my dreams.

In January 1986, I arrived at Zurich airport with my luggage containing my most valued possessions, including my piano books.

There was a baby grand piano in my new home. I played two compositions from my last piano recital in 1979 from Franz Liszt's *Suisse* collection, *Églogue,* and *Au Lac de Wallenstadt,* long before I met my fiancé. Tears welled up in my eyes.

My heart is bursting with joy.

My priority as a new Swiss resident was to learn Swiss German, a German dialect spoken in Zurich. I wanted to understand what people were saying and integrate into my new environment. Within two years, I succeeded.

In June 1986, we married, and I became a Swiss.

I am in the right place with the right person.

I started as a research and development (R&D) specialist at the European headquarters of a global chemical company. The corporate language was English, but the social language was Swiss German. I was one of four women out of 200 R&D employees working in Switzerland. My job was to develop plastics for the food packaging industry.

I'm not excited.

However, I wanted to work and demonstrate my scientific capabilities. I set a professional standard for writing research reports, and although this was the right thing to do, not everyone was excited.

My R&D boss summoned me.

"Slow down."

What! Why?

"Look at your job as a hobby. You're married and will have children. Later, you will care for your family vs. having a career."

I can't believe this. A hobby?
This is not your decision, it's mine.
I am wondering if I am in the right place.

Unbeknownst to me, the European R&D Director had a new job for me and became my first sponsor in the company.

I am excited to learn more.

"Your talents are precisely what we need for the Human Resources (HR) Development Manager for Switzerland, the Middle East, Africa, and Eastern Europe."

What! HR? What did I do wrong?
I am a research scientist, not a social worker.
Is this my fate?

"This is your first assignment in HR, and in a few years, you can become the HR R&D Business Partner in Europe. I've done both jobs and will support you."

I'm saved!

After settling into my new office, I met my new HR boss. "I am so excited to have you working for me. If you do as I say, everything will be fine."

What!? I'm not amused.

I soon had a new HR mentor and sponsor, the Vice President of HR Europe. He taught me the company culture and allowed me to work with the European leadership team headed by the European president.

My first assignment was to train the European leadership team to run their executive management meetings better.

I can do this. And I did!

I also facilitated strategy development and implementation sessions with European business leaders. My biggest clients were the Business President for Hydrocarbons and Energy and the Global Technology Director. I supported their business teams, traveled with them worldwide, and led their leadership meetings.

I realized having a Ph.D. and working for a technology-based company had its advantages.

I love the influence I have.

However, some of my HR colleagues were jealous of my opportunities.

"You're lucky. It has nothing to do with your capabilities. It won't continue."

Why are people jealous? My protective shields are up.

Several years later, I became the HR R&D Business Partner in Europe. I was pleased to work again with like-minded scientists and loved the opportunity to select, develop, and mobilize R&D talent for the company. I worked closely with their leaders to transform them into strong, compassionate people.

The jealousy from my colleagues continued, and my shields got stronger.

"You don't have the HR education to do this job."

I am acquiring the competencies.

After seven successful years as the HR R&D Business Partner, I wanted a new opportunity. A job opened as the Global HR Director for two business joint ventures (JV) between the U.S. and a Middle East partner.

I am confident and ready for the assignment.

I applied and got the job.

Why am I the only person interested in this job?

During the next two years, we had to develop the HR strategy, policies, and programs so the JVs could operate independently in eight countries around the world.

In the beginning, everything went according to plan, and everyone was pleased.

But I have a funny feeling in my stomach. What is not right?

I learned from a former colleague the Middle East JV partner suddenly had a problem. They wanted more control over the JVs and appointed a VP to oversee the JV activities, one for each JV. I was expected to inform them what I was doing daily, and they would report back to their home office.

Is Big Brother watching?

Suddenly, the VPs piled on additional work that had top priority. I felt they expected others to do the work for them. The office climate shifted. I was told what to do and closely watched as I did my job. After a fifteen-year successful HR career, I was frustrated and felt disrespected.

I am in the wrong place.

I was unhappy with the work environment. I started to look for a way out and interviewed with another company for a new job.

I was afraid to take time off or call in sick when I felt unwell.

This is an impossible situation.

Although my body reacted to the situation, I ignored the headaches, severe menstrual cramps, and weight gain. I took medication to reduce the pain. When I came home, I needed several glasses of wine to relax before falling asleep.

I'm ignoring the signals from my body.
I'm barely surviving.

I was afraid to be stabbed in the back. My protective shields got stronger.

For the moment, I'll continue rowing and focus on the work to be done.

One of my critical goals was to implement new compensation and benefits plans for the JV employees in Germany. Approval from the Works Council was imperative. Before my trip, my boss expressed doubts about getting the approval.

I am confident and have no doubts about this.

I was greeted warmly by the Works Council. I previously worked with them and established a level of credibility and trust. We had a productive discussion in German about the new compensation and benefits plans. Within 30 minutes, they were approved.

I returned to the office. My boss was extremely happy. But the VP for the JV was not. Unbeknownst to me, he tried to establish a relationship with the Works Council a week earlier using his position and was unsuccessful.

"I don't like your attitude."

What!? I am delivering the required results.

My intuition tells me a storm is brewing.
There are strong egos in play.

I took a week of ski vacation to consider my next steps. I was exhausted and wanted to escape from my job.

I am not willing to nurture other people's egos or do additional work.
My cup is empty. I have nothing more to give.

A few days later, I told my husband, "I will speak to my boss on Monday."

We met the following Monday morning in his office. I felt like all eyes were watching me except for the VP. He was nowhere to be found.

Does everyone else know what is about to happen?

I felt sick to my stomach and couldn't stand the smell of cappuccino in the room.

I sense what's happening.

"I don't have good news."

Was I expecting anything different?

"I'm sorry. I did everything I could. I've been on an extensive tour of both JV partners to find a solution. I told them the wrong person was leaving. They didn't care. Your services are no longer required."

Bang! You could hear a pin drop.

I am not showing him my feelings, nor am I shedding a tear.

My devastation turned to relief. He generously compensated me for my departure.

I packed up my stuff and walked out the door, never to return to the office again. I was more affected by the news than I thought.

I am exhausted and hurt.
It's not right or fair.

I went home and the tears came.

The price is simply too high!

I am finally free and no longer being controlled.

I needed to reprogram my thinking and adjust my priorities. All my life, I have been passionate about my work. At times I could not say no.

There is more to life than just work.

I took an extended break from corporate life and canceled the career discussions with the other company. The headaches stopped, and I slept better.

It was time to put me first. I realized although I thought I had a lot of self-confidence, I also depended on external recognition and sponsorships from others. I loved my career and my job more than I loved myself.

It's now time for self-love and more diversity in my life.
I am free to choose what makes me happy.

I focused on doing what seemed obvious to me.

I immersed myself in horticulture and learned about the wisdom of nature. Gardening is my biggest passion. I especially love nurturing my English roses. My garden grounds and rewards me with its grace and magnificent beauty.

I received a golf license to play in Switzerland and Europe. It requires multiple competencies, including intellectual, interpersonal, and intuitive skills, and connects me with nature and with others.

And, I had the piano tuned to again play music that makes my heart sing.

In 2016, I met a yogini on the golf course. She inspired me to start my spiritual journey, develop well-being lifestyle strategies, and find self-love and happiness.

For the first time in my life, I started to meditate regularly. I always knew meditation existed, but I didn't think it was for me.

I'm not stressed!

I was in my 50s and intuitively aware of health issues as I watched my parents' health deteriorate.

I searched for complementary ways to merge the well-established Western approach to health and well-being with Eastern wisdom traditions.

I learned about living an Ayurvedic lifestyle and about healing my life through the chakra energy system.

In 2022, I felt an urgent need to travel to Bali for a Chakradance retreat to move my chakras and transform my life. It indeed changed my life. I was inspired by other women who had started their well-being businesses and knew I had to do the same.

I am now ready to drop my protective shields and share my talents again with the rest of the world.

My focus shifted, and I realized how my life and work experiences had prepared me for my next steps. I created a business and lifestyle plan to implement my newly gained knowledge, use my facilitation skills, and be in nature.

My new life's purpose was to facilitate well-being programs and share my wisdom with others. I mustered all my courage to start a well-being business, *Wisdom Unleashed with Charleen Michel – Paths to Self-Discovery.*

THE SELF-LOVE PRACTICE

BE YOUR SPONSOR, MEDITATE, AND PRACTICE SELF-LOVE

Listen to the wisdom of your body, find antidotes for stress, meditate, and regularly take a close look in the mirror as you ask yourself:

Who am I?
What do I want?
What is my purpose?
What am I grateful for?

I invite you to join me for a short introduction to meditation and a free 20-minute meditation experience.

https://www.wisdomunleashed.ch/service-page/meditation-masterclass-free

EXPERIENCE CHAKRADANCE

Stress from corporate life is stored in our bodies and shows up later in life as chronic illnesses, such as rheumatism, high blood pressure, and weight gain.

Chakradance is a powerful movement healing modality and helps us release the stress in our bodies through chakra-resonant music, spontaneous dance, art creation, and guided meditations. We learn to take off our masks, drop our shields, release limiting beliefs, and let go of negative emotions. This experience is awakening and life-changing.

I highly encourage you to experience it yourself.

I invite you to join me for a short introduction to Chakradance and a free 20-minute Chakradance experience.

https://www.wisdomunleashed.ch/service-page/chakradance-masterclass-free

ASK YOURSELF, "AM I IN THE RIGHT PLACE?"

It is important to periodically validate the question, "Am I in the right place?"

Be aware of your feelings. Are you happy with your work environment and what you are doing?

- Ask yourself, "Who am I? What do I want?" as you continue your journey to personal success and self-discovery.

- Prepare yourself with a strong resumé or CV, and actively explore other career opportunities for validation.
- Have the courage to follow your intuition and listen to the wisdom of your body as you do things that make you feel good while practicing self-love. Headaches, menstrual cramps, lack of good sleep, and body aches and pains are warning signs.

DEVELOP DAILY ROUTINES TO SUPPORT WELL-BEING

Good quality sleep is essential to rest, relax, and rejuvenate. We often get immersed in our jobs and work long hours to achieve results. It is better to get a good night's sleep every day rather than sleep in on the weekends to release stress, calm the body and mind, and reduce the risk of chronic illnesses.

Here is an example of my daily routine.

- Each day I rise and shine with the sun at 6 a.m.
- I meditate for 21 minutes early in the morning to start the day with a calm and still mind. Afterwards, I do some yoga.
- I have a light breakfast and get ready for my day.
- I eat my main meal at lunchtime when my digestion is strong.
- After lunch, I get out in nature and take a walk with my dog.
- At the end of the day, I meditate or practice Chakradance to release the stress accumulated during the day.
- My husband and I cook a light dinner and eat by 7 p.m.
- I turn off all electronics by 8 p.m.
- I like to read a book or listen to music in the evenings.
- I turn off the lights by 10 p.m. and go to sleep.

PAMPER YOURSELF

- Go to the hairdresser.
- Get a manicure and a pedicure.
- Have a weekly body, facial, and hand massage.
- Buy yourself luxurious body care products.

- Wear clothes that make you feel beautiful.
- Use aromatherapy to calm your mind. Lavender is a great choice.
- Take a vacation and personal time out from work.

CONNECT WITH LIKE-MINDED PEOPLE

Having friends and connections with like-minded people is the best nourishment for the body, mind, and soul.

- Enroll in a spiritual practice, like yoga and meditation.
- Join a writer's circle.
- Go out for lunch, enjoy a cup of afternoon tea, and chat about whatever is on your mind and in your heart.

Working in the corporate world gave me valuable experiences to learn and grow as a person. Working today as an entrepreneur gives me the freedom and independence I have been seeking all my life. I realized I could be happy doing whatever I wanted if I put my heart and mind into it while practicing self-love and self-respect.

"Ask your Soul what makes you feel alive, happy, healthy, and personally satisfied. Follow Your Passions, Practice Self-Love, and Live Your Dreams."

~ Charleen M. Michel, Ph.D.

Charleen M. Michel, Ph.D. worked with global corporate clients for many years as a Human Resources facilitator and moderator to achieve their business and career goals. She made decisions to get ahead in life based on her intellect and quick reactive mind.

In 2016, she started her spiritual journey and learned the value of self-love. She discovered paths to use her intellect and mind to know herself better, make better decisions, and listen to the inner wisdom of her body, mind, and soul.

Charleen is certified to facilitate complementary healing modalities, including:

- Chakradance™*
- Chopra Meditation™**
- Chopra Ayurvedic Health™***

In 2023, she started a sole (soul) proprietary business called Wisdom Unleashed with Charleen Michel – Paths to Self-Discovery. Meditation is a cornerstone of her life and her business. Her mission as a spiritual alchemist is to guide others to discover their inner wisdom and transform their lives.

She grew up in New England and is a bona fide Chemist, starting with her university studies and extending into her kitchen and garden.

She speaks Swiss German fluently and has integrated into Swiss Culture and Society. Since 1986, Switzerland has been her home. Her heart and soul reside here.

Charleen loves to be in nature, nourishing her garden, playing golf, and realizing her dream of living in the Swiss Alps. She and her husband, Lukas, enjoy cooking and caring for their dog, Vivienne.

* Chakradance™ is the registered trademark of Chakradance Pty Ltd.
** Chopra Meditation™ is a registered trademark of Chopra Global LLC.
*** Chopra Ayurvedic Health™ is a registered trademark of Chopra Global LLC.

She expresses her heartfelt gratitude to her husband and her good friend Alexandra, who supported and encouraged her to write this chapter.

Connect with Charleen for deeper conversations:

Website: https://www.wisdomunleashed.ch/

Facebook: https://www.facebook.com/WisdomUnleashedCM

Instagram: https://www.instagram.com/wisdom_unleashed_cm

LinkedIn:
https://www.linkedin.com/company/wisdomunleashed-with-charleen-michel

CHAPTER 6

SINGLE, CHILDFREE (OR CHILDLESS) WOMEN
THE TRANSFORMATIVE POWER OF LOVING YOURSELF FIRST

Holly M. Rapport, MPH

MY STORY

July 4, 1996: Break up with the guy I thought I was going to marry, have children with, and start a family.

May 19, 1997: My mom dies of cancer.

Double whammy mourning ensues.

I remember the car trunk slamming shut as tears were running down my face. My boyfriend and I were breaking up as he dropped me off at the Amtrak station, and I was in shock.

Happy Birthday, America! Someone, please shoot a firecracker at me and blow me up. My mother was dying, and here I was with this guy breaking my heart.

What the actual fuck?! I was going to marry you and have our children and start a family. And my mother is dying, and you're just gonna peace out?

It was an explosion of sadness I could barely comprehend because I was also dealing with the dread of my mom never recovering from her illness. Twenty-six years old with my life ahead of me, but this was a disaster. By the way, we broke up that day, and I never heard from him again. It was harsh and heartless.

I've spent over 25 years working through the grief and pain of losing my mother and him basically at the same time. Along with other grief I accumulated, in early 2023, my therapist diagnosed me with chronic grief.

Is there such a diagnosis? I had no idea. Whew, it feels good to have my feelings validated!

In working with my practitioner, I realized that the major heartache I've been managing is that I'm not a 'common person' nor a 'typical' woman. It hasn't been permissible for me to be myself for real, and I'm always apologizing in one way or another for being myself. I'm guessing this might resonate with you, dear reader.

Picture this: I was writing in my journal at the library, and a woman came into the room I was in. She looked like she was in her 30s and was holding a baby. She was walking around, showing the baby different pieces of art on the walls. First thought: *Oh shit. I hope that the baby stays quiet and calm!* I crave quiet, especially when reading or writing, so I silently prayed for good behavior. When I looked up from my computer, the baby and I caught each other's eyes. I smiled and felt a familiar pang in my stomach.

- I wasn't ever one of those girls who dreamed of having babies or had lots of dolls, though I've always loved little ones and babysat as an early teenager.

- I did expect to get married, but it didn't necessarily go as far as a four-person household dream (aka one husband; two kiddos kind of scenario).

- I did meet a guy who I thought I'd marry, and that was the one time where I thought, *yeah, I want children with him.* But I'll get to that later.

But that adorable baby in the library and that pang in my middle. Familiar, yet not all the time. That pang happens every once in a while. That 'what if' feeling of *that could have been me. I could've been a mother. I should've been a mother. Or is it just a hunger pang?* Kidding.

I didn't have a baby. I've never been pregnant, never tried. So, you could call me childfree. Or childless, depending on your personal definitions. I define childfree as a woman who does not want to bear children. She made that choice for herself and her body. Childless is a woman who wanted children but could not, for whatever reason, such as infertility, her husband's sperm, no partner, or IVF didn't work.

It's so interesting how those two words feel different. The energy isn't the same when you say them. Childless feels 'less than'—I do not have what other women have, and I'm less than because of it; I'm less of a woman because I couldn't give birth even though I tried. It feels negative and sad. It also feels ostracizing and lonely. Childfree feels energetic and positive. Like having the freedom to do whatever, whenever. It doesn't feel constrained— you get to follow your path without compromising. Childfree allows for more sleep, not arguing over the TV remote, traveling to your heart's desire. Or just staying in bed all day reading!

I've often thought of myself as childfree, yet I've realized recently that it's more like I'm in the middle, in the liminal space in between. It's more complex than picking a side, being in the middle. And it's because I don't think I ever really chose to have kids or not. It just sort of happened.

As I mentioned earlier, I don't remember consciously thinking I wanted to have children. Growing up, my parents were in love, and I was surrounded by couples with kids. My parents' closest friends were lucky to be happily married with two kids each. We all grew up together, enjoying long weekends, holidays, vacations. That was the norm—I don't remember having close friends with divorced and/or single parents.

Mr. Break-up on July 4th in my mid-20s was the guy I thought I would marry. We were super compatible on paper: both Jews, tall, lean, attractive, smart, creative, educated, athletic, and family-oriented. He was a journalist; I was in book publishing. This was it—I could marry this guy and have children. My maternal grandmother would be happy because she expected all of her grandkids to marry and procreate. I was her first grandchild and her favorite. She used to whisper to me, "Holly, you're my favorite," thinking I'd feel special and loved. Sadly, I felt uncomfortable and confused, sigh. Being her favorite and the oldest also meant grandchildren, and soon.

A year into the relationship with him, my mother was diagnosed with a rare type of cancer. The doctors didn't know how to treat it, and it was messy and traumatic (understatement). Also, I was only 25 years old when she was diagnosed, and they gave her three to six months to live.

My mother and I were very close (we spoke every day), and I never imagined my life without her. Even in my 20s, I lay in her bed, and she stroked my hair, and we talked through whatever was going on.

"Mom, I've got [x, y, z problem] what should I do about it?" And she always listened and tried to help.

"Well, did he actually say that you're not pretty enough to date or too strong or too this or that, or are you just making that up in your head?"

I was living my best life in NYC, dating the man of my (supposed) dreams, working in book publishing (real dream!). The cancer diagnosis turned my life upside down. I was young, naïve, and in total shock. I couldn't conceive of losing my mom or living without her. Then the break-up and she passed away.

"Holly is going to have the hardest time out of everyone with this loss."

My mom said that to her best friends right before she died. Which was pretty substantial considering my mom was a twin. But she knew how dependent I was on her, how much love we had for each other, and how enormous the loss of a mother is to a daughter.

I took three weeks off of work and sat shiva, slept, and tried to make sense of it all. Through the years, I went to therapists, energy healers, and massage therapists, went hiking, and practiced yoga to work through the loss. I didn't consciously realize it was a double loss (at the same time!) until one of my friends pointed that out. "Holly, do you realize that you had two losses, and now you're actually mourning both?"

I continued to date through my 30s and 40s, but nothing stuck. Truthfully, in hindsight, I was picking the wrong men and not getting too attached. And then, a few years ago, I realized I hadn't really healed from these losses and the behavioral patterns they created. Not moving through the grief at the time they occurred (likely because I was young and inexperienced) really affected my life.

And I never considered having children with any of the guys I dated after my mom passed. When I was 35 and single, I had those common conversations women have with ourselves at that age.

I wonder if I can still have children.

Could I do this by myself? Maybe I should go to a sperm bank and get pregnant. Wow, that sounds sexy AF!

As I considered my options, two of my friends got separated and basically became single moms because their husbands weren't supportive. They struggled because they weren't used to doing it alone, delinquent child support, etc. Being a witness to this scared me off. I also realized I didn't have my mother to lean on, help with babysitting, give me advice on childrearing, and all that. So, I decided not to go through with it.

I didn't consciously daydream about being a mother. Nor did I crave it like other women I knew. I was having a (mostly) great time being single and free—not having to compromise and doing what I wanted when I wanted. Yet I missed my mother, became an aunt, and dated less in my 40s. I started management consulting in public health and healthcare with the federal government in Washington, DC, and worked there through the COVID-19 years. It was incredibly chaotic, stressful, intense, and rewarding. I was proud of how I was giving back to my country in a meaningful way during a time of crisis. And then I crashed and burned out. In the Fall of 2020, I moved to the beach in New Jersey to start anew, rest, and recover. I took a timeout to grieve what I thought was long gone (the dream of a husband and children). The reality is that I can still find a life partner; I can't procreate at this point in my mid-life.

I get it—there's a lot to unpack here. More than I can get into in this book chapter. Society says we're not smart enough. Productive enough. Pretty enough. Paired-off enough. Over time, these impossibly high expectations can make women—especially those like us who are single and childfree—feel isolated, ostracized, and "othered." In an attempt to be truly seen, we push ourselves to the point of exhaustion—or ten steps past it—by chasing someone else's ridiculous standards instead of creating an intensely rewarding life of our own.

I've been right where you are. Overwhelmed by work, my circumstances, and my emotions—stuck and burned out. "Othered" by society, my community, and even some of my friends. Like you, I found it challenging to find the right community, resources, and tools that supported my goals and aspirations.

This holistic approach allowed me to be present in my own self-care and healing journey, one that doesn't end where I am "healed" but rather one that appreciates the lifelong, life-giving process of being gentle with myself first—so I can share greater compassion with the world beyond.

By embracing this incredible mind, body, and spirit work, I found my authentic self and true well-being while striking a healthy balance between inner peace and bold, beautiful power.

AND I'M HERE TO HELP YOU DO THE SAME.

THE SELF-LOVE PRACTICE

Permitting myself to grieve has helped me in so many ways. Mostly, I've realized that how I feel about myself and where I am in my life dictates how I react to others. The way other people feel about me is their business.

I've worked through my grief of not being a "typical woman" in our society, feelings that it's not permissible to be myself as a single, childfree (or childless) woman, and not apologizing for it. The patriarchy doesn't like female strength like this, AND we can work together to push through and assert our voices, our leadership, and our importance in this world and our local communities.

I'd like to share initial three thoughts I hope can help heal the dull ache behind these weighty labels of childfree and childless:

1. If you're feeling the pressure to fit society's unrealistic standards for women, first know you're not alone. I'm right there with you. Additionally, we are a multi-generational and growing demographic who can lead and support each other through love and acceptance!

2. Secondly, remember that your worth in this world is not determined by motherhood. You can allow yourself to feel the emotions of your experience. Whether that's grief, anger, longing, or a mix of a million emotions you can't even name. Then tell yourself, "I'm enough, just as I am." Tell yourself again and again until it sinks deep.

3. And finally, find a community of women who get it. It's so much easier to practice self-love and self-care when you have a group of women around you who pour genuine love and care into you. For me, my life changed drastically (and for the better) when I started intentionally surrounding myself with other single, childfree (or childless) women.

TOOLS FOR THE WAY FORWARD

These suggestions can be a meditation or journaling series of exercises to help you reframe your thinking, move through your grief, and practice healthier behaviors. When you read through this list, see what resonates in your mind and body, and take your next steps. All with the intention to love yourself first. You deserve it!

Challenge Societal Expectations

- Educate yourself about the diversity of human experiences. Recognize that there is no one "typical" woman, and societal expectations are often based on outdated stereotypes within the patriarchy. I've published some writings on my website at www.hollywellcommunity.com that I hope will be helpful.

- Understand that your relationship status does not determine your worth or whether you have children. Being single and without children is not a curse nor a forever if you do want something more. You are a unique individual with your path to follow and special gifts to share.

Seek Support

- Connect with supportive friends, family, energy healers, or a therapist who can provide a safe space to express your feelings and help you work through your grief.

- Consider joining or starting support groups or online communities where you can find women like you so you all can feel more seen, heard, and respected for who you are today.

Practice Self-Compassion

- Treat yourself with the same kindness and understanding you'd offer to a friend going through a tough time. Be patient with yourself as you work through your feelings. When you tell yourself something negative (e.g., I'm alone; no one loves me), take time to think about how you would react if a friend said that to you about herself. Would you lash out at her, or would you hold her with love and kindness and help her through it?

- Practice being gentle with yourself. Meditation (sitting or walking) can help hone in on your thoughts and move through negative chatter. Challenge any thoughts that make you feel inadequate through positive affirmations or mantras you can say over and over again to transform your thinking.

Set Boundaries:

- No is a complete sentence!

- Practice saying "no" when necessary (and it feels right to you) and establish healthy boundaries with people who try to pressure you into conforming to societal norms. This includes at work, where there are times that single, childfree, and childless women are expected to take on extra work because we don't have dependents or a partner. That may be true; however, we have full lives that are just as important, and it's up to us to set those parameters.

Cultivate Self-Love:

- Practice self-love and self-care regularly, aka every day. This may involve activities like stretching, walks in nature, baths, breaks from technology, or simply treating yourself to something you enjoy.

- Remember that self-love is an ongoing journey, and it's okay to have ups and downs along the way. This goes back to being gentle with yourself.

Give Back:

- Consider volunteering or getting involved in causes that are meaningful to you. Helping others can provide a sense of purpose and fulfillment. It's a big win-win and brings love and peace into your community and the world.

- Volunteering is also a great way to meet like-minded people who become acquaintances, friends, and partners. It enriches your life in so many ways and the lives of those you're helping.

Remember that self-acceptance and self-love are ongoing processes. It's lifelong, and that's a good thing! If we remain curious, we're always learning and growing at any age. It's natural to have moments of doubt, but by practicing these strategies consistently, you can gradually move through the grief and embrace your authentic self as a single, childfree (or childless) woman. Your worth is not defined by societal expectations but by the love and acceptance you have for yourself.

Holly M. Rapport, MPH, is the Founder + CEO of HollyWell, a holistic health coaching and healing organization where independent women come to heal, grow, and thrive. Holly has a Master's in Public Health and is trained and certified in behavioral science and health education, health coaching, yoga teaching, reiki and intuitive energy healing, and human-centered design. While HollyWell's holistic health coaching program can benefit any woman ready for better health and change, it's especially helpful for single, childfree (and childless) women who want to move beyond feeling left out and "othered" and into a place of phenomenal growth, health, and discovery. Holly brings her multiple-modality experience and expertise to collaborate with each of her clients with compassion and accountability.

Holly has had many careers, including book publishing, television, health research, sports event planning, health coaching, and management consulting for federal health agencies. Her vision is to build an inclusive community for all women to come together, learn, grow, and collaborate to build healthier, vibrant lives full of peace and love! She currently lives in Asbury Park, NJ, where she enjoys beach time and live music. Holly loves to travel, spend active time outdoors in nature, hang with family and friends, read books, practice yoga/Pilates, volunteer, watch tennis and movies, explore art, and anything to do with NYC.

Connect with Holly:

Website: www.hollywellcommunity.com

Email: holly@hollywellcommunity.com

LinkedIn: https://www.linkedin.com/in/hollyrapport/

Instagram: @hollywellcommunity

CHAPTER 7

YOU ARE NOT BROKEN

FINDING LOVE IN THE PAIN POINTS

Madrone Kalil, Ph.D., End of Life Doula

MY STORY

Night falls on the community of women I have traveled a thousand miles to gather with on this summer full moon. We have each lit a candle that will burn through the night.

We process quietly in our goddess garb to the fire ceremony grounds. It's a beautiful sight, the candlelight of almost 60 women walking in the twilight. We form a circle around the fire ring. The wood is stacked tall and gorgeous, with flowers tucked between the logs. The fire is lit by two women using flint ('How badass is that,' I think to myself!).

The large mother drum starts to sing at full moon rise and does not stop beating, not once, until moon-set. Other drummers join in, rattles shake, dancers begin to move around the raging fire, and our intentions and prayers are sent as we give our whole being to open up our sight in service to others, the Earth, and ourselves.

During the night, I drop to my knees and begin rocking, forehead close to the ground, arms outstretched, fingers running through the sandy earthen dance floor. I'm in the universal grieving pose surrounded by the tallest ancestor pine trees and held by sixty-five acres of sacred land. Tears begin to fall. I start to speak—to chant. I am not broken. I am not broken. Women from the community circle gather around me rattling loudly. One has a large frame drum beating fiercely behind my body. I can feel it in my back and up my spine. I'm supported in their presence. No words. I am seen.

On the last day, I conjure enough courage to let my voice out in a most needed and forgotten manner. I scream three times from the core of my being, keening with the river in the arms of a dear friend, wrapping my spirit with love as the movement of the water carries away some of the suffering. I am awakened.

I claim my power standing in the center of the circle, declaring a new name as a sign of my re-birth. Feeling like a phoenix rising from the ashes, I am now Madrone.

Each summer for over a decade I attended this retreat, co-creating multiple ceremonies for our week-long gathering. We showed up for ourselves, open to being vulnerable and ready to cross important thresholds for healing and growth. My experiences in this community and on the land enabled me to see the world in ways I was not previously accessing. I believe we are born with this sight, but ceremony can facilitate the "switching on." The women in this community taught me the power of ceremony to shift our reality. I wouldn't be the spiritual ceremonialist, community weaver, or facilitative leader I am today without their guidance.

Ceremony has provided a safe space to engage in self-love and healing work related to my chronic low back pain. Through the power of ceremony, I remembered that I wasn't alone, regained hope, practiced self-reflexivity, felt validated, and more. Ceremony helped me see the many gifts in my chronic pain, as dreadful as it may be.

We are all storytelling beings. Stories are how we make sense of and understand the world. In this chapter, I offer you a glimpse into my chronic pain story and the power of ceremony to nurture self-love, lifting us up even when we feel gutted and hopeless. I'll share some thoughts about pain vs. suffering, giving voice to our invisible pain, and honoring mystery. Finally, I offer a self-love ceremonial practice for your chronic pain journey. As with most journeys, there are lessons here related to many human experiences, so please take what resonates and grow.

Often, I feel like my spirit is stronger than my body, and it has been this way for thirty-three years, since I was sixteen, when, as I say, my back left me. I have four degenerated discs in my low back, which means the fluid in my discs does not absorb shock. The importance of these small fluid sacs between our vertebrae is tremendous: discs absorb 350 pounds of pressure per cubic square inch. My degenerative disc disease is genetic. I have spent many years grieving this part of my life, trying to convince myself that

I'm not broken. I live life managing my chronic pain, and when it flares, I cannot walk without assistance for a full week or more.

I'm here to share that grieving is a form of self-love.

PAIN VS. SUFFERING

"If you have a body, you are an athlete."

~ Bill Bowerman (Legendary track coach
at the University of Oregon and Nike co-founder)

Training with chronic pain made me an endurance athlete. Through physical therapy, massage, exercise, acupuncture, and more, I've worked through the pain to avoid surgery and prioritize spiritual expansion and adventure in my life. My back pain has been a great teacher through the years, and ceremony has freed me from the suffering associated with chronic pain.

As an End of Life Doula, we're taught there's a difference between suffering and pain. Suffering is the unpleasant sensation of varying degrees in the *emotional* and *mental* body. It's a human condition and is not obligatory—we don't have to suffer. It's very real, but we can work with it; we can shift out of suffering and into a new understanding.

Pain, on the other hand, is a different beast entirely. It's an unpleasant sensation that we experience of varying degrees. We can't always stop our pain. Perhaps you read that and are now thinking, *yes, you can!* This brings up a point of tension for me over the years that I'd like to discuss. The conversation goes something like this:

"It's so great that you can backpack and walk so many miles!" I say. "That's not something I can do this lifetime. I mean, I love being in nature and going on long walks, but I couldn't carry a pack and sleep on the ground and still walk in the morning."

"Oh, but you can!" They respond enthusiastically and meaning well. "You can do anything you put your mind to. You can heal yourself! You're capable of fully healing your body."

Those of us with chronic pain are skilled at staying open for a miracle while simultaneously navigating the reality of being in relationship with what is happening in the present. Ceremony, magick, and ritual have all illuminated for me that miracles exist. (Just so you know, I spell magick with a *k* to denote it from "top hat magic" with the rabbits and all that. Magick is a form of conscious will.)

And yet, the truth is many people strive to bypass having to feel pain. This sometimes leads to a mentality that you can fix everything, a viewpoint that can be a disservice to people with chronic pain. It just makes us feel bad. It sends the message that there's something wrong with us because we *should* be able to make our pain disappear. It negates all the work we do in physical therapy and with other healing modalities when they're not a cure-all.

Take my hand and follow me down this philosophical rabbit hole for a minute. We know that every entity dies, and because of this, we also know that we very literally cannot heal everything. If we could, we'd be immortal. When we believe we can heal everything to a fault, we may well be accessing deeply held fears of death and suffering, our fear of existing in a world that has pain. We risk enough-ism thinking, *If only I am spiritual enough, I can avoid physical pain.* Ceremony helps us love every *body* regardless of whether your body has limitations, needs to go slow, or needs support.

GIVING VOICE TO INVISIBLE PAIN

Ceremony has helped me hone the skills of my external voice (e.g., asking for support) and recognize my limitations. Chronic pain offers no choice because it is invisible—just like not all disabilities are visible. Sometimes, I wish I was wearing a body cast so people could see I was hurting or wish I had a sign that said, "It's a seven out of ten for pain in here today" to signal sympathy or empathy. There are so many scripts in our world, especially for women, dictating the importance of super-human independence. Yet, we know no one can do life all by themselves. We are riddled with contradiction.

I have accepted that I am magick, not despite my limitations but because of them. Many of the experiential activities that make up a good ceremony are designed to help us dive deeply into who we are and explore our life's purpose. These rituals have given me practice using my voice to directly and clearly ask for what I need from others and from the universe/divine/spirit. The practice of setting strong intentions is key for working with chronic pain as well as creating a powerful ceremony. For example, I used to think to myself, *My back is killing me,* vs now I say, *This is temporary; breathe through it.* In ceremony, we practice setting clear intentions to manifest what is best for our higher good. The voice we give our pain matters.

CHRONIC PAIN AND OUR MIND

Our external voice is essential for our ability to thrive and to be seen. Ceremonial practice has also helped me become extremely attuned to my internal voices. The voices that say things like "Push through this" when you know you shouldn't and those that cheer on thoughts that promote disaster mind. Our language and internal thoughts become so important when we're in acute pain. The whole time I'm in a flare-up, I'm in my head thinking, *I hope I walk again; I've walked after this pain before; I can do this.* As I begin to regain my strength, I am like a child learning to walk again, moving slowly, with focused attention. These flare-ups are a journey with the life, death, rebirth cycle. They are aspects of training to be in our conscious body.

Ceremony offers glimmers of full freedom because in the power of ritual and community, my pain often disappears. It's made less by my endorphins and the energy of the collective. I've done what seems to be impossible: dancing all night to ceremonial drums, walking on fire, and so much more. My practice with ceremony taught me to raise the focused energy of my pain and apply it toward the healing of the planet and others—turning suffering into healing generations past and future.

HOLDING MYSTERY

Through ceremony I've learned valuable teachings about honoring mystery as a gift rather than fearing it as an unknown. This helps me to be able to compartmentalize the fear of a "flare-up" when I'm traveling or adventuring here or overseas and to jump into living more fully. To be clear, I still sometimes cry, get sad, am exhausted from it all, or worry. It takes strength to ask for help, and it takes courage to risk living your life fearlessly. I've worked tirelessly to be okay with the mystery of not knowing what activity will push me over my limit and weaken my ability to function autonomously.

For years, I spent time trying to figure out the 'why' of it all. Over time, I've had to let that go and accept my back pain journey as a tough lesson/ teacher in not needing total understanding but to simply accept the reality of the moment. The over-analytical brain still creeps in on occasion. This usually appears in the form of shoulding myself—*You shouldn't have moved so fast after getting up,* or *Why did you bend down so quickly,* when in reality, I won't ever know what caused my flare-up. My choices are to do the best I can using all my tools or to stay in the cave and not venture out.

Here's some food for thought. Consider how much easier it is for me to stay put. It's easier to not move my body and face little risk vs. inviting movement that can bring possibility, healing, changes, new experiences, and, yes, even flare-ups.

And here is the lesson chronic pain teaches us about life: it takes considerable bravery to embrace the risk(s) involved with movement and change.

May we all grieve fully to make space for more self-love to arise.

Here is a healing self-love practice you can use for any type of chronic or ongoing pain, physical or emotional.

THE SELF-LOVE PRACTICE

THE LIGHT AND THE DARK CANDLE CEREMONY

You will need:

- One candle in a safe container to burn
- A larger sized rock
- Bowl filled with water
- Smaller rocks or pebbles (10-20)
- Some yarn, ribbon, or string to make a circle
- A quiet space with low lighting
- Journal or something to write on and a pen
- Drum, rattle, or chime, or a way to play a song
- Optional—Oracle deck

Setting your space

Place your candle, water bowl, and a large rock in the center of the circle you form using the yarn. You don't have to be sitting inside the circle.

Intentional Symbolism

- The circle represents your community.

- The rock represents you—a strong taproot surviving all the ebbs and flows of your walk with chronic pain.

- The water bowl is reflective of how water holds us for healing. It is, of course, literally cleansing, but it also displaces weight when we enter a body of water, making our body lighter.

Centering

Take three deep breaths, letting out sound on the third one. Do what feels best to center and ground yourself (call in the elements, play music, sing a song, say a prayer, drum, rattle, etc.).

- To begin, I invite you to write a short love letter to those places in your body that have chronically held your pain(s). When you're finished, read the letter out loud.

  Make a note of what bubbled up. What did you voice in the letter? What did those pain points in your body communicate as you wrote to them?

- When you're finished reflecting, place the large stone (symbolizing you) in the bowl of water.

Next, we're going to do a magickal working together. We'll light and blow out a candle multiple times, signifying the challenges and gifts of pain as a threshold or rite of passage in our lives.

Think of your journey with chronic pain as the alchemical process of being like fire, getting blown out, and finding the energy to spark up again and thrive!

First Candle Lighting

Think about what pain point will be the focus for this ceremony.

Say the following out loud: *I light this candle in honor of my strength to endure.*

Light your candle.

- Ask yourself, what vulnerabilities come up for me when dealing with my pain? What have these vulnerabilities taught me about myself? What wisdom was gained?

For example, with my back journey, I might explore, "What does this pain in my core say about my life's path and my security or insecurity about being supported in life?"

- Take five minutes to journal some vulnerabilities that come up related to your chronic pain.

- Next, take the pebbles and put one in the water for each wisdom you've gained through reflecting. *Speak these out loud.*

  These wisdoms help you see the gifts you have received from living with your chronic pain.

- Ring a chime, rattle, or drum for a minute to shift to the next round.

First Candle Dousing

- Sometimes our health is a mystery, making it a complex and difficult road to walk. When you blow out the candle, remember the darkness is filled with all potential. Think of what you love about the mystery of the unknown. *Blow out your candle.*

- Journal about a time(s) when you have felt abandoned, alone, or angry with your chronic pain journey.

- If you feel daring, take a pillow and release these feelings through a scream or Irish keening (wailing and moaning).

  This kind of releasing helps with the stress your body holds, helping you feel better. It can feel weird at first, but just "fake it till you make it" and see what happens. If able, you can also punch a pillow to release.

- Ring a chime, rattle, or drum for a minute to shift to the next round.

Second Candle Lighting

- Think of a time you have navigated pain obstacles on your path and were successful or accomplished with a goal to overcome or manage pain.

- Think back to that moment and give yourself a hug. *Light your candle* in gratitude for how your light shone brightly.

- Ring a chime, rattle, or drum for a minute to shift to the next round.

Second Candle Dousing

- Think of an intention for your future.

- *Speak your intention out loud with conviction. Blow out your candle.*

- Remember that you now carry this flame/light in your heart.

- Draw an oracle card to see who might guide you on your continued journey.

Closing

Pick a song and play it, sing, grab a drum or a rattle. Be with musical rhythms for 5-10 minutes. Whatever feels right for you.

As you listen or play, reflect. Look at the pebbles in the water and celebrate yourself for all the important spirit work you have just done. Acknowledge how much love you have for yourself to honor your walk with chronic pain so intentionally through ceremony.

Notice how the pebbles/wisdoms surround and support the larger rock representing your strong taproot, made up of all you have experienced growing and stretching yourself as a human being learning to love yourself exactly as you are, pain points and all.

To continue the conversation we have started here, please visit my website and download a free giveaway with simple ways to support yourself as you navigate chronic pain flare-ups. It also includes a short coaching recording that you can use for support when you need a light at the end of the tunnel. Reach out, lean in, and let's spin some magick as we co-create a space for you to be you fully!

A lover of mystery and believer in magick, **Madrone Kalil** (She/They) is a community weaver who has led sacred circles and ceremonies for the past eighteen years as an animistic wild witchy womyn! She has years of experience working with the healing powers of nature. Led by her Celtic roots, one thing is for sure; she loves creating rituals and facilitating restorative circles as a safe space for your transformation.

Madrone is the founder of Taproot Journeys LLC, where she supports clients as a certified End of Life Doula for humans and animal companions, is a death and grief coach, retreat and workshop facilitator, educator, certified breathwork facilitator, certified funeral celebrant and spiritual leader, Warrior Goddess trained facilitator, qualified Sundoor Firewalk guide, creator of Threshold Circles and Flagstaff Drumming into the Seasons.

Why Taproot Journeys? Madrone was inspired by the taproot as the strongest in a plant's growth or development. They provide stability as the first anchor in the soil. Taproot Journeys offers you opportunities to explore how your taproot has been nurtured or neglected and how you can cultivate roots of resilience. Read about how others have benefited from growing their taproots on my website: https://www.taprootjourneys.com/testimonials

Madrone holds a Ph.D. in Communication Studies, teaching university courses in interpersonal and inter-natural communication, gender and nature studies, team leadership, and race and gender in media. This gives her a unique and informed perspective as she leads and facilitates communities, helping them open more fully to themselves.

She lives in the snowy mountains of Flagstaff, Arizona, with her wife and fur kiddos. When she isn't manifesting something magickal, she is likely traveling, spending time with loved ones, out in nature, or binge-watching something thought-provoking.

Connect with Madrone:

Giveaway: https://taprootjourneys.com/life-changing

Website: https://www.taprootjourneys.com/

Facebook: https://www.facebook.com/taprootjourneys

Instagram: https://www.instagram.com/taproot.journeys/

Linkedin: www.linkedin.com/in/madrone-kalil

Email: Madrone@taprootjourneys.com

CHAPTER 8

TANTRIC BREATHWORK

HOW TO HAVE SPIRITUAL SEXUAL EXPERIENCES

Alyssa Anaya, M.Div.

MY STORY

THE HALFWAY HOUSE

Is *Andrew okay? He doesn't look like himself today,* I thought to myself as Andrew stared blankly into the distance. All the clients were on hardcore psych medications, and the sunlight on their skin made them appear extra pale and lifeless. They moved in slow motion, somewhere between sleep and awake.

The sun streamed through the windows of the living room so brightly that you could see every bit of dust suspended in the air. The old Victorian house in the mission district of San Francisco that the clients called home had a cozy, stale feeling.

"Raise your hands in the air! Reach up, up, toward the sky, stretch, stretch," I said. One client rolled his eyes, and the other six had their eyes closed, still half asleep as they reluctantly floated their arms slightly upward. They barely stretched. They knew that all they had to do was be in the room to get credit for the morning movement I was guiding here at the halfway house.

Here I am again, taking it personally, feeling insecure and afraid that the clients don't like me.

I swallowed my insecurities and leaned into my stretch, luxuriating as my body opened. This was one of the more enjoyable parts of my job as a counselor for adults with co-occurring disorders: mental illnesses and substance use disorders. They were usually sweet, or at least civil clients, unless, of course, they were psychotic, which was rare.

Though it was pretty challenging, there were reasons to like working there, including helping people in real need get back on their feet. Especially since I, too, have addictive genes and, in a way, felt at home there. Like the clients, I walked through my life longing for something more.

Leaving the halfway house after work that day, I walked a block down the street and ducked into a shaded area next to an apartment building. No one was walking by, so I pulled out my mini blown glass pipe and smoked some weed. *Ahh, sweet relief.*

On a cloud of cannabis high, I focused on the beautiful murals painted on the side of the building. *I wonder how the artist got so lucky to paint murals and get paid for it.* I enjoyed the vibrant colors of paint, flowing designs, and slowly walked toward the train to go home.

I used cannabis to numb myself. Don't get me wrong—I believe in the herb's medicinal qualities—but it was a crutch that was not beneficial in this case. It came from my desire to escape what was challenging in life.

On this particular day, I used it to cope with my job. The clients were a type of shadow because I felt akin to them in a way that scared me.

Both of my grandfathers were alcoholics. Addiction runs through my family lineage and has touched every one of my family members in some way. For me, addiction is the other side of the coin of spiritual longing. The way I have transformed unhealthy substance use into what I would call healthy spiritual desire is through breathwork and meditation.

THE BEGINNING

One day after work, I came home to a blinking message light on my old-fashioned answering machine. When I pressed play, the voice that spoke touched me somewhere deep inside.

"Hello Alyssa, this is Evalena Rose. I am returning your call about my tantra workshop. Call me back if you would like. Be gentle with yourself; be kind to yourself; you deserve it!" she said.

Who is this woman? I like her deep, calm voice. She sounds so warm and caring. I stood there, feeling goosebumps on my skin, my entire being resonating with the soothing sound of her voice. I decided right then and there, *I'm taking that workshop.* Little did I know where my longing would take me.

Tantra is an ancient spiritual tradition originating in India, encompassing practices aimed at achieving union with the divine, often involving meditation, yoga, breathwork, and the transmutation of energy, including sexual energy for spiritual growth.

Neo-tantra is a modern adaptation of tantra that emerged in the West focused on personal growth, self-discovery, and enhanced sensuality. The exercises described in this chapter are considered neo-tantra.

THE TANTRA WORKSHOP

I drove an hour and a half up from San Francisco to the retreat center in the foothills of Sonoma County, where I knew no one. I had a bit of culture shock that began in the opening circle. I always lived in cities and hadn't yet been exposed to this level of crunchy granola hippie-ness. One of the 30 women in the circle sipped a greenish-gray smoothie in a glass jar. *I wonder what is in that smoothie that made it that disturbing color? Could it possibly taste good?*

During the break, the "smoothie woman" processed something urgently with a long, gray-haired woman, in hushed voices still in the main room. *What are they whispering about? I wonder if they are partners.* I wasn't yet used to this, the importance of each woman's emotional process, with just a touch of drama sprinkled on top.

We learned tantric breathwork on the first morning. It was the foundation for everything. At first, it felt unnatural, and my body was stiff. *I wonder if this is ever going to end.* I was breathing in and out in sync with a perfect stranger while looking into her eyes, then another, and another. After a while, my entire being relaxed, and I began to open.

The women were kind, fun, and laughed loudly. There was a self-acceptance many of them exuded that was still foreign to me in my 30-year-old, socially awkward body. We all committed to spending one weekend a month for six months together, learning tantra. We were healing and opening to ourselves together.

There was homework: to practice breathing for about 20 minutes every day. I was inspired and did it almost every day, not because I was disciplined but because I began to get glimpses of that which I longed for.

KUNDALINI OPENING

Not long after I took that initial workshop, I was at home, alone in my studio just after dusk, practicing tantric breathing. My experience transcended anything I'd known before.

My whole body relaxes. I feel my breath deepening, and I'm making loud sounds as I exhale. I'm gently caressing my body, and every touch feels electric, awakening. I'm riding the edge between wanting and having everything I've ever wanted.

The energy fills my body. My pelvis undulates, and I feel energy moving up my spine. I am a bit dizzy and more deeply fulfilled than ever. This is it, this! I am in an altered state of bliss, one with all that is, eternally peaceful, and incredibly turned on.

I allow my fingertips to slide slowly up my thigh and underneath my own underwear, barely touching my labia, just enough to feel how wet I am. The sublime sensation of my own juices on my wet yoni sends a jolt of energy through my entire being. I am love, lover, and beloved; I am human and divine, and this is IT.

I don't need to touch myself anymore. It's an energetic ecstasy I'm experiencing, no need for physical stimulation. I am on fire energetically, and it is all-consuming. I am surrendered to the oneness and more fulfilled than I've ever been in my life.

The next day, I went into work feeling fantastic. The feeling of oneness with the universe still resonated in my being, everything felt more effortless, and I had a sense of abundance inside. I found an increasing harmony with both my clients and coworkers. I wasn't fully aware of what was happening to me. I just knew I felt good.

Later, I realized that I had had a kundalini opening, a.k.a. kundalini rising. All of the tantric breathwork opened my energetic pathways to a deeper level of ecstasy, and from that day forward, I've had countless energetic and full-body orgasms.

Once these pathways are open, physical orgasms become full-body orgasms because the orgasmic energy flows throughout the nervous system to the entire body. Full-body orgasms are a profoundly spiritual, sexual experience. Difficult to put into words as many spiritual experiences are, they take sexual experience to a level I never knew existed. All orgasms are profound, yet full-body orgasms include a shift in consciousness to oneness with all that is. This lasts anywhere from a few minutes to a few days.

LEARNING

The monthly tantra workshops continued. We did several embodiment practices, such as getting naked in front of a small group of women, who encouraged us to love our bodies with genuine adoring comments like, "Your thighs are beautiful!" and "Your breasts are so elegant!" (after breastfeeding and getting saggy). This was heartwarming and did help me feel more comfortable in my own body.

We did LOTS of guided breathwork. Primarily slow, undulating breaths while looking into the eyes of a partner. This practice resulted in a magical falling-in-love feeling of awe of the other person. I remember breathing with a middle-aged woman named Veronica, who had brown eyes and brown hair. *She is exquisitely beautiful and wise. I feel so loved in her presence. I wonder what she's thinking about me. She looks like the most loving person I've ever encountered.* My insecurities melted away with the breath.

We also laid on the floor and did intense emotional release breathwork. I opened my throat chakra and yelled, cried, and released, and then had the most exquisite waves of bliss.

"Tears are really joy, finally coming home."

~ Savanna (singer/songwriter),
from *"She Moves Me"* on *"Breath of Earth, EP"*

The full-body bliss always came after the release, like clockwork. It was a cycle I learned to recognize—breath, tears (release), bliss. Sometimes the release was sounding or screaming. As soon as I deeply let go of whatever I held, my energy shifted into profound peace and joy.

There was much more on the relational level, starting with exercises where we practiced speaking our physical and energetic boundaries to each other. We were also invited to say the hard things to each other. One practice was called "Withholds." Withholds are things you feel towards another but haven't had the courage to say. They are anything that needs to be cleared to be fully present with them.

LOVE

There was a woman in the workshop whom I found myself enamored with named Candra. She was shiny and overwhelmingly attractive to me, and I definitely had a crush. One sunny afternoon, we were outdoors practicing the withhold exercise. I nervously approached her. *My heart is pounding out of my chest. I am so afraid to tell her; what if she gets mad at me because she's in a relationship with someone else?*

"Umm, hi. I have a withhold. I really like you. I think I like you more than friends. I know you're in a relationship, which I completely honor. I just wanted to name it."

Long pause. Candra is looking right into my eyes. I am sweating.

She says, "Thank you."

"Thank you" is what you're supposed to say for the exercise. You're not allowed to dialogue. We namaste and bow to each other and walk away, following the rules of the container.

The following month, Candra echoed my desire to experience more than friendship together. We immediately sat down on a hay bale and started doing tantric breathwork together while looking into each other's eyes.

I feel the deep stirrings of energy, love, and cosmic oneness spread throughout my body. I am so open to the core and feel like my essence is pure light in her presence. This is amazing. I can't fall in love. She's not available. But I feel like I'm falling in love. It's okay; I don't have to do anything about it. It just is.

Outside the workshop, Candra and I continued getting together for private "tantra dates," which means sitting and breathing, opening our kundalini energy together. Because we were both in romantic relationships with other people, we honored our partners by not being sexual, which included no kissing and keeping clothes on.

Our teacher spoke about going slowly through the "gates of intimacy," which meant not rushing into sex or a relationship. This was a beneficial guideline and one that we honored with reverence.

Candra and I did fall in love. We reached incredible states of ecstasy together by breathing and not doing anything physically sexual. Eventually, with our partner's blessings, we did a ritual and opened the relationship. After six months of tantra dates, breathwork, and energetic opening to each other, we finally kissed on the lips. It was like fireworks.

We then went a few more months before getting the blessing from our partners to have sex. It had been nine months since we first breathed together on the hay bale when we surrendered to our love and had mind-blowing spiritual sex.

Over time, we separated from our other partners. We had many deep heart communications among all four of us, several rituals, and ended up all staying very close friends.

Candra and I married and had a child together, whom we're raising to this day. Over time, we transitioned into a platonic relationship. We still live together in harmony with our daughter and our family.

Also, to this day, I practice the middle path with substances: everything in moderation. My occasional desire to feel high or escape what's hard is easily remedied by a few minutes of tantric breathwork or meditation. Now I know that at the heart of all longing is spiritual longing. I am evolving my family lineage with spiritual practices.

WHAT HAPPENED NEXT

Within that first year of learning tantra, I got promoted to assistant director of the halfway house in San Francisco, fell in love, and moved to a better home. All of these "upgrades" were due to my inner shifts as a result of tantric breathwork.

I now teach tantra to hundreds of people every year, helping them open their kundalini energy to achieve greater depths of fulfillment. My lineage of tantra comes from my teacher and mentor, Evalena Rose, who I will forever be grateful to, for transforming my life with her teachings.

THE SELF-LOVE PRACTICE

TANTRIC BREATHWORK

Tantric breathwork is a practice that involves conscious and controlled breathing techniques, often used in tantra to enhance awareness, energy circulation, and connection between partners during intimate experiences.

We're breathing and moving our energy up our spine to awaken our kundalini energy. Kundalini energy is the life force, the energy that runs through you and through everything. By doing this specific breathwork, we open our pathways to increased life force flow.

SOLO TANTRA BREATH

1. **Create ambiance.** Go into a quiet space in your home where you will not be interrupted by pets, children, phones, etc. Put on slow, peaceful music you enjoy. Light a candle or lower the lights.

2. **Get comfortable.** Make yourself comfortable sitting, ideally cross-legged on a zafu or meditation cushion. Sit on the first third of the pillow. Add pillows under your knees if this helps you be more comfortable. You can also sit on a chair or even lie down. The important thing is that you're comfortable enough to relax. Wear loose-fitting clothing so you can move easily.

3. **Breathe - tantric breathwork has three main components:**

   • **Breath.** Begin by deepening the breath, breathing extra slowly, as in slow motion, into the bottom of your belly. Breathe in through the nose and out through the mouth. Exhale fully and completely.

   • **Movement.** Undulate your hips, gently rocking them forward and backward. Open your chest a bit on the inhale and round your back a little on the exhale. This is a natural movement; your body already knows how to do this. It's similar to the undulation of having sex.

   • **Sound.** Allow yourself to make an audible sigh or a gentle "Haaaaa" sound on the exhale. The sound vibration opens the throat chakra and expands the kundalini energy throughout the body.

4. **Work up to 20 minutes.** If this is your first time doing breathwork, set a timer for two minutes and stop there. The next day, do it for three minutes. Then five, ten, and eventually 20 minutes. Any time of day that works for you is excellent—morning, afternoon, or evening. If you can't do it daily, three times a week will still have positive results. Forty days of regular practice will result in profound, positive internal and external shifts in your life.

You may experience tingling in your hands or feet, your body shaking, or spontaneous movement when you breathe. These are a normal part of kundalini awakening; they are Kriyas. The energy is clearing out blocks and opening you to new pathways of pleasure and spiritual experience. Enjoy!

SPIRITUAL SEXUAL EXPERIENCE

Bring tantric breathwork into the bedroom with a lover, partner, or spouse. It's the best foreplay! When breathing with another, face each other and synchronize your breath while looking softly into each other's eyes.

During lovemaking, take breaks from kissing to breathe together. When the eros (erotic energy) rises, consciously bring in the tantric breath. Breathe and take a long time, letting your sacred sexual energy fill you before touching one another's genitals. Touch each other in slow motion.

Do everything in slow motion, with your entire presence. Don't strive for orgasm; enjoy every moment as it is. When you treat your partner with reverence in this way, spirit enters, and oneness ensues.

Alyssa Anaya is a certified sacred sexuality practitioner and tantra guide based in the San Francisco Bay Area. For over 20 years, she has been studying, practicing, and teaching tantric traditions from around the world aimed at helping individuals and couples unlock their potential for deep intimacy, sexual fulfillment, and spiritual connection.

Alyssa holds a Master of Divinity in spiritual counseling and is currently pursuing a doctorate in human sexuality from California Institute of Integral Studies. She has undergone extensive training from renowned teachers Evalena Rose, Sofia Sundari, and Lindy James to become a qualified practitioner of sacred sexuality and tantric arts.

In her private practice, Alyssa works with clients to help them overcome sexual and intimacy challenges utilizing tantric breathing, meditation, and mindfulness techniques. Her approach aims to empower individuals and couples to move beyond limiting beliefs about sexuality into realms of deeper fulfillment and transcendence. She also facilitates tantra workshops under the name Reverence.

Alyssa's work honors the sacredness of sexuality by bringing the divine in through breathwork, meditation, and ritual. She works with clients in coaching sessions focused on creating self-awareness, improving communication skills, reconnecting with the body's erotic potential, and establishing a sense of reverence in one's intimate relationships.

Alyssa views sexuality as a pathway to heal wounds, awaken creativity, deepen bonds with others, and experience higher states of awareness. Her life's work is dedicated to guiding others on their journeys towards embracing the totality of themselves and living each moment with full presence and passion.

For a visual on tantric breathing, you will find a video on her website here: http://www.reverenceoftheheart.com/resources

Connect with Alyssa:

Website: https://reverenceoftheheart.com/

Facebook: https://www.facebook.com/ReverenceOfTheHeart

Instagram: https://www.instagram.com/reverenceoftheheart/

Email: alyssa@reverenceoftheheart.com

Phone: 707-861-8692

CHAPTER 9

SAYING YES TO ME

COMMITTING TO SELF-LOVE FOR AMPLIFYING LIFE

Heather Westling

*"The hardest part of the journey
is believing you are worthy of the trip."*

~ Glenn Beck

MY STORY

Wow! What a view! I never thought I would be seeing this at all. I love this view. Just think, you were going to be inside a cold cement building with four walls for ten-plus years, a metal bed, sounds of slamming metal doors, and no privacy while looking out a two-by-five window with a barbed wire fence confining you.

I walked along a trail, with tiny rocks paving the way, roots from the trees bursting through the path, and the sidelines filled with green trees, wildflowers, and rocks. The fresh, crisp air hit my face, and I heard the crunching sound of pebbles underneath my feet from each step I took.

I arrived at the top of Devil's Courthouse, where there was a mini half wall made of rock. The view was expansive and priceless, with fresh mountain air. The mountains in the distance were never-ending, and the different ridges showed the depth of each. There was a metal map that pinpointed a few of the main mountain ranges.

As I stood up there, taking in the panoramic view, I was taken back to how I got to this place. There were so many reasons I should've never been there.

I am so glad I took this risk and followed my heart, intuition, and dreams.

I lived with my parents back in Tennessee. I had lived on my own for a little over a year prior but then moved back in with them. A part of me was feeling that I would never get out of their house, that I'd always be stuck there with them.

I was going through a dark time and was on a six-year probation (the story behind that and what empowered me to say yes to me and freedom, you can read in "Shaman Heart, Sacred Rebel, Chapter 8, Breaking the Chains: Seeking Freedom From Confinement and Living Your Life").

"I can't wait till I get through this probation. I am ready to move out of my parent's house and be on my own. With my own personal space and freedom."

When probation was completed, I felt freedom. I decided one day that I wanted to work at a veterinarian's office and began a job at an animal hospital as a veterinary assistant in North Carolina. I finally moved out of my parent's house and purchased my own place. I felt more freedom and personal space. I accomplished this by believing in and loving myself and by doing personal work.

I was scared out of my wits of being free, even though this was something I longed for. After a while, I began to be less fearful and went about my days.

I was going to work and began an online school to become a Veterinary Technician. This drove me towards freedom. After a couple of years, I developed a lack of motivation and lost interest in the Vet Tech Program. I began to develop a passion for my true life in the legal field. This was a detour to strengthen my ability to not react to triggers or become angry with feelings of becoming a ticking timebomb.

I lost interest in the Veterinary Technician program completely, and work was becoming a job. I began to have similar feelings, like *I no longer need to do this.* The same situation happened when I was working in law enforcement. My soul was preparing me for my true dream.

My true dream is to work in the legal field. I wanted to work in the criminal law field. The first time was back in 2012 when I graduated from the Sheriff's Department Academy. After a couple of years of being on patrol, I resigned.

I'm not meant to be an officer on the streets. I am meant to be somewhere else, but where?

It was to work within the court infrastructure. I completed so much healing work around the traumas from the past that I was empowered to go back into it.

I realized the vet job was a temporary placement until I was not triggered as easily by anything law-related. When the show Cops came on, I watched it, and it had no effect on me whatsoever. I knew then I was ready. Then, things began to spiral into a downward motion with the vet job and to rise up into the legal field.

When I spiraled into depression, I felt "off." I talked to the head veterinarian and asked for a week-long sabbatical. I went back to my parent's house because I felt scared and unsafe to be by myself. In the past, when I had my apartment for a year, I stayed on my own and self-harmed by cutting.

I recognized the pattern and behavior of self-destruction. I gained this awareness by doing deep personal work. After the week's sabbatical, I returned to work. When I entered, my mind just shut down. My body and soul knew what the day would entail: people not doing their jobs and the loss of passion in this field.

Mid-day, I talked to the hospital manager in the office.

"Hey. I need to talk to you."

"What do you need to talk about?"

"I just want to thank you for the opportunity to work here and the experience. However, I need to put in my two-week notice. I am not feeling right, and my mental health is shot."

"How about taking a longer sabbatical, and when you're ready to return, let us know."

"No. I'm only staying for two weeks. Plus, I'm starting school in April for Paralegal studies, and it's an accelerated course. I don't know how much work it's going to be. When my two weeks are up, I am leaving. I can't stay here."

"Well, I wanted to talk to you about your performance. I have received many accolades for your hard work. And since we have some money in the budget, we are giving raises. You would be making this amount starting next month."

"Thanks, but I won't be working here anymore. This is becoming toxic, and my mental health is not good. I don't feel right."

"Just take the rest of the day off, and when you come back in two days, let me know what you decide."

Two days later, I was triggered at work. I started to relapse to an old pattern and went off on a co-worker and doctor. I stormed outside for a few minutes and cried angrily.

I can't do this anymore. This is becoming toxic to me. I am aware of this old pattern and behavior, and I don't want to be like it was nine years ago. I need to think of myself and my mental health.

I went back inside and to the hospital manager's office.

"I can't wait for the two weeks. I need today to be my last day."

"Are you sure? Why not take some personal time…"

"No. Today needs to be my last day. I can't do this anymore, and I am scared I may hurt someone. I'm scared I may do something that would get me in trouble, and I don't want that. I am starting school in April."

"Ok. If that's what you need to do, I'll respect that."

He typed out a resignation letter for me. I read and signed it. It was stating how I am pursuing my dream in the legal field. *Maybe I should stay? Just extend my sabbatical for a couple of weeks, then come back? The pay is good. Or is he saying this to get me to stay? Does he really care? He showed empathy, but is it true? Am I crossing my boundaries if I say, 'Yes, I'll stay?' Ugh.*

I signed it and left. Knowing I was not returning. Walking to the car was hard. I felt many emotions and thoughts, but it was for the better. I cried when I got into the car and screamed.

I can't believe I did this. Was this meant to be? Why are you doing this? Can't you just suck it up and get through it? You were just offered a raise! Yes, but is it worth my mental health? My mental sanity?

I avoided my co-workers because I did not want to deal with them. All these emotions started showing up when I looked at South College for their

Paralegal program in December. When I said yes to that, my soul knew I needed to leave the toxic environment. The veterinary field was not my dream. It was a temporary dream to strengthen my self-love.

I had no reaction or anger when I watched Cops. I never was able to watch that show ten years ago. But now, I can watch it. Is that what I'm supposed to do in my life? Yes, I will have to fight harder than most people because of my felony, but there are felons out there who are lawyers. This is what my purpose is. I can do this!

My decision to leave the animal hospital was from my intuition and boundaries. I had previous experiences where I ignored those feelings, and bad shit happened. I was no longer going to ignore the feelings and suck it up. I was aware of what might happen if I didn't and did.

Should I just stay since I would be making more money and have benefits? Maybe I should suck it up, butter cup? Am I being a crybaby and a weakling? I think I should have stayed because of the pay and benefits. But is it worth my mental health?

I didn't have time to sit with it and see if I could just do part-time. I knew I had to leave permanently. I cared and loved myself too much to destroy myself again. I came too far to destroy my life and health. This freedom was what I longed for for so long. I fought hard like a boxer in a ring defending his title.

Great. What am I supposed to do now? I am lost and have no idea what I want to do. Should I look for a part-time job somewhere? I don't want to go back to that toxicity of an environment.

I looked for a part-time job and found one. I knew this would be temporary. I took a pay cut, and it was worth it. I am working towards my main dream of what I am called to do, working in the legal field and being a voice for those who are lost. I began to feel I had a life and could do the things I was passionate about. I felt passion about teaching the tools that support and make me stronger.

The amount of schoolwork is intense. A part of me is glad I left when I did. Even working part-time there, I would still be in the same mental health status. My soul knew if I stayed, I would probably spiral back into a mental breakdown and start self-harm again. I listened and followed my intuition.

Saying yes to myself has not always been easy. I hit some speed bumps along the way and learned the hard way. This time, I listened. It was for the better. My mental health is better, not burned out, and stronger. I was aware of my behaviors that would have led to negative consequences.

I was shocked by my level of awareness about feeling "off." If I had stayed because of the pay raise and benefits, I felt I may have done or said something to get me into trouble, either with the manager telling me I was on suspension or police showing up and escorting me out in handcuffs, which I knew I didn't need.

This was preparing me for something better. I worked hard to be where I am today, and I didn't want to screw up. I put up with limited freedom for so long and fought for full freedom. I am back on the path where I know I belonged.

THE SELF-LOVE PRACTICE

As I continued to do my self-love practice routinely, I noticed changes within myself. I listened more to that gut feeling and was not going to be in situations where I was losing it. I have had horrible mental breakdowns because I was sucking it up. Let's just say it was not worth it.

Staying with this practice made me more aware of my physical, emotional, and mental states. This made me stronger and more confident when boundaries were crossed. When I have questions about a situation, I follow this practice to receive guidance on what my next steps may be.

This self-love practice is completed at night before sleep. While sleeping, the dream state offers you insight into what you need to receive. If you can't remember your dream, there are ways to recall. Have a journal near your bed, and in the morning time, write down what you dreamed about and what thoughts or songs pop up when you wake.

Create a sacred space with an altar, with no distractions. This will be your sacred meditation space. Decorate your altar with what you feel called to put on it. Have at least one item to represent you; place a cloth, statutes, candles, crystals, feathers, incense, or whatever you feel should be placed on it based on your intention.

If you cannot light candles or have smoke sensitivities, you can create it your way. Use your imagination to create a candle in the mind's eye. The following steps are a guide to this self-love practice:

First, take a shower or bath to help wash away the energies of the day. Light a candle to make it more relaxing, and imagine the flame burning that no longer serves you. Imagine the water being white light, washing and cleansing your body. When done, extinguish the flame.

Second, light candles and incense in your sacred space and take a deep breath. Play some meditation or drumming music. This is to help you focus on your intention for this meditation. Close your eyes, take a few more deep breaths, and call in whoever you feel called to: elements, God/Goddess, Creator, spirit guides, animals, Mother Earth, etc.

Third, after calling in, state your intention or question for this mediation. This meditation could also be turned into a ritual. Follow your intuition. It may be you need to sit and listen or need to burn something. There is no time frame on how long it needs to be.

Fourth, when you feel it is complete, thank whoever you called in and yourself, and extinguish the flames. Head to bed and sleep. The intention through meditation is programmed in the subconscious mind. Avoid much action afterward, such as cleaning, folding laundry, checking Facebook or Instagram, talking on the phone, etc. The dream state will give you messages in visual form. Journal when you wake up before starting your day.

This is helpful when you don't have time during the day for yourself. It's a way to release all from the day and to refresh your mind, body, and spirit in resting form. To feel rejuvenated the next day. It is a way to connect within and feel what is coming up. A time to release and listen. A time for you.

Heather Westling, "Grace Eagle Heart," is a Shamanic Ordained Minister, certified Holy Fire III Reiki Master/Teacher, Karuna Reiki Practitioner, Shamanic Breathwork and Toltec Sacred Journey Breathwork Facilitator, Personal Freedom Coach, and Elemental Priestess.

Her knowledge and wisdom today of what works and what doesn't have shifted her life. The journey in life continues to grow and expand in ways that were never imagined. Heather shares her wisdom and tools for those who feel confined and limited. She understands the struggles when you want to live life, but the traumas hold you back.

From her experiences with these tools, she sees how powerful she can be. Her traumas don't make decisions or hinder her in life anymore. She makes her own decisions based on her heart and intuition. She knows what it's like to not live your authentic life. Take the risk to do the things you are called to do. This empowers you in your life.

Heather continues to do her personal work, diving deep within. Her willingness made her stronger and more empowered. When she thought *this was the best it was going to get,* other opportunities showed up. She traveled to Mexico in January 2023 and became an author in a collaborative book project.

She became stronger, more aware of her patterns, and took back her power. Her traumas no longer control her emotionally or mentally.

Heather is strongly connected to Mother Earth and loves bringing in a ceremonial touch. She enjoys being out in nature and loves animals and gardening.

Even in the darkness, you still have the power.

Website: www.sacredlifesjourney.com
Facebook: Sacred Life's Journey - www.facebook.com/sacredlifesjourney
Instagram: https://www.instagram.com/sacredlifesjourney/
LinkedIn: https://www.linkedin.com/in/heather-westling-069545119

CHAPTER 10

NATURE'S HEALING WINGS

A GRATITUDE PRACTICE TO EMPOWER SELF-WORTH

Lydia Greenwoods

MY STORY

I strayed across the road from our house to the park, plopping down under my favorite tree. I heard my sister, Gracie, giggle. Her boyfriend, Matt, gripped Gracie's jaw and yanked her face to his. "You're lucky you have me. No one else would put up with you." He groped in her bag and pulled out something.

"I need money." Snatching her hair, he hissed at her. She closed her eyes and their lips met. Next thing, Matt was shoving Gracie face down onto the ground. "Now you look as good as you taste." He sniggered while she coughed out grains of soil.

"Like roses?" Gracie joked, fluttering her eyelids while twisting her mother's ring off and on.

"Yeah, whatever."

More kids Gracie's age arrived in the park and started flicking lit matches into the air and burning twigs. Matt kicked Gracie. "Hey, isn't that our science teacher watching us? She's your sister, right? Get rid of her."

Gracie stomped over, "Stop spying. You're my sister, not my mother."

I lowered my head, "Sorry Gracie. Didn't mean to, but it's my job to protect you."

"No, it's not. I'm sixteen and can protect myself. Besides, I'm moving downstate with Matt after the summer break. You won't have to worry about me anymore. Now leave us alone." She snapped her nails against my cheeks before running back to Matt.

She threatened this before, but now that she is older, she could do it. I've tried so hard these last four years to look after her. How do I stop her?

I thumped my head against the tree, drumming my pen on my notebook.

Matt yelled, "Let's light my fireworks to celebrate the summer holidays. No more school!"

Gracie stood motionless. Matt sneered at her.

I jumped up. I knew Gracie wouldn't say anything. She was like me at that age, afraid she'd lose her boyfriend. He is so abusive. I couldn't bear for her to suffer like I did. But what do I do? I'm only six years older. I'm hardly qualified.

Matt punched Gracie. "Chicken? I'll do it without you." He thundered off with fireworks under his arm.

Gracie scraped her fingers through her scalp. I crept over to her and tried to speak but my vocal cords tightened into knots.

I'm only a trainee teacher. Will they even listen to me outside of school? Maybe a parent will come and say something.

I scrunched up my eyes as Gracie dug her nails into my arm. We shivered while Matt played with fire.

Gunpowder, smoke, and noise crackled down around us. "Gracie, I don't know how to stop this. Please come home." I begged. She nodded and we slunk away.

Bird song outside my window woke me. Gracie was already in the park with Matt. He elbowed her and darted off when I approached. "Need any money for today?" I held out my purse. Gracie bit her lip, took the money, and bolted over to Matt. He dragged her to a bench out of sight.

She was right not to want me around. She blames me for our parents. I blame myself. I should have stopped them that night. I knew the roads were icy. Now they're dead.

I drifted towards my tree. Grumbling, I rifled through the pile of bills. Pushing them aside, I frowned while an ant crawled across my fingers, clasping an egg twice its size. It tilted its head up at me. Placing my thumb near the ant hill, it scurried down. My notebook and bill pile slid off my lap and I closed my eyes, soaking up the sensations.

Later, Gracie joined me under my tree.

"Have you been crying? You okay?" I asked.

"Stop interfering. You can't fix me. Just like you can't fix yourself." She grumbled, gripping her wrists.

I draped my arms over her. Kids nearby were snickering and throwing stones at cans. I offered Gracie a notebook and felt tips from my bag. "I like my notebook. This one was Mom's. She once told me drawing helped her see the world differently."

Gracie jammed her hands into her pockets. "I'm useless at art."

"No one is useless; besides, it doesn't have to be pictures. You could write words or poetry or feelings." I mumbled.

Gracie flung the notebook at me. It lay dormant in my lap. All my tomorrows will be worse if I don't do something about this today. And yet, I sat there. Shadows stretched down to meet me, and grey clouds skidded across the sky.

A tiny tweet trilled in the tree far above. A rustling of leaves drifted on the breeze, and with it, a brown bird clattered to the ground beside us. It lay on its side, barely breathing. We both jumped and stared at it. Gracie pointed to a nest high in the branches. Peeping floated through the boughs.

I gingerly placed my hand on the bird's chest. It opened its beak but made no sound. "There's blood on its wing. I think it might be broken." I wrapped my jacket around the bird.

"Lydia, will it die if it can't fly? What will happen to the babies? They're helpless. You have to fix this." Gracie plucked at my arms.

"I don't know. But I'll get my first aid kit and the bird crumble from last week's science experiment." I laid the bird in Gracie's arms and she started to hum.

I only had a basic knowledge of animal wellbeing so I hoped it was enough. I showed Gracie how to drip-feed the bird, and she giggled when it nipped her finger. Then we hunted for grubs and worms for the chicks.

Gracie climbed the tree to the nest. "Lydia, they're letting me feed them. They're ripping the worms from my fingers! They're so big. They're trying to fly." Gracie sang above the loud tweeting.

"That's a great sign. They'll still need lots of feeding but should be able to survive on their own soon." I called up, sighing gently.

In the morning, I heard the door slam. From the window, I saw Gracie running to Matt in the park. He pinned Gracie's arms behind her, flung her to the ground and ransacked her bag. Scrambling to catch up with him, she stuffed things back into her bag and cried out to him.

I shook my head and then went to check on the bird. It was still breathing and I held her in the sunshine. Gracie returned later and I said, "I think the bird will heal faster if she's warm at night. Please, will you help me make a nest box?"

Gracie picked at a strawberry, squashing it to a pulp, then smudged it against the bird's beak. I showed her my nest box design from my notebook and she snorted. "You need a framework first. I learned how to do this in shop."

By sunset, we had a snuggly box for mama bird. Gracie smiled and drew a hummingbird flying over yellow honeysuckle on the lid. A bee landed on it. "It's looking for pollen from a box." Gracie laughed and tossed a flower at me.

"Let's wedge the box into that limb so that mama can hear her chicks but the dogs can't reach her," I suggested.

"Good idea."

After dinner, Gracie said, "I'm going out with Matt." She didn't wait for me to respond. Night after night she came back late, barging into cupboards and doorframes. But each morning, she hauled me out of bed to feed mama and her chicks. Blueberries speckled the bushes around us which we munched on till lunchtime. Fragrant roses clustered into a riot of color while the days rolled across the mountaintops.

One afternoon, as Gracie was holding mama bird, Matt stormed over. "Come on. Let's hang."

Without looking up, Gracie murmured, "Maybe later."

Wow, Gracie. I'm proud of you. I scribbled in my notebook. Matt glowered at me and I lowered my eyes quickly. I chewed on the end of my pen. An ache between my ears made me wince.

Matt growled and then marched off. Gracie let out all her breath at once, "You still have Mom's notebook?"

"Yes, in my bag." I smiled as I handed it to her. She read through the notes and then stopped at a picture of a bird. She picked up a pen and drew a tree behind the bird, adding little hearts around the border. Gracie showed her notebook to mama bird as she rocked her in her lap. "See this? It's you and your babies flying free." I felt like bursting into song.

Sitting with our birds the next day, Gracie opened a new page in the notebook and doodled words. They crisscrossed into a colorful mosaic as the tree branches above us swayed in time to an unheard symphony. Gracie dug her toes into the soil and flicked it at me. I held my breath and her nose wrinkled as she laughed.

The summer melted like golden honey dripping off sunflowers. Mama bird blinked her yellow-rimmed eyes at the chirping of her chicks. They were thriving. Was that because of Gracie? She seems so much more confident, even happier. Perhaps mama bird had given her a sense of purpose. Maybe as Gracie heals mama, mama is healing Gracie? I know Gracie has more to offer the world than being someone else's punching bag. Perhaps she sees this too?

I leaned against the tree. Gracie snuggled mama bird into the nest box. She kissed her head and then murmured, "You're going to make it. You have to, for your babies' sake."

That night I looked through my notebook. Things were getting better. I hadn't realized that until I read back over the months. Maybe, I don't need to think about yesterday's pain or worry about tomorrow. Maybe, I need to be grateful for small forward steps. I closed my eyes listening to Gracie humming in her bedroom.

At breakfast, Gracie beamed, "Today, I'm going to reunite mama with her babies." Her hair whooshed around her face as she raced to the park

"Lydia!" She howled. "The nest box is gone!"

I charged towards her, my heels flapping.

Gracie's head flopped back and forth. She tore at her clothes and ripped pages from her notebook. My heart began to bleed.

We accosted people all day, but no one saw anything.

Eventually, the screeching chicks forced Gracie to sit on the tree limb and feed them. "How could someone do this to them? To their mama? To me? They're murdering nature!" Gracie shrieked at the top of her lungs. People stared. Her eyes wobbled in their sockets and she beat her legs with her fists.

"I have to look again. Someone must know something." Gracie trudged towards the picnic area and disappeared.

I shuffled through the dark park. A damp drizzle clung to my clothes. Tripping into a hole, I tumbled sideways, bashing my knee on a rock. Fractured pain punctured my leg. I collapsed. My body coiled around a cold stone, and my cheek clashed on its slimy surface. A frosty wetness dulled my bones. I struggled to a sitting position, then felt an arm wrap around my shoulder.

"Lydia. I can't find mama."

"Me neither," I croaked back. My leg had stopped throbbing.

"I feel so lost without her. She needed me and I let her down."

"No Gracie, you cared, and you gave her a fighting chance." I stuttered.

"Everything in my life leaves me." Gracie's raspy voice grated against my ears.

"Not me."

"Because you can't. I know you don't really want to look after me."

"No, please. I want to. I need to. I know you blame me for killing our parents. I have to make it up to you. I must protect you. There isn't anyone else. Just us." I clutched at my throat. Tears drenched my shirt till I shivered.

"Lydia, you egg! I don't blame you. I hate you being my mother. I'd rather you were my sister and we could do things and be free. I know you've done so much for me since they died. I'm sorry I wasn't grateful." Gracie leaned over but lost her balance and fell on my knee.

I groaned loudly.

"Lydia, you're hurt. Come on. Let's get out of this rain." Gracie helped me hobble home. We stayed up with hot chocolates, sharing memories of our parents, crying and laughing.

Late the next morning, I heard Matt's voice at the door. I rubbed my knee, grateful it was just a bruise.

Gracie squealed. "Lydia, look. Matt found the nest box. Mama's alive!" Mama bird was snuggled in her arms.

"Hooray!" I stroked Gracie's head.

"Yeah. Your 'precious' bird squawked all night." Matt complained.

"Wait. What? When did you find her and where?" Gracie demanded.

Matt pointed to me. "That tree where she sits and watches us. It was just a joke. You were supposed to come to me for help."

"Did you take her? On purpose?" My voice was quiet but as high-pitched as a siren.

"What's it to you?" Matt snarled at me then turned to Gracie. "You should be grateful I brought it back. Could have left it anywhere. Teach you to ignore me."

Gracie's teeth crunched and her fingers curled into a ball. "You were jealous of my bird?"

"What? No." Matt stumbled backward as Gracie stamped her feet up and down.

"Get out! I can't believe I wanted to live with you. Get out!" Gracie roared.

Matt reversed out the door and scurried up the street.

Gracie crumpled into my arms. "Do you think mama will be okay?"

"She will be now." I held Gracie tightly.

A few days later, we were under our tree with Gracie cuddling and cooing to mama bird. "What do you think of my poem?" Gracie asked as she read from her notebook.

"Flowers will bloom whether you see them or not,

Bird song will still dance in the trees.

The sun will still shine with all that it's got,

Every new day is yours to seize."

"I love it," I whispered.

Mama bird pecked at the notebook, then pushed against Gracie's chest. Breaking free, she flew to her chicks, who were tweeting and beating their wings.

Gracie twirled us around until the spinning world caught up with us and we toppled to the grass. Then Gracie's grin faded. "Matt has moved to his father's house. I was so desperate to be loved. I thought I needed him for that. I'm sorry I let you down."

"Gracie, I'm the one who let you down. Please forgive me." I stammered.

Gracie laced our fingers together and held them against the tree. She broke away only to fling her arms around my neck and squeeze me. She planted our notebooks against our hearts, then clasped my hand in hers. "I love you, sis."

"I love you too, Grace."

THE SELF-LOVE PRACTICE

A GRATITUDE PRACTICE TO EMPOWER SELF-WORTH

Daily journaling has many benefits. It allows us time to slow down and breathe, taking a moment for ourselves amongst the chaos. It creates space to reflect on thoughts and feelings and to notice things in ourselves that we may have subconsciously ignored. Journaling can be anything we need it to be. Some days we may have lots to say, others, a couple of words. It could be a detailed account of the day, with things we are grateful for, or a moment that made us smile. Journaling includes both positive emotions and challenges because it is easier to untangle our emotions when we take the time to identify them. Journaling helps us reflect on past decisions and the results. It can be a letter of hope, a guide, or a reminder of happy moments. Spending time with ourselves allows a deeper understanding of how we think, react, and what we need. It helps us to better love ourselves and others, motivates us to make new, informed, inspired choices, nurtures our well-being, and helps us to respond more positively to life's obstacles. The more we write, the more we observe and the more connected we will feel to ourselves and the people and world around us.

Week 1

Go outside/open a window. Close your eyes and listen to the sounds. Breathe deeply.

Daily, observe surroundings. Watch a tree dance, birds fly, rainfall, or shadows flicker. Write one thing that you see, hear, smell, touch, and taste. Write more if you wish, or draw pictures. At the end of the day, when you have completed these, you will feel a sense of accomplishment and gratitude for taking this time for yourself.

Week 2

Sip a hot drink/enjoy some chocolate. Savor the tastes.

Daily, think about a moment that day that made you feel something positive. Write down at least three words that describe how you feel at this moment. Praise yourself for taking this time.

Week 3

Imagine placing your thoughts on their own leaf and letting them float down a stream. Observe them from a distance, acknowledge their existence, and let them go.

Daily, write at least three things you are grateful for and why. Notice how often you feel grateful; praise yourself every time. Incorporating gratitude into our daily lives can help us be more mindful of beautiful things and moments in life we otherwise may overlook. If you do this consistently, life will feel fuller.

GRATITUDE SUGGESTIONS

Friends/family

Pets

Delicious food

Good sleep

Time for journaling

Health

Small happy moments

Achievements at work/home/life

Upcoming events

Sunshine/air/water

Music/art/dance/laughter

Desire to improve.

Faith

Week 4

Check in with a friend or family member. Ask them how they are. Help them with their challenges. This will generate a sense of connection, value, and self-worth. It will also help distract you from your worries.

Repeat your favorite week's activity that helped you the most. Write down why it resonated with you and how it helped. What were your reactions? What are the results?

Lydia Greenwoods is the author of Nature's Healing Wings; A Gratitude Practice to Empower Self-Worth from the book The Life Changing Power of Self-Love. An Essential Guide. Lydia's writing encompasses healing through nature. A passion she lives with daily and encourages others to incorporate into their thinking, writing, and being. She writes fiction and nonfiction and is embarking on the journey of publishing a children's book about animals who save their homes from the destruction caused by humans.

Lydia works with charities saving endangered species and raising awareness and funds. She helps teach us how to be good stewards of this fragile earth. As an environmentalist, her knowledge of healing always incorporates our natural settings. Lydia emphasizes that often the easiest route to healing is to spend time outdoors, soaking up the sounds, smells, and sights. This will enrich our thoughts and show us the magnificence of the creation around us. Being grateful for such an intricate, fragile life opens our hearts to praise, love, and worth both of ourselves and the life around us.

Lydia recommends writing outside, regardless of the weather, so that nature can flow through us and cleanse us anew. Writing down our feelings, observing nature around us, incorporating how we have responded to situations, and then periodically reviewing what we keep in our journals gives us the opportunity to learn from challenging situations, identify progress and growth, and foster our self-worth as we see small forward steps in our life.

For more information and personal connection, go to https://www.Facebook.com/LydiaGreenwoods We'll share ideas. Encourage each other. Discuss goal setting. Understand the consequences of various path choices. Celebrate victories. Lydia offers individual guidance and suggestions but be prepared to get outside and sometimes get wet.

CHAPTER 11

SYNERGIZE SCIENCE WITH SOUL

HOW I BRAVED A ONE-IN-A-BILLION STATISTIC

Candra Anaya

MY STORY

Any second, the two loves of my life would arrive home and my words would obliterate the ordinary from our lives.

My daughter, Lil' G, I called her, completed our triple goddess family with her other mom and me. She was 17 months old, and while she didn't understand our words, she absorbed our energy like a sponge. Since day one of her existence, the vocal exchange between her two moms created thousands of echoes that embraced her as she grew into formation inside the womb. The frequency of our voices was otherwise internalized until she developed her ability to hear. How many times did she sense me lay my hands on Love's belly while singing *Patience,* or *Sweet Child O' Mine?* How much of our laughter reverberated in the womb Lil' G knew as home?

I agonized, knowing there was nothing I could say to lessen today's blow. What I could do, though, was make damn certain Lil' G was in the safest place in the world surrounded by her familiars. I imagined us nestled into the pillows of our lush, purple velvet couch where we breastfed Lil' G a thousand times before. I'd wrap her in her favorite blanket, the one with soothing pastels that her goddess-mother hand-knit, and delicately pass her over to Love, who would cradle her to the breast. Sitting down, I'd wrap my arms around my family, and once Lil' G was happily nursing, I'd whisper the news in the calmest tone I could possibly muster. Embodying the eye of the hurricane, I'd create calm for us, even amidst the devastation.

Spontaneously, I flashed on Lil' G's birth. I sang softly to Love in the operating room. A curtain barrier divided us from Love's lower half of her body and the surgical team delivering our baby. Suddenly, we were sprayed by what felt like rain, and the doctor shouted, "STAT!"

Instinctively, I reached up to wipe my face dry, and red blood covered my fingertips. My chest erupted; my heart swept away in a stampede of panic as I registered whether this was Love's blood on my cheeks or our daughter's.

Holy fuck- there's no guarantee either one is coming out alive.

I was spinning, but I was sitting, and everything started whirling, faster and faster, until all the objects blurred into one. *Oh god, no! I'm gonna black out.*

Love's despairing voice cracked sharply through my terror, a lightning bolt that jolted me back into my body. "Please!" Love begged. "Please keep singing to me!"

I followed the sound of her voice, focused back toward her face, and allowed my vision to readjust. Her almond-colored eyes were almost entirely blacked out by her pupils, her surgical mask sprinkled with the same drops of blood I was spattered in. *I have to. I HAVE TO.* Yanked by the force of my pure will alone, I burst back from the verge of fainting and began singing to her once again. If I could find my voice then, I could certainly find my voice now.

The sound downstairs of a key fiddling with the lock on our front door brought me back to the present moment. Next, the familiar chimes gently jingled, alerting me our door had opened. Only 16 stairs remained between my old life and my new reality.

"Hi, honey, we're home. Any news?" Immediately, Love called from the bottom of the staircase.

Every single fiber of my being screamed. *Do not answer her.* The monster I was about to deliver needed to be wrapped up neatly with a pretty little red bow on top. If I spoke out loud too soon, my perfect delivery would surely unravel. I opened my mouth to say, 'I'll be there in a minute,' but all that came out was the exhale of a breath I didn't realize I was holding.

"Honey?" Her voice was getting louder now as she neared the top of the staircase.

"I'm coming," I managed as I stayed hidden in the bathroom.

Every cell in my body roared. *Sit still!* Why am I standing up? Slowly, I inched into our bedroom. The weight of the news I was about to deliver was like cold, hard cement blocks glued to the soles of my feet.

Love had Lil' G on the changing table. With a clean diaper in one hand and a dirty diaper in the other, she glanced up as she saw me enter the room. Her focus remained on the task at hand, and I sensed from her tone that her patience was dwindling. She asked a third time now if I had heard from the doctor. The tiny voice I was trying to muster shrank even smaller against the sharp edge of her impatience.

"I want to sit down. I—I want to talk to you," I choked out.

Love snapped her head back up, her words like darts, "Why won't you answer me?" Unknowingly, she aimed. "Just say it. Do you have cancer? Yes or no?" Mistakenly, she fired.

Our gaze locked, my silence as loud as a bloodcurdling scream echoing through a forest at midnight. Love blinked one elongated time as if she closed her eyes and opened them again, she'd see a different reality.

"Oh my God," Love whispered, her words penetrating the silence. The word *God* lingered in the air like an echo in the halls of an empty cathedral. "Oh my God," she repeated, scrambling to touch me.

Love grabbed me with such familiar urgency, the way she does when we make love. She clutched me in a desperate embrace, handfuls of my flesh in her palms as though the touch of my familiar body would somehow erase this foreign nightmare we were thrust so violently into. She crumbled in my arms, and I couldn't tell whose chest was heaving as we both broke in unison. Startled by our sudden uproar, Lil' G began to wail. Our happy triple goddess family was reduced to a chorus of primal cries—unrecognizable sounds from a guttural level of angst we never knew existed until this very moment. It was impossible to distinguish whose grief was whose.

In this new reality, cancer clutched onto us, beginning an excruciatingly slow and deliberate kill.

• • •

The following afternoon, Love and I passed Lil' G over to her gramma and headed down to San Francisco to meet with the brain surgeon. He cleared his entire afternoon schedule, allowing us as long as we needed to ask him anything and everything. The magnitude of the sheer weight alone kept us quiet for the majority of the 90-minute drive to the most prestigious hospital on the West Coast. Our hands remained interlaced— her right and my left—unwavering in their grip.

Dr. E spent the better half of two hours answering every single question we were instructed to ask by my general practitioner and those of our family members. When I hit my tolerance of hearing the fifty different ways I could die from brain surgery alone, I took a deep breath and broke the unspeakable agreement Love and I had made.

"If I decide to say, 'Thanks, but no thanks,' to brain surgery, how long will I live?" I couldn't bring my eyes to meet Love's.

Dr. E spoke confidently yet gently. I wondered how long it took him to master that balance.

"Well, every individual is unique. Taking into consideration your particular variables of the tumor positioned against both your brainstem and your carotid arteries, I'd say about two years."

I stifled a scream that sounded a lot like, *but I don't DO Western medicine.* It became crystal clear in that moment that it no longer mattered what I did or didn't do. Death's door was wide open. I was simply in the waiting room, leafing through magazines until I was called.

On our drive home, we made the colossal mistake of searching the word *Chordoma* on the internet. As we drove north across the Golden Gate Bridge, I couldn't help but recall it was hardly two months ago since we were driving home from the same hospital on the same bridge, only last time we searched for *Multiple Sclerosis* on the web, as I was just given that diagnosis. Doesn't it go against a universal law or something to have more than one life-threatening disease thrown at you at a time? There was no longer a need to worry about my long and debilitating future with MS as it slowly leeched the life out of me. I mean, cancer would take me out so much sooner.

I scanned the statistics for Chordoma. *Extremely rare. . .Bone cancer. . .Only 8 in 10 million diagnosed annually. . .Average life span, five to seven years. . .*Hold up. Five to seven years is the average? I'm pretty sure marrying a major immune-compromising diagnosis like Multiple Sclerosis to Chordoma is gonna land me in the below-average statistic. So even if I do consent to this atrocity they call *brain surgery*, and I survive the plethora of ways it could kill me, it's statistically likely I won't even live to see Lil' G's first day of kindergarten?

Oh, hell no! I slammed the phone down on my thigh, pledging out loud to never read the statistics for Chordoma again. I looked out over the bridge, the city slipping away as we barreled homebound. What I didn't say out loud was the immediate thought that rode the waves of heat that flushed my cheeks. An inner strength ignited, boiling up from a new depth in me I was meeting for the very first time.

Screw the statistics—every last one of them. They haven't met me yet. I moved heaven and Earth to have my daughter, and there isn't a snowball's chance in hell I'm going to be anywhere other than alive and by her side for her first day of kindergarten.

In the whirlpool of horrifying thoughts that spun around in my mind, this one was a lifeline tossed to me. I clung to it with all my might. I promised in my heart right then and there that I would live to see Lil' G start kindergarten. The vow I made was a contract for life—literally. I had zero hesitation in signing my name on the dotted line.

• • •

Later that week, in the dead of night, when my loves peacefully slumbered in our family bed, I tip-toed into Lil' G's future bedroom, closing the door behind me. I knew exactly what I needed to do. I lay on the floor, comfortably sprawled on my stomach, the shag of the rug cushioning my body. Imagining I was laying directly on the earth, I turned my head and rested my cheek down as though my ear could listen to our Great Mother whispering directly to me. I closed my eyes, summoning all the magic I learned over the past two decades of studying various ways prayer and intention impact our brain waves. The holy union of spirit and science has many names. For the sake of ease, I'll call it Truth. I allowed all the wisdom I held in me to collude with all the magic that exists around me. Together, we mixed until I had the perfect recipe I needed to whip up nothing shy of a downright miracle.

When I felt sufficiently moved, I propped my head up, opened my journal, and penned myself the most glorious love letter from my soul. I told myself—my full self—body, mind, and spirit, exactly what I needed to hear in order to make a full recovery. Equal parts spiritual and physical, I co-created my ultimate healing in a meditative place and then wrote exactly what I channeled. Before I knew it, I grabbed my phone, tapped *record,* and read myself this mother of all love letters. I could feel the words resonate in my being profoundly. Each word was a tiny seed, taking root as though my very cells heard the call. My chest became warm and full; my mind relaxed and at ease. The fear I grew accustomed to living within slowly dissipated until all that remained was the comfort of the longevity of my soul's existence: who I was before this lifetime, who I am now at the core, and who I will remain, even as life and its unpredictable challenges fluctuate.

Once I was done recording, I slipped back into our family bed and nestled in with Love and Lil' G between us. I put on my headset and tapped play, curious how well my love letter had been recorded. Before I knew it, I felt myself transcend to that glorious place between waking and dreaming, where all that exists is the Truth of unconditional love. From this eternal state of soul recognition, I fell deeply into a peaceful slumber.

The next morning I woke for the first time in months feeling serene and empowered. Lil' G lay sleeping next to me, and Love was sitting at her altar meditating on the other side of our bedroom. I reached over and laid my hand on Lil' G's heart chakra. Instantly, I flashed forward several years and imagined waking up for her first day of kindergarten. I was alive, and I was there to witness her once-in-a-lifetime milestone. I smiled softly at Lil' G and whispered, "I promise." And for the first time in months, I knew I meant it.

• • •

Unbeknownst to me, I was literally rewriting my destiny on that fateful night. I listened to the recording of my love letter every single night during my first year of cancer treatment. No matter how brutal the physical initiation became with multiple brain surgeries and months of radiation, I had the consistency of my love letter reminding me of my resilience. As of the publication of this book, it is ten years later. I am 100% free from cancer, all brain tumors, and any progression of MS.

THE SELF-LOVE PRACTICE

WRITING A LOVE LETTER FROM YOUR SOUL

My love letter meditation became the number one instrument in my toolbox, as my soul directed me to co-create my ultimate healing through my strongest brain wave frequencies. Today, I am prepared to teach you. On my website, https://candraanaya.com, I offer you a free step-by-step guide wherein you glean a potent and personal way to write your own love letter to use in a guided imagery meditation focused on your specific issue at hand. I provide a series of prompts for you to insert the words and images that resonate most deeply with your soul. You'll be armed with a fully fleshed-out, personalized script that leads you directly to the brain wave frequencies where co-creation occurs. From here, you will read and record yourself on a device as simple as a cell phone and implement a routine to listen every night for a minimum of 40 nights, at which point, you can keep listening or go through the process again to select another issue you'd like to heal.

At any given time, we're both students and teachers, both human and spirit, making millions of unconscious decisions daily as dictated by our soul through our brain wave frequencies. Imagine what your life can become by learning how to make any one of those decisions consciously. Be a student of life today and be an instructor of your life tomorrow, as making even one out of a million decisions consciously is enough to affect the outcome of the whole.

Seriously, my friends, this is life-altering wisdom you're being offered. My ever-self-lovin' soul's goal is to gift humanity with as many healing instruments as it takes to effectively instate a full-on love revolution. It all begins with the self. Let's be trailblazers and rock a self-love revolution for the ages. Say yes! Go to https://candraanaya.com for your free, life-changing script, and together we will do this one self-loving choice at a time.

Candra Anaya is a renowned freelance writer celebrated for her unfiltered autobiographical essays and her heartwarming and humorous advice column, *DearQueer~ Gayly Giving Advice Straight from the Heart,* as read on Medium.com.

Candra left her first written mark on the world at age 12 when her story about racism won first place in the state of California in a creative writing competition. At 14, she was published nationally for the first time in *American Poetry Anthology.*

What sets Candra apart is her extraordinary commitment to self-healing when faced with life-threatening adversity time and again. With over 30 years of experience, she is a Certified Clinical Hypnotherapist, Reiki Master, and hands-on healer. Candra utilized her specialties alongside Western medicine when faced with a one-in-a-billion statistic. She conquered Chordoma, a terminal cancer, and stopped the progression of Multiple Sclerosis.

Candra's triumphant battle against impossible odds is an inspiration to her community, who awaits her debut memoir, *Invincible.* Her writing has garnered a loyal following, thousands of whom witnessed her remarkable recovery through her writing online. The intimate details of her in-depth journey are woven together in her highly anticipated memoir.

Candra wins the hearts of straight and queer folks alike with her rousing advice column, *DearQueer.* Her feedback is evidence of her innate ability to uplift and educate readers through raw truth dipped in genuine care and delivered with a dollop of sweet sarcasm. She's the gay Mom you want to confess everything to who will embrace you with arms wide open.

Candra has been featured in Sebastopol Times, Sonoma West Times, and Medium.com where *DearQueer* is published monthly.

She lives happily in Northern California with her family, their magical Siberian Forest cat, and her favorite ficus tree, Angel.

Candra welcomes your contact.

Website: https://candraanaya.com

Medium: https://medium.com/@candra-anaya

Facebook: https://www.facebook.com/candra.anaya

Instagram: https://www.instagram.com/candra_anaya/

CHAPTER 12

COLLAGED DREAMS

CREATING A LIFE YOU LOVE PIECE BY PIECE

Beverly LaZar

MY STORY

The candle flame flickered in the darkened room, illuminating my face in the mirror. I sought my eyes in the reflection and gazed into them. After a few moments, I heard a clear voice say: *He will never give you what you seek. He cannot; it's not his purpose. He can't give you the love you so desperately crave because your lesson is to learn to love yourself. You need to create a life for yourself.* I answered: *How can I love myself when I don't even recognize myself anymore? How can I build a life for myself when I don't even know where to begin?*

At that moment, I knew, deep in my bones, that my marriage was over. I was sad, yet also relieved. My then-husband and I were separated and spent the last tumultuous year dancing around the inevitability of divorce. I clung to the only life and identity I knew, terrified of the unknown.

While it would take us a few more months to file for divorce, that night it became clear it was time to accept the ending and start anew. I needed to shift from self-abandonment to self-love.

Like many women, in marriage and motherhood, I put everyone else's needs before my own. Driving my kids to their dance practices, volleyball games, and speech and debate tournaments, we were perpetually on the go. Working late most nights at home after teaching each day, stacks of papers to grade, and lesson plans to write wore me out.

I also handled most of the grocery shopping, cooking, cleaning, and laundry, thinking *I make less money than him; I need to pick up the slack.* "Yeah, sure sweetie, buy that ski pass. Go have fun; you need it after working hard all week," I'd say to him while (not so silently) seething on the inside.

A classic martyred mom by my own doing, my artist self was dying. When I buried my voice to be loved or simply to keep the peace, when I busied myself to the point of exhaustion, my creativity dried up like the desert. Bit by bit, my starving soul insisted on more creative nourishment. In these moments I collaged, and certain images emerged and repeated.

Tall evergreens dripping with moss. Lichen clinging to wet rocks. Mushrooms growing out of old rotting stumps. Brilliant flowers blooming in lush gardens. Orcas diving in the deep. Ocean waves rolling, crashing into shore. Kelp beds swaying in the sea. Images like these infiltrated my dreams and art for decades.

It was an odd juxtaposition, as I was living in the high desert of New Mexico. Yet, my soul longed for something in these images so much I would return to them, again and again, for over two decades.

When I initially reflected on these images, my Piscean self exclaimed to anyone who might listen, "I'm a fish in the desert! I'm drying up and I need to get out of here. I need to move to Washington."

I dreamed of greener, wetter lands. Tearing up magazines, I created collage after collage with images of the Pacific Northwest. I tried to convince my then-husband to move, "Come on, let's go to Washington, it's so lush, so abundant. We could have a better life there."

"No, the skiing isn't as good as it is here. Besides, I don't think I could handle all of that rain," he replied. My heart sank, feeling anchored in New Mexico.

I'll never have the chance to live my dream. I didn't want to leave my marriage and family. As it turned out, in 2017, he declared his need for separation. As hard as that was, I remain grateful to him because I would've stayed stuck much longer.

In 2018, after our divorce was final, I thought: *Here's my chance to get out of here and move to the Northwest.* Part of me knew if I left then, I'd be running away from the pain of my divorce rather than creating a new life. I waited. My heart needed time to heal.

Post-divorce, strutting around in my cheetah boots, working out at the gym, and training in karate, I grew stronger. I gained confidence in taking care of my own house and bills. My kids were older and responsible for their own needs. I felt more free and independent than ever.

Still, I jumped into another long-term relationship with a sweet man. Yeah, yeah, I know. I kept seeking love from another instead of myself. Considering building a life with him, my Northwest dream faded into the mists once more. There I was again, orbiting a man instead of becoming my own sun.

Meanwhile, gardens, forests, oceans, and whales persisted in my art. My soul longed for a different kind of life, even when I tried to convince it otherwise. Over time, the call became too loud to ignore. A few key things unfolded that led me to end my relationship (amicably) and create the life I imagined.

In March 2020, an email from my school read, "We will be closing for a few weeks until more information about COVID-19 is known and it becomes safe enough for us to return."

Who knew a global pandemic would cause us to remain in the cocoon of our homes for the next year? Although worried about the state of the world, I allowed myself time to rest and reconnect with my passions. Music, specifically by a K-pop group from South Korea, provided healing and reignited my passion for creating.

The summer prior, my then 17-year-old youngest child introduced me to the music of BTS (Bangtan Sonyeondan), having found them during a time of personal crisis. From then, and continuing through the pandemic, we spent countless hours huddled together on the couch watching their music videos, concerts, and variety shows. In time, my youngest revealed, "Mom, they are the reason I'm still alive."

Sitting alone in my bathroom, I sobbed along to *Singularity*, when V (aka Kim Taehyung) crooned the lines "I buried my voice for you," and "Have I lost myself or have I gained you?" *Ouch*. I knew that pain all too well. "But in the end," he promised, "spring will come someday." With those words, they became my lifeline, too.

When my eldest came back home from school to live with us during the pandemic, she joined in our BTS obsession. We rocked out together, staying up all night streaming live concerts from Korea. Inspired by our favorite artists, my kids and I drew, painted, photographed, collaged, and wrote. We slowly began to heal from our past, individually and collectively.

During this time, I also chose to heal my emotional eating habits. I joined the Women Food and Forgiveness Academy, led by Marcella Friel. In a Zoom call with the group, Marcella asked us, "What are you really hungry for?"

From deep in my soul, I answered, "A more authentic, creative life."

She followed up with, "What does that look like to you?"

I answered, "I want to create a life I love instead of using food as a consolation prize. I want to live in Washington. I want to make art, write, and teach workshops." I imagined what that life might look like living in the Northwest, spending my days making art and writing, taking long walks in nature, and teaching workshops online or in person in beautiful retreat centers. Creating a life not just of my own but one of my dreams seemed a little more possible.

I'll never forget the day everything changed. November 2020. Sitting in my bedroom, on my favorite cozy brown thrift store chaise, roaming the internet, I came across an ad for a teaching position in Washington.

The hair on my arms stood on end as electricity surged through my body. I jumped up and raced across the house to show my eldest the ad. As I headed down the hallway, she was already hurrying toward me. "What's up? I was just coming to check on you. I felt an energy burst in the house like the roof was going to blow off!"

"Check out this ad," I blurted, "for a teaching position in Friday Harbor! I'm so qualified for this."

She replied, "Mom, you have to apply."

Immediately I came up with a bunch of reasons why I shouldn't, "I don't have a Washington license. It's the middle of the school year. How could I afford to pull this off?"

She wouldn't take my excuses and encouraged me, "Mom, just try. You never know what could happen or how it could work out. It's what you've always dreamed about, living there."

"You're right," I answered. *How could I encourage my kids to chase their dreams but then ignore my own?*

Becoming a self-supporting artist, writer, and workshop leader takes time, at least for me. Securing a teaching job in public education allowed me to make the move and keep a roof over our heads while I manifest the rest of my vision.

I didn't get that first job, but I kept at it. After months of prep and testing, I held a Washington teaching license. A few interviews later, a school district close to Seattle offered me a job. It wasn't Friday Harbor, but perhaps even better (It was!).

Within days an old friend contacted me unexpectedly, asking if I was still planning to move and needing an apartment. She and her partner were moving out of theirs in Magnolia, just northwest of downtown Seattle. She said, "It's in a great neighborhood, near the water and a giant 500-acre park. Coming from New Mexico you need to live here; it's very connected to nature."

When I searched for images of the park and waterfront online, I cried. The images could've come straight out of my collages. Long-held dreams were finally becoming reality. Before I knew it, I was headed to the place that called to me through my dreams and art.

There are times I hardly believe I pulled off a cross-country move later in life. Thank goodness for close friends and family who supported me through it all. On August 1st, 2021, I steered the fifteen-foot U-Haul crammed with all of our belongings out of our driveway while my dear friend, kid, and pets followed in my red Subaru hatchback.

After three arduous days on the road, we arrived in Washington. Rumbling along I90, I drove out of a long dark tunnel into brilliant sunlight, a fitting visual metaphor for my life at that moment.

Making my way west across the floating bridge over the wide expanse of Lake Washington, my hands shook as I gripped the steering wheel. Excited and terrified, I sang along with BTS's song *Idol,* belting out, "You can't stop me lovin' myself!"

A bit later, driving into our new neighborhood, I caught a glimpse of Puget Sound peeking through tall madrona trees. Once again, I wept. We were here, in the land that called my soul home for so long.

It's easy to forget how far I've come and focus on what I haven't yet achieved. I'm still working to balance my work and home life while carving out time for creative practice.

Reminders of how far I've grown pop up when least expected. The other night on the phone, my eldest said, "Mom, I tell people all the time how proud I am of you for going out there, for creating a life that's your own. You're very different now than you were in New Mexico."

Curious, I asked, "Really? How so?"

She answered, "You are much more confident. You are more you now than before the divorce. Even though you might not be doing all the things you want yet, you are thriving out there."

She's right; I am thriving. By tending my relationship with my creative self, I know, love, and trust myself a little more each day. I learned how to manifest a dream into reality piece by piece. I'll continue taking steps to fully build the authentic, creative life that I've imagined for myself.

THE SELF-LOVE PRACTICE

If you're feeling disconnected from your creative soul, one way to know and love yourself is to make some art and then spend time reflecting upon it. Sometimes we struggle to express what is in our hearts and minds. Creating images allows expression of what we might not be yet ready to voice. Image is the language of the soul. Once our image is made, we create time and space to sit with it. As we dialogue with it, we open to insights it may reveal.

I recommend starting with collage, a favorite art practice of mine. They're made by cutting or tearing up paper and then gluing it together to form new images. I love collage because it can be completed easily with materials you have on hand. You can use photographs, colored papers, and various ephemera like stamps, tickets, or boarding passes.

I recommend starting with a pile of magazines. If you don't have any magazines at home, you can often find them at thrift stores, in free piles at libraries, or through local buy-nothing groups online. You can also ask family, friends, or coworkers to share any they may have.

You also need scissors, glue sticks, and a backing to glue the images onto. For the backing, I often use small (4 x 6 inches) watercolor postcards, a page from my sketchbook, or thin, recycled cardboard (such as cereal boxes). You can work any size that feels right to you. I often work smaller because I know I can finish it fairly quickly. If it's too big, I might abandon the project midway.

Once you have your stash of magazines, allow yourself some time and space to discover which images excite and delight you. Don't think too much about it. Work quickly. As fast as you can, go through the magazines and rip out anything that pleases your eye.

Tear images out quickly, as slowing down to cut carefully creates too much time to overthink your choices. Perhaps a certain type of image catches your eye, or maybe colors pop off the page. Just notice them, tear them out, and toss them into a pile.

When you reach 10-20 images, look through them more closely. Notice what colors and types of images repeat, if any. Select a few images to begin with. Experiment with layering images on top of one another. Play with relationships between images. I like to experiment with unusual sizing of objects, such as tiny humans on a giant flower or a giant insect on a human.

I also play with pairing things that don't normally go together, for example, fish swimming through flames. You can even create a collage from fields of color alone to make your collage more abstract. Have fun with this! Play is the keyword.

Notice what repeats, what tugs at your heart. Experiment with cutting holes through layers, revealing images behind. After you have your composition laid out, glue the papers to the backing. Glue the background layers first, then add any other smaller images in layers on top.

Take some time to look closely at the collage you created. Jot down what you see exactly as you see it. For example, you might have an image that includes a large bee sitting on a woman's head with some red dots floating around the edges of a blue background.

We might be tempted to view this image and say, "I had this dream about a giant bee that stung me, and it hurt so much I saw red dots in front of my eyes."

Instead, try writing phrases like "red dots float across a field of blue" or "a giant bee hovers on the woman's head."

Don't try to analyze what you think the collage means; just play with describing what you see. Play with the relationships that you notice, such as "only when red dots float across a field of blue, then what stings hovers over a woman's head."

What you're doing when writing this way is having a dialogue with your image and opening up to multiple meanings of this image. You can take the words you jot down and rearrange or rewrite them in different ways. Repeat them for emphasis, "What hovers, stings, what hovers, stings."

Be open to multiple interpretations. For example, my Pacific Northwest collages could be interpreted as "I want to move to Washington."

While true, why stop there? What else could I learn from them? By playing with writing about them in different ways, over time, I might see them differently. Themes of longing for creative fertility, a more sustainable life, or a desire for abundance might emerge.

I might gain insights into what needs to rot and be composted, like fallen trees in a forest, for something new to grow. I might ask, "What is rotting, and what is growing?"

The list of insights grows when we continue to work with an image or series of images. Keeping your image(s) visible and close to you (both physically and emotionally) and writing about them over time allows space for new insights to reveal themselves. In working with a series of images, look for patterns, ideas, layers, and repetitions.

I learned this style of dialoguing with images from my mentor, Linney Wix, in graduate school for art education. As you begin to build a relationship with your images this way, you will learn more about your mind and longings. This creative practice is a way for you to carve out space to know, honor, and love yourself. Who knows what might be possible for you, you might find yourself on a new creative adventure.

Beverly LaZar is an artist, writer, and teacher. Midwife for the creative process, she holds space for others to know, honor, and love themselves through artistic practice.

She has an MA in Art Education and has taught art workshops in a variety of media for over twenty years. She especially loves collage, bookmaking, photography, and mixed-media visual journaling. Join Beverly for collage workshops and creativity circles online at Soul Song Studio. She dreams of facilitating workshops in beautiful places.

Additionally, Beverly has been a Guidess (mentor) with the Women, Food, and Forgiveness Academy since March 2022 and has participated in the Academy since May 2020.

Beverly lives in Seattle with her 21-year-old trans, non-binary child, their dog, and two cats. Her 25-year-old daughter lives in Tucson for graduate school. She loves walking through the park, sitting on the beach, feeding the crows, and taking photographs of all of it. Music, especially by BTS, brings her joy; she attends as many concerts as possible. Beverly and her BTS fan friends are planning a trip to South Korea in 2025, another dream in the making!

Connect with Beverly:

Website: http://soulsongstudio.com/

Facebook: https://www.facebook.com/soulsongstudiobeverlylazar/

Email: soulsongstudiobeverly@gmail.com

Additional resource:

Women, Food, and Forgiveness Academy:

www.womenfoodandforgiveness.com

CHAPTER 13

MY JOURNEY FROM TRAUMA TO SELF-LOVE

LIBERATING OURSELVES AND OUR UNIQUE GIFTS

Michelle Vesser

MY STORY

From my earliest memories, I knew that the unspoken pain of unprocessed grief hovering in every corner of the house lived within my dad's smooth tan nightstand.

Waking again, cold to the bone, legs bent unmoving, my four-year-old heart filled with trepidation; I smelled the terror and death in the air. I breathe into the tension in my body. When I breathe again, my bed's soft sheets and warmth bring me back. The confusion of where I am clears as night turns into day, and words swirl within me.

If people really know who I really am, this is what will happen to me.

It's quiet, my three sisters nowhere in sight. As I walk down the hall, there's an impulse, a young girl's intrigue. My heart beats faster as I enter my parent's bedroom. I close the door and sit on my dad's side of the bed.

I open the drawer. The familiar smell meets me as I see the colorful stripes of his worn army metals and the swastika armband he took to not forget. Goosebumps ripple through me as I reach for the white envelope. There's a familiar weight to the pictures inside.

Slowly, I look at each black-and-white snapshot. Nothing has changed in their stillness and horror. I take time with the one with naked bodies piled six men high in a barren concrete room. They are nothing but skin and bones.

In another, there are men in thick coats in a train car, arms and legs splayed out lifeless. The one that catches my attention the most is of a man on the train tracks. I look closely at the expression on his face. There is a resolve. His legs curled up to his chest, his shoes too big for his shrunken body. It's as if I can see his soul and all he lost in this interrupted life.

This ritual of sitting by my dad's bedside table is etched in my cellular memory. He grew up in the Jewish orthodoxy of Brooklyn and was a U.S. Army medic in WWII. His division helped liberate the Dachau concentration camp. This discounting of human life during the Holocaust developed into a quest to learn how to keep one's light, joy, and curiosity alive through the worst of human cruelty.

How do we peel back the layers of trauma and tragedies we live through as humans to find the full expression of ourselves and the self-love that can be enlivened on the journey?

Yet there was little Mishi, curled up and crying at age five, asking God, "If you are really there, please make sure I don't wake up in the morning."

Life was difficult for me. My parents were wonderful people, yet with both ancestral and personal trauma, they lacked the capacity to support me emotionally. I was often told, "You are too emotional and sensitive."

These words closed me into my inner world. I also had two older sisters who had airs of always being right and commented on how I was in the world. To complicate matters, I was born with physical deficiencies. This required me to wear corrective braced shoes at night (I had to crawl to the bathroom), have tooth extractions, braces, and do crazy eye exercises.

I also had learning disabilities. The school system deemed me less than and sent me to the back of the class to work with phonics or in remedial classes throughout my 16-year education. I internalized everything.

Not fitting into the human material world and not wanting to live became a theme in my life. I did make an inner pact:

I will not take my life. However, I will welcome my death whenever it comes.

There was another deeper voice within me, the one that knows, that urged me to leave the house for the aliveness of the wild world. Flowers glistening with raindrops in our neighborhood or the old walnut grove near us with a riot of squawking, rushing life that welcomed me. The soil, plants, and creatures there gave me a place of belonging, acceptance, joy, and wonder.

That was my dad's healing, too. He also made a pact: "If I were lucky enough to survive this horrific war and have a wife and family, they would see the world differently than I did."

And we did. The six of us packed into a VW camper and explored the U.S. during the summers.

Yet daily, my inner life held these two strong voices vying for control in the confused state of being me.

You don't belong.
You see the world's magic.
You are dumb.
You have your way of connecting with the world.
You were born at the wrong time.
Your uniqueness opens people to new possibilities.

As my life unfolded, the Earth-connected voice desperate for joy and belonging became bolder and took risks, adventuring to places of beauty and wonder. At the same time, a professor encouraged me by his example of working overseas to "follow my heart" in the work I pursued. Eventually, I lived in earth-based cultures, first as a Peace Corps volunteer in the Philippines and later in Mexico and Nepal.

Returning from working overseas, I stopped by a rural educational center I heard about and wandered down a wooded pathway.

I wonder what this place will be like?

As I came to the main area, a kind man pointed me to a rock stairway. As I moved down the steps, I gasped and had to stop and take it in.

Oh, my Goddess, what a magical garden. I've never seen anything like it. There is so much wildness, beauty, and abundance. And that huge oak tree is calling me.

I knew I was home. The world of gardening became my life. I loved tending the earth, growing nourishing food, and creating beauty.

My life in the outer world was blessed in many ways, yet my inner world continued to haunt me. I often curled up at night crying in my self-tending cave. The deeply etched fear of persecution, being discounted, death, and feeling less than interrupted my sleep. Although I was gardening full-time and married at this point in my life, the pattern continued.

The battle of voices continued to play out in my mind. I spiraled down and found my way back. Finally, in 1995, while working in Nepal, I cracked. My emotions imploded. I was trapped in a current of sadness, anger, and confusion; I couldn't bear it.

I wanted out, out of the situation, my body, my life. Laying in our room in a traditional Nepali house, I knew that I was in trouble. I wanted nothing more than to put a pillow over my face and end this inner torment.

In the confusion, another voice came through: *What would it be like for this small village if I took my life here?*

Imagining this brought me back. That night, I made a second pact. *I'll leave this project, return to the U.S., and find someone to help me.*

The next morning, I left, choosing to love myself, and began a journey of healing and discovery that continues today.

Stepping into this sacred "yes" to allow support in and move beyond my pride and shame, a miraculous energy arose. Gifted people began to appear in my life. The first miracle was Beth Stauffer. I hold her as my spiritual mother; she truly gave me back my life.

It was overwhelming for me to think of working with a therapist. I realized I put roadblocks and coping mechanisms in place and needed an outside perspective to navigate them.

The greatest gift Beth offered to me was her unconditional love. Now, mind you, she was quirky, tall, slender, and always barefoot. She had stones everywhere, and she would go to her screen door in the middle of a session to smoke a cigarette. Yet she had a profound ability to hear the inner voices within people. Each tool Beth used allowed unheard, unseen, or unappreciated parts of me to have a voice and to be free.

We were catching up when, out of the blue, she said:

"Got it, it's your six-year-old. Come sit by me."

I walked over to the ottoman in front of her chair.

"Tell me what happened in school for you at that age."

"Oh, I can remember everyone laughing at me. I kept raising my hand to make animal sounds. I was excited each time but only said 'bark bark' or 'meow meow,' not making real sounds. The teacher would pick someone else. The third time, everyone started laughing. I was so ashamed, I didn't understand. That's when I realized I was different and not one of the smart kids."

"Okay, watch my pen."

My eyes moved back and forth, following her figure eights–faster and faster.

She was saying things quickly.

Then,

"Whoosh, that was a good one," Beth whisked her pen up several times.

I could feel the energy release.

"Now, walk your six-year-old out of that classroom. She has been stuck there for a long time. Take her to your beautiful garden."

I was amazed how, with these pen movements, Beth occupied my conscious mind while she worked with my unconscious to shift old beliefs. This hypnotherapy technique was powerful for me.

At the time, I didn't understand the gravity of the gifts she offered me. This was one of the most difficult things I've ever done—to look inside. I was afraid to face all the pain and demons I held. What I found week after week, as Beth connected with different parts of me, was that working with her was the greatest gift I ever gave myself.

She always brought new tools, Neuro-Linguistic Programming, hypnotherapy techniques, the museum of old beliefs, and more. She was excited, as I still am, about different practices to tend our inner landscape. Slowly, my life began to change. My time with Beth brought me an inner acceptance and a deepening self-love.

Instead of being overwhelmed with my inner world, I saw each challenge as an opportunity to free myself and pursue different somatic and spiritual practices. Each took me deeper into a liberation and expression of my most authentic self.

At one workshop, riddled with anxiety, I stood up first in front of the group. My heart was racing. The facilitator helped me explore and release my fear of being ridiculed and speaking in public through inquiry and breathe work. Amazed, within fifteen minutes, I was completely relaxed and at ease. This experience propelled me to create a course on healing foods, gardening, and herbs, which I taught for the next ten years.

In time, I intentionally leaned into my past traumas.

What was I thinking walking onto a prison yard?

The guns, heavy gear, stark buildings—my heart jumped from the bang of the large metal gates closing behind me. I saw the garden across the yard. The men were happy we came. As we entered the garden, they welcomed us with fist bumps and handshakes. Then, we circled up to start our meditation.

Witnessing these men change when treated with humanity and care and given a connection to land and plants through a prison garden program showed me that our hearts are always whole and healing is possible for us all, even in the harshest circumstances.

My aversion to dying and death was also calling for change. It was always a place of pain and discomfort for me. In time, I stood beside someone who had recently died, tenderly washing and adorning them with beautiful clothing, fabric, and flowers. This brought a sacredness to death that opened my heart in unexpected ways.

Walking out after guiding a family to tend the body of their loved one, I thought:

My heart is so full; Michelle, look at you! You're bringing all of you here— your spiritual, emotional, and practical skills. They are all welcome. You're giving families tools you didn't have. What a blessing it is to do this work.

Never in my wildest dreams would I imagine becoming an End-of-Life doula.

As I write this, I'm leaning toward transforming my educational trauma, where I repeatedly heard I couldn't write and was not "smart." Over time, I learned that writing and editing are very different things. Writing isn't about grades and getting by. It's about expressing what touches and inspires you in the world.

I've realized that when we come to this Earth school, we are given some complicated scripts to work within our lives. We pop into these strange circumstances of our family, religion, cultural context, and the educational system we find ourselves in.

We adapt to everything around us. As we move forward in life, obstacles arise. They can harden or inspire us to look within healing layers of pain and protection. This clearing opens pathways for our true essence and unique gifts to come into full expression. We often become wounded healers using our painful experiences to support others.

I now love all the parts of me. I love that little girl who sat on my dad's bed, seeing the harshness of life so early, and who didn't connect with the material world. She led me to create an alternative life, living close to the land and being of service along the way. She is no longer stuck by that bed. I've journeyed back to many frozen memories, held my young ones, loved myself, and freed the joy that always lived within me.

RADIANCE - LORRAINE GANE

When you come to the door
of your new self,
you will know it is time
to let go of the shadow
who walks behind you
with the box of old books

In the place behind the door,
there is no room
for anything
but your shining heart
free of all your fears,
the grievances you carried
for so long

In the place behind the door,
your deepest longing
will greet you on the path
to a high meadow

Sit on the soft grass.
Let the great dome of sky,
widening rays of sun
and all the faces of heaven
show what you have become.

THE SELF-LOVE PRACTICE

SOUL RETRIEVAL

Soul retrieval invites you to come back from your future and connect with younger parts of yourself. You know more than anyone what has happened in your life. With loving care, you can ask them what they need, breathe together, hold them, and take them from these places of pain and trauma.

An important first step is to know that this practice is not intended to re-traumatize.

Free - Soul Retrieval Meditation Audio:
https://www.everythingsacred.co/inner-landscape

Find a comfortable place to either sit or lie down.

Have a pillow to hold your younger self.

Grounding and Rising Motivation:
Take a moment and center yourself.
Take several deep breaths, releasing any physical tension you might be carrying.
Take several more deep breaths, releasing any emotional tension.
Take several more deep breaths, releasing any mental tension.
Raise your motivation to do this work for yourself and anyone who can benefit.

Step 1: Exploring your emotions
Breathe into your body and see where you are holding tension or contraction.

Where is it located? _____
Breathe into it.
Name the emotion held there. _____

Let yourself feel the emotions; don't push them away.
Fully experience the feeling. You don't have to stay long. Once you have experienced them, move on.

Step 2: Tracking into our Emotional Landscape
Ask yourself: What is the emotion underneath that? _____
Be curious, breathe.
Where is it located in your body? _____
Allow yourself to feel this completely.

Repeat Step 2 again.
Eventually, you will come across an old emotion, or an image will present itself.

Step 3: Working with Old Emotions
Ask: Do you remember when you first felt this way?
See where this younger you is. Take in the situation.

Step 4: Coming Back from Your Future
Now, see your present self walking into this place to be with them.
Tell them you have come back from your future.

Ask your younger self what they need.
(They often want to be held – if so, hold the pillow as if it were your younger selves.)

Take time to be with your younger self. Breathe together.
Let them know you understand more than anyone what they have gone through.
When trauma happens, a part of you gets frozen and left behind.
Have them see that everyone has grown up and is gone, that they got stuck here.

Step 5: Liberating Yourself
Share with them: You don't have to stay here any longer. We can leave or transform this place. We can magically go anywhere (to the ocean, mountain, or a favorite place).

If they are ready to go, ask if there is anything they want to take with them.
If it's in a house/building, when walking them out, stop and feel the wind and see all the life around them. Then, take them to this nourishing place.

If they are not ready, stay with them and rest.

Step 6: Enjoy your time together.
Once at the nourishing place, take time to be with them.
Let them know they are free and never have to go back to the place again.

Step 7: Bringing them into your heart
Once you feel complete.
Take some breaths and bring them into your heart.

Spend some time in gratitude for all the work they have done.
Send out heart streams to anyone who can benefit from your work today.

Now that they are with you, you can connect with them regularly.
Check in with them daily, go on walks, and love them up.

Michelle Vesser is guided by her deep connection with the natural and spiritual worlds. She created *Everything Sacred: Tending the Inner and Outer Landscape,* bringing her passions as a spiritual counselor and mediator, an End-of-Life doula, home funeral guide, grief counselor, and other work to be of service.

As a spiritual counselor, Michelle loves leading you into your inner landscape and assists in releasing stuck emotions and reconnecting you with your radiance and gifts. She holds many modalities: Inner tracking, Soul Retrieval, Inner Child Work, Feeding Your Demons, Ancestral Trauma, Brain Working Recursive Therapy (BWRT), and Tibetan Elemental Practices.

"I leave our sessions feeling uplifted, resourced, and with new tools for deepening relationships and personal expression. Michelle brings her unique combination of expertise and curiosity, and I've always been met with compassion."

~ CS

Her offerings as an End-of-Life doula are an accumulation of her life. She brings practical, calm, and loving care to individuals and families in this sacred time. Her emotional and spiritual experience supports them through their final illness and last breath. She also offers guidance in after-death care, Tibetan end-of-life practices, and grief support.

"Michelle helped me experience my brother's death in beautiful and meaningful ways. She enabled me to connect with him in his passing, so I did not feel so helpless or alone. Michelle is a natural and profound healer, and has helped me to understand my own capacity for healing."

~ ZS

Michelle brings the heart essence of her Tibetan practice to all her offerings.

She lives in Sebastopol, Ca. with her loving and supportive partner Barry.

Connect with Michelle

Email: michelle@everythingsacred.co

Website:
www.everythingsacred.co
www.socoelda.com

Facebook: www.facebook.com/michelleeverythingsacred

Free Soul Retrieval Meditation link:
https://www.everythingsacred.co/inner-landscape

CHAPTER 14

MY SELF-SOLUTIONS TO GETTING UNSTUCK

RESOURCES IN POST-TRAUMATIC HEALING, RECOVERY, AND RELEASING FEAR

Laura Spinner, LCSW

MY STORY

Oh my God!

Disassociating, I was floating out of my body.

Not again, it's happening again; why now? Not here, not now. Ground, Laura, ground. Don't run and hide. Don't shut down. What is wrong with you, girl?

Terror knifed my heart, the intensity and surprise of it all scaring the shit out of me, as there was no apparent reason for my reaction. I was revisiting an old story that again presented itself, demanding my attention.

My eyeballs continued to spin in my sockets. Looking at my body from above confused me. At one level of consciousness, there was still a part of me saying, "It's all good. You are safe." I also feared I would remain that way.

I continued to drift out of my body and stuck there; horror seemed to freeze my organs.

The smell of hospital alcohol triggered this experience in the hallway of the hospital where my granddaughter just had surgery. An encounter with an unexpected trigger set off the post-traumatic response.

Using diaphragmatic breathing, tapping my arms, and applying deep pressure to my abdomen with my hands helped me love myself through the seconds-long experience. Using tools that worked, I grounded.

The smell of alcohol triggered visceral, biological, and neuro-cognitive reactions, leading to a physical and emotional out-of-body experience. Self-love and self-trust helped me use my tools, which always grounded me and brought me back to the present.

Letting go of the old habits of pushing back and burying fear deep in my subconscious, I invited the feelings and memories to come forward. I chose not to ignore and deny the memories, and a scene from many years ago surfaced as I walked toward my granddaughter's room.

I allowed a memory of a vicious hospitalization at age twelve to surface. I allowed it to play from beginning to end, loving myself through yet another healing experience.

Allowing another replay is necessary. You must experience this again to heal even further and to ground in your body.

Courage and confidence increased as inner knowing guided me to where I needed to go. Self-love affirmed that all the positive tools I needed to integrate were easily accessible. Saying "welcome memory" out loud ushered in the recollection and more learning and healing.

I have already died once.

At twelve years old, my parents were gone. I was facing bleeding out again, and I was alone.

I remember screaming, "Help! Help!" but no one came.

Sitting on a bedpan in a hospital bed, isolated, fear constricted my heart. Bright red life force energy, the very liquid our body depends on to keep our heartbeat going, spurted across the room in a powerful arc.

It's your fault. If you'd kept your butt on the bed and waited for a nurse, maybe the bleeding wouldn't have started. You probably injured yourself by not waiting for help.

Ashamed, I lowered myself from the pan to the bed. *Pull your pants up, girl. Cover yourself!*

Spurt, splat. Spurt, splat. The rhythm of the blood loss parroted my heartbeat, sprinkling the wall like an artist flicking a paintbrush and scattering red paint droplets. The difference was the artist's creation would bring life-fortifying energy.

My creation promised death.

"Oh my God, I want my mom!" Panicked, I hit the bedside call alert for the fiftieth time, but still no one showed.

Neither my screams for the nurse nor the light flashing outside my room solicited the help I desperately needed. No one was covering my room, as emergency room procedures on me just hours ago were thought to have stabilized me after I had a crisis on the road.

No one's going to come. I am going to die again. This time I'll stay dead. Death in the hospital. In the middle of doctors and nurses. They won't come because they aren't watching. They think I'm safe.

Crying and screaming, I relived the trauma of bleeding out in the back of Mom's station wagon the day before while experiencing the trauma of bleeding out in my hospital bed.

Yesterday, catapulting down the highway on the way back to the hospital, I bled out and flat-lined in the back of the car. Miraculously, paramedics arrived in a minute or two, responding to a police radio for help. Defibrillating me, the team saved my life.

"Laura!" Someone's shout startled me and brought me back to the present and my hospital bed.

The voice was loud and clear over my hysterical screaming, "It's not stopping."

June, my roommate, just out of surgery called to me. Her name in large letters on the chalkboard, along with her orders, jumped out at me.

As my piercing calls for help echoed in the room and down the hallway, June swung her legs over the edge of the bed and sat up.

"June, June, I'm sorry," the apology, garbled during my sobbing, roused June even further. "No, June, no! You can't go."

Wobbling, June pushed herself up with her right hand.

"Help!" The crimson spurts continued in a regular rhythm.

The arcs are weakening, but not so much blood. Oh God, I am bleeding out. Oh God, oh God, oh God. Another attempt for nurses, but my scream failed.

June, I can't help yelling! I am dying.

And I was.

Groggy from surgery, June protected her casted arm cradled in her hospital sling. With eyes as big as saucers and flickering back and forth between her and the wall, I watched this angel rise.

Not much time left. Not much red hitting the wall anymore.

With superhuman strength, pushing her IV in front of her and moving as fast as she could June went out the door and down the hallway. Her face was drawn tight in pain, but she walked with determination.

June countered, "If I don't go, you will die."

Before I knew it, "Code Blue" vibrated the hallways. Staff flooded the room, piled on top of me, and cinched a tourniquet on my leg, compressing a main artery to stop the blood flow. My legs were tied to the bed, and needles were jabbed into my soft elbow area and buttocks.

IVs, tranquilizers, and anesthetics flowed into my body, but not quickly enough. I was conscious, staring into the faces of four people as surgeons shoved tools into my ankle. Searing pain racked me as clamps were jammed into my ankle, closing the severed artery while I was fully conscious.

I spent the next few days with June as a roommate.

"June, how could you get up to help me?"

"I don't know. I saw your face, and I could tell you needed me. Your face told me I had to move fast. I don't even remember feeling anything but adrenaline and a rush to go get help."

"June, I love you. You saved me."

Several days later, both sobbing, we hugged as June was wheeled out to go home. June was there for me when my parents couldn't be.

Days later, my foot was not healing. The radical surgery created a gaping wound. Three weeks passed. My lonely days created a deep, welling sadness and sense of abandonment, even though Mom was in and out as the hospital would allow. Depression and giving up took over my being.

June "saved my life" again.

Somehow, she rode the El and other transfer trains from her home in downtown Chicago to the hospital to see me, sneaking into my room.

"Hi, Laura, here!" A little white suitcase full of every piece of jewelry, bubble gum plastic, dime store trinkets, garage sale treasures, and gifts June had collected since she was little plopped onto my lap.

"Oh, June, all your treasures? For me?"

She valued me.

A loving relationship saves lives.

This comforting memory grounded me and brought me back to the present as I neared my granddaughter's room.

Returning to my body, one more very significant memory surfaced with the smell of alcohol. At two years old, for one of my surgeries on my leg, I was put in a cast and placed in a crib built like a cage. The top had a lid that swung down and locked tight, jailing me in my bed.

Bounce, bounce, bounce: tiny me jumping, holding the bars, and watching my parents wave goodbye. My bouncing was furious and nonstop.

"We will be back."

Babble. Pleading babble. If I had words, they might have been, "I need you, can't you see me bouncing? Take me home."

My lullaby was screaming children. Some of my roommates were thrown off burning tenements by parents hoping they could save their babies. Many were burns and broken bones.

I didn't understand.

I could see, hear, and smell, but I didn't understand. My senses were overwhelmed with distress.

My parents left me.

I didn't understand.

No one came when I cried.

I didn't understand.

No one came when the baby in the crib next to me, hysterically shrieking in pain, died while I tried to help by holding her hand. I tried to soothe her (and myself) by babbling my preverbal rendition of Mom's "Suzie Snowflake."

I didn't understand.

Terrorized, I buried the memory.

All of us have experienced traumatic incidents. Tools that help us deal with anxiety, stress, and post-traumatic reactions begin with building trust and a powerful love of self.

Individualizing the tools and exploring many modalities of healing are very important. Coaching and facilitating self-exploration in identifying tools and modalities of self-healing is a required commitment, allowing people to grow that love for themselves.

THE SELF-LOVE PRACTICE

First, grow your trust and self-love as you deal with post-traumatic stress and/or stress and anxiety. Make a sacred space in your home. Place your art, sacred objects, concrete affirmations, and/or nature items there to honor you. Spend time there honoring yourself.

Second, take time to notice your feelings and where and what they bring up in your body. Have an individualized positive self-affirmation ready, maybe written on a pocket-sized card with a visual. As I reached my granddaughter's hospital room, I recited my mantra.

"You are Divine Perfection."

"I love, I am loved, I am love. I love myself."

I lock in the messages by reading them out loud and hugging myself. Deep pressure can also help ground and instill the messages you are gifting yourself. Your mantra, an active, positive "I am" statement, may be different from mine and may change in the future. The mantra can change based on your needs at the time.

Third, use bodywork and movement to interrupt negative self-talk or repetitive shaming perseveration (thinking fixed on not being enough, not having any worth, being a failure).

Jumping jacks for deeper fear to flight/fight/freeze/fawn responses in the body is a movement that can ground you, and address your need to break up intense feelings and repetitive negative thinking.

Play soothing music (you can YouTube alpha beta delta theta brain waves and choose sound healing) or sounds to soothe and calm yourself.

Dancing and crossing your midlines (right-left midline, top-bottom midline, and crossing both midlines at the same time) also interrupt negative perseveration and integrate positive self-talk and feelings while grounding.

Fourth, diaphragmatic breathing is a good tool for the relief of anxiety and post-traumatic stress. Lying down, place a stuffed animal (or a small special object) on your lower abdomen. As you breathe in with your nose, allow your lungs to fill up and drop down into your abdomen or belly area. As your diaphragm relaxes, your lower abdomen or belly will rise like a balloon.

Pause a second, not really holding your breath but just taking a one, two-count pause on breathing in before slowly releasing air through your mouth. As you breathe out, feel the warm breath flow from your mouth out into the world. Toning while breathing out also helps bring calm and a sense of power and creativity. Whatever noises want to come out is a true gift to yourself.

Fifth, get away from the screens and go outside, offering yourself the gifts of nature in self-love. Furry four-legged friends, winged ones, creepy crawlers, swimmers, and other life abound in the elements and beauty of Mother Earth.

Sitting near water creates calm and deepens healing and self-love. Creating outside allows your loving spirit to grow. Make fairy houses out of flowers and twigs. Nestle up to an ancient tree and feel its bark. Watch the activity around you and gift yourself with outside fun or rest, whatever is needed. You may need to move, sit and read, or fall asleep in the sun or shade. Nature heals.

Finally, there is strength in vulnerability. If you find yourself needing support, finding the right coaching and developing your ability to provide your own self-care in the manner and when you need it are two key elements of reinforcing your self-trust and self-love. Encourage yourself to meet a coach like me who is licensed in many modalities and who can help you with your memories and develop your own custom-tailored solutions that promote loving yourself through all of your fear, anxiety, and post-traumatic stress experiences.

Getting unstuck is possible.

Be patient with your process.

Becoming vulnerable with the right kind of nonjudgmental support will empower you to make sense of nebulous, haunting memories real enough to deal with and release their grip over time.

Falling in love with yourself and taking time to get to know yourself is a lifelong process.

My earliest hospital experiences remained buried in my body and soul until I was fifty-four. Unbeknownst to me, the strange, hopeless emotions I equated with failure were throwbacks to early childhood. I needed custom-tailored interventions in many modalities to access them. Even doing inner child work by itself in traditional therapy was not enough.

You may find some of these instances true as well.

I would cry when leaving my parents' home into my late fifties.

In staff meetings as a supervisor, I froze and experienced brief out-of-body experiences when threatened and overwhelmed while in large groups.

I felt safest being with my children and husband, even though I worked hard and was very competent on the job. Feeling safe was at home but not "out there."

At forty-eight years old, I found the key within to become unstuck.

I worked on personal issues in therapy and consultation with mentors, teachers, and therapists to stay fresh and neutral in my work as a therapist/healing facilitator. My choices of involvement were good but not specialized enough to address where I was stuck and what I did not understand within myself.

I began adding other modalities of healing for my health, growth, and development. Some of those choices were play, hypnosis, past-life regression, yoga, meditation, creative arts, meditative dance, spiritual consultation with local soul and spiritual healers, fire walking, sweat lodges, Shamanic Breathwork, earth-based healing, and equine therapy.

Lucky for me, a group of devoted partners and colleagues helped me trust and love myself enough to become unstuck and regress to age two. My breathwork family was there to help me relive, process, and put adult language to what I experienced back then.

My spiritual support, especially from the Aahara Spiritual Community in Springfield, Illinois, was key in setting the stage for bringing this trauma into life in a form I could heal.

The kickoff catalyst that led me to love myself and explore life enough to find healing modalities, friendships, and a spiritual milieu to fall in love with myself and cultivate self-love while on my life journey occurred at age forty-eight. A very significant, loving moment catapulted me into really exploring myself and finding healing.

My friends who were healers and I were traveling together. Anxiety about a workshop sign-up ravaged my body. They playfully threw me onto a bed, jumped on top of me, smooshing me in a big hug, and asked, "Do you love yourself?"

It was the first time anyone had ever asked me such a powerful question.

This critical moment and question launched me into a phase of life that focused on my commitment to and pursuit of *The Life-Changing Power of Self-Love.*

I can nail the cause and childhood trauma and bring up the experiences so I can adequately take care of loving my entire self, including the child or young adult within. For example, I can say, "That is two-year-old fear, that is twelve-year-old fear, that is seventeen-year-old fear, that is fourteen-year-old fear, that is my current fear."

Identifying when past trauma is heightening and magnifying current feelings of worry is a great tool—noticing the feelings and their expression in the body leads to self-initiation in applying individualized, self-loving tools. Many times, in self-love, I even credit an out-of-body experience as a productive tool necessary for channeling and use it for insight and divine messaging.

I'm open to embracing and loving my power and receiving in the moment rather than faulting myself for not being whole and moving into terror.

My treasure box of individualized tools that helps me heal, ground, release the fear and perseverative anxiety, and become unstuck is constantly growing and changing. I love my treasure box, just as I loved that little white suitcase as a twelve-year-old child.

I am valuable and a gift to myself. You are, too. I hope you answer yes to the question, "Do you love yourself?" My answer is, "Yes, you do, and you are powerful."

Laura Spinner, Licensed Clinical Social Worker, has over forty-five years of psychotherapeutic experience in mental health, education, chemical dependency, child welfare, and private practice settings. She has built and supervised programs in two mental health centers and one chemical dependency treatment setting.

During her thirty-one years in the school setting, Laura created a successful wraparound program meeting children's and families' needs. Her third specialty license is as a Brain Gym Instructor through Breakthroughs International, and her certifications as a Reiki Master Level 4, Shamanic Breathwork Facilitator, and Touch for Health Practitioner Level 4 provide depth to her skills in physical, cognitive, emotional, and spiritual support. Laura also has further training through Epona Quest in facilitating groundwork in equine therapy.

Laura's interest in social work and the healing arts began at age twelve when she realized loving relationship is the true healing property during one of her many major surgeries. She has survived three death experiences.

Laura has a life partner of over forty-eight years, two sons, and one grandaughter. A son and her granddaughter have also survived major medical incidents.

Her favorite activities include kayaking, swimming, bicycling, camping, horseback riding, nature, family, pets, and friends. She loves and has experience in drama, music, reading, and writing. She's had a houseful of children and animals for the past four decades.

Gratefully, she acknowledges all the mentors in her life. Licensing in Brain Gym through Breakthroughs International guided her. Thanks to Paul and Gail Dennison and Breakthroughs International.

Thank you to Helen Cox at Options Center in Peoria, Illinois, and Carol Ann Erickson and Movement Exploration, for teaching the importance of helping others notice their needs and facilitating my professional growth. Thank you to my spiritual communities for supporting my spiritual growth.

"Here's Laura's website if you would like to connect with her: https://www.lauralcsw.com

CHAPTER 15

IT'S NOT ENOUGH TO QUIT
DISCOVERING THE BEAUTY IN BEING

Natalie Petersen

MY STORY

I discovered I was pregnant on the upstairs bathroom floor of my grandparents' home outside Memphis in May 1997. Truth is, I was less afraid of actually being pregnant than of the consequences of the father being black.

I was 22, and my childhood best friend, Chrissy, waited outside the door.

"We're sisters forever," she promised in a whisper. "No matter what the test shows, I'm not leaving your side."

A mixed-race baby was *not* going to be accepted in my family; we both knew that. I held my breath as I waited for the test strip to reveal the results, memories of lessons of race, blacks, negros, and all the reasons why whites were superior and should remain separate, bouncing off the walls of my mind.

In one particular instance, I recall my grandfather teaching me how to use a shotgun from the second floor to defend against greedy, colored thieves who were sure to come upstairs looking for more to steal.

I was 10.

That same summer, I was discouraged from attending a church day camp when it was discovered there were kids of color attending.

There was no doubt.

These thoughts joined an ugly symphony of chaos in my mind already in progress. Just months earlier, my father died by suicide, sending my world into a tailspin. Love, family, and stability were confusing at best, and I stepped further into parenting my alcoholic mother through the unfathomable anguish of losing her beloved to his own hand and subtly leaving her to believe it was her fault.

Despite the din and drama, I was determined to begin grad school that fall. Though I wasn't entirely sure it was what I wanted to do, it was the next right step in my academic journey, and I had the support and encouragement of family and faculty to assuage my doubts. I was good at school. It'd keep me busy, at least.

"I'm pregnant."

The "++" on the test strip was undeniable, and my world pitched.

"Can I come in?" asked Chrissy.

We sat on the dusty bathroom floor together for some time before gathering up the go-ahead to move.

I would have an abortion, I decided.

Several weeks later, I ventured alone to Planned Parenthood, telling myself over and over I was making the right decision. Terminating the pregnancy was a procedure, a difficult but necessary course of action given plans and the potential for familial backlash.

I recall waiting alone, questioning the collage of inspirational posters on the ceiling of the small, cold clinic room, a distinct background noise of voices of judgment and self-loathing humming in my mind at the same octave as the fluorescent lights. The sheet I lay under smelled of bleach and failure, and the taste in my mouth was disgust.

Recovering in my bed later that day, an ice pack resting on my tender and confused midsection, I shook with anxiety. *You're a whore,* I thought in condemnation. *You deserve the pain.*

• • •

Except for securing the perimeter from intruders with firearms, setting boundaries as a concept of personal limits was not a topic in my home growing up. Neither was femininity, sexuality, self-love, or self-care. It wasn't that these ideas were withheld from me; rather, boundaries and bodies were matters the Bible decided. According to my parents and their parents before them, you only have sex if you're married, and if you have sex outside of wedlock, you can be sure you'll go to Hell. Masturbation? Sinful. Makeup? Suggestive. Structure? The husband is the head of the household, and everyone else falls in line.

And so, when I lost my virginity at the age of 17, I did so as an act of defiance and a warped sense of control. Confused and insecure, lust became my superpower, and I used my blossoming body and sexuality to manipulate situations of want and animal attraction. Conservative upbringing in the rearview mirror as I fled to college, sex became my currency. I began trading my body for attention, feigning control as I worked a room, a bar, a party, or any gathering, for a man to engage me in the non-verbal dance of supposed boundaries and the thrill of risky behavior as he crossed them.

God, I loved being wanted. I made a game of my boundaries being broken. And I was always winning.

Over the next ten years, I began a career and grew a lifestyle of living beyond my means and outside my body. The industry and circles in which I found myself running were ideal for indulging my escalating addictions to alcohol, sex, and drama. Everyone was doing it, and I did it well. I dangled off the ladder I climbed, my body distinctly disconnected from my mind, disconnected from my soul. I developed panic disorder and thought it was proof of my worthlessness. I was put-together, sassy, and well-spoken on the outside, but inside, I was vulnerable and deteriorating.

• • •

"You have cervical cancer."

The doctor gave matter-of-fact instructions to return to her office to create a plan of action.

Of course I have cancer, I thought. I wanted this, wanted the diagnosis of my body not being enough to hold up against the disease of my choices. I was nothing but in control of my own demise.

"Cut it out," I told my oncologist several weeks later. We scheduled a radical hysterectomy. I'd leave my ovaries in the event I wanted children, but the decision was based more on my desire to avoid menopause at such an early age and return to partying and playing house with my new husband and less on the chance I could someday be a mother.

I spent a week in the hospital by myself, and the day after I returned home, I threw a party and drank to blackout to drown out the voices battling in my head while sober in recovery.

• • •

"You're pregnant."

I was in the back seat of a co-worker's car racing down the interstate when I heard the words, and I screamed. Everyone in the car screamed.

My husband and I decided to try and start a family many months earlier, and after researching, meetings, soul searching, and interviews, we engaged an agency that introduced us to our gestational surrogate. After two tries, fertilized egg implantation succeeded.

Having cemented an agreement that I didn't deserve to be a mother, that the miracle in progress was just what money could buy, I was drunk the entire pregnancy. Though I accompanied our surrogate on every doctor's visit and spent hours nesting and creating a nursery and safe landing for our child, I recall the days being filled with anxiety of needing to get sober and get real.

I drank more than ever. My breastmilk came in surprisingly quickly after beginning hormones and pumping, but I squandered most of the precious juice, dumping the plastic baggies, knowing the contents were poisoned with my addiction.

The morning of my son's birth, I was still intoxicated from the night before. My head throbbed in overwhelm, and the bright lights of the delivery room made me nauseous and gave me nowhere to hide. I held one hand over my eyes, and the other took our surrogate's hand as my son was taken from her womb. She smiled up at me and whispered, "Congratulations, Mama."

"I don't deserve this," I silently replied.

Several hours later, I fed my newborn baby from my breast for the first time. He latched on without issue, and the woosh of love and milk leaving my body to nourish him left me sobbing.

I'm poisoning him, I thought to myself. *You don't deserve this, you selfish bitch. How can you think for one second you're strong enough, woman enough, to take this responsibility and do right by this tiny human now in your care?*

I breastfed for four months before the dark thoughts consuming my mind became too much. I began again on antidepressants, washing them down with wine and refusing to stop long enough to acknowledge the questions growing in intensity.

Where's your breaking point, Natalie?

• • •

In the wee hours of the morning I decided to quit drinking. I knew I was careening towards disaster, and the possibility of leaving my son to live without a mother broke my heart wide open. I didn't deserve him, but he didn't deserve the chaos.

"Why do you drink so much, Mommy?" he began asking.

"Mommy, maybe you can take a break tonight," he wondered out loud. The worry in his sweet voice stung, and his innocence and vulnerability amplified a heartbreak I knew all too well.

In fact, my past had come looking for me. As a teenager, I begged my own parents to stop drinking. But I lost my family to alcoholism, my father to suicide, and my mother to anguish. In the wake of the fall-out, I established agreements with myself that I wasn't enough to save them, wasn't worthy of being a woman, wasn't strong enough to stand up for my own love, wasn't fit to become a mother, didn't deserve any blessing or beauty or soul connection.

I saw myself in my sweet son. How incredibly sad.

If I was going to alter the trajectory of my lineage, break the cycle of heartbreak, and recover the woman, mother, sister, and partner I somehow knew I was, I would have to excavate through layers of loss, denial, abandonment, subordination, sabotage, and much, much more. I would have to go deep to save my soul.

• • •

In putting down the booze, I gave myself many things, and the early days had me high on how crisp the edges of life were when I gave my body and mind a chance to breathe. My physical self shifted, too, as a lifetime of drinking was shed and the weight of the alcohol lifted from my bones. I dove head first into self-help books and deep conversations with others who I hoped could help me bring clarity to the confusion I swam in for so long.

My relationship with my son shifted as he recognized my commitment to sobriety was real. But soon he saw me struggling mentally. A massive, dirty blanket of shame quickly enveloped me, and I was suffocating in a new way.

Up before the sun every morning, I stalked a solution, became obsessed with finding relief in the pages of someone else's story, hellbent on locating the switch that would turn me on and set me free.

Exhausted and experiencing anxiety attacks on a near-daily basis, I willed myself to sleep to quell the cacophony.

It's too late.

I'm too far gone.

I'm fine. I'll survive. And at least I won't wind up killing myself or someone else as I barrel down another bottle of booze. The trials I've survived are testimony to my toughness, and that's enough.

Can't quitting be enough?

Drinking drowned the voices and self-abuse, but sober, I was swept up in a tsunami of regret, guilt, and shame, the likes of nothing I'd experienced. I would never be free of the storm created by my careless decisions, blatant misdeeds, and selfish games.

I was severely disappointed in myself, enraged at my father, resentful of my mother, and just plain mad at my situation. I carved timelines of my trials in notebook after notebook, mentally wound my way through the maze of my life, backward and forward, and sketched pages of words and poems and questions of self-doubt, self-criticism, and self-sabotage. I bloodied my hands beating the prison walls of my choices. I was sucking for air.

And I was suicidal when I extended a hand and reached for help.

I boarded a plane to Kansas City and into the arms of my mentor and best friend, Andi. It was with her in a field with her horses, the cold

Missouri winter wind whipping around me, that I opened my arms and my heart and accepted my own love. I surrendered to the truth that my life had become unmanageable, and I committed to do whatever it took to retrieve my soul.

Athena, one of Andi's beautiful herd, stood stoic as my witness as I lifted my hands above my head, tears running down my face, and prayed to my Source.

I promise to live, for myself first, and for those who love me. Give me strength. Give me courage. Illuminate the dark with the light of forgiveness. Wrap your arms of unconditional love around me as I embark on this journey of healing and release from the chains of shame that bind me. Set my spirit free.

THE SELF-LOVE PRACTICE

Be. Do. Have.

Andi's guidance was simple. Out of order, a person living a life of 'doing' will surely burn out. 'Having,' and she will find herself always wanting.

But 'being'—well, therein lies a beautiful secret. Consider this model in reverse:

The **Have-Do-Be** human is caught thinking: *When I HAVE enough time, money, and support, a different living situation, or a marriage, or a promotion, then I'll DO the things I've always wanted to, and then I'll BE happy and successful.* She judges herself and others. She thinks, *the problem is I don't HAVE yet. If I had what that person has, I'd certainly be as successful as them, but I don't, so I'm not.*

And then there's the grind of the **Do-Have-Be** human. His thoughts whirl with something like, *the more I DO, the more I'll HAVE. The more I HAVE, the happier I'll BE.*

The problem is, the more we do, the more there is still to do, and the more we have, the more there is still to have. We become defined by what we do, so we become driven, busy, and tired. The more we have, the more there is to lose, so the harder we work.

We all know that the link between having more things and being happier is a myth, but we grind anyway—and burnout, stagnation, resentment, exhaustion, languishing, and even collapse soon manifest.

In both the Have-Do-Be and Do-Have-Be set-ups, we're caught in the spin cycle of life seeming to happen TO us. We "just can't get ahead," and we start many sentences with, "As soon as I…"

It's only in realizing that life happens FOR us that the opportunity to **Be-Do-Have** unfolds in all of its potential.

To 'Be' creates the context for how we think, feel, and act, giving us access to what we're really after. When you allow yourself to 'Be,' what you must 'Do' shows itself, and you 'Have' all that you desire.

In 'Being' followed by 'Doing,' you will reach your greatest potential, and only then do you begin to face obstacles, both real and perceived, standing in the way of your 'Having' your greatest desires manifested effortlessly and with joy in your life.

It's not, 'What do you need to HAVE before you can start,' or 'What work do you need to DO,' but 'Who do you want to BE?'

And please believe you have the capacity to experience any state of being at any time, not just when things work out perfectly, or you achieve exactly what you're after.

I invite you to participate in a simple exercise I personally used in the early stages of my own soul recovery to bring the Be-Do-Have model to life. Grab a journal, and dig in. Let's make this real.

1. **Think of one of your biggest goals right now.**

   Write this goal at the top of the page. Create three columns labeled "Be," "Do," and "Have" consecutively.

   For example, I have a goal of an open and supportive relationship with my son.

2. **In no particular order, note the states of being, the actions, and the results you assume will come from realizing this goal.**

   In my example, I am honest, non-judgmental, available, loving, and intentional. I engage my son in conversation, I listen to understand, and I curate experiences in which we can share our love and see the world. I'm rewarded with opportunities to support my son and sweet memories of unforgettable moments together.

3. **In this state of understanding and openness, stay quiet and meditate on your potential.**

Allow yourself to sit with this page of thoughts for a while. Life's not going anywhere. If you really give yourself time and space to come from an empowered and intentional state of being, actions will start to show up with ease, and your ability to both take them and allow them to work will increase.

Remember, we are human beings, not human doings. When we embrace this, our lives really can blossom in profound and fulfilling ways.

It's taken ceremony, guides, therapy, and revisiting extreme memories to release pain and attend to severe wounds, but being has become easier for me. It's taken time. In being in a flow state without a label or an association with anything, any emotion or judgment, fully receiving, giving, and in balance with the energy that I am, I find myself vibrating with love for myself and the world around me.

It matters not what's going on around me as my place in this space rolls out in front of me naturally. I'm calmer and lighter, and I find myself taking the next steps without questioning them, doing what feels best when it feels right. With each next right step forward I take, the having takes care of itself.

I look in the mirror each morning and ask myself, "Tell me, Natalie, who do you want to be?"

I want to be a woman.

I want to be a mother.

I want to be a sister.

I want to be a partner.

I want to be honest.

I want to be love.

In all my glorious Human Being-ness, I am free.

Gifted with a fierce passion for #COMMUNICATION, **Natalie Petersen** is a Communications Coach and Consultant whose calling is partnering with human beings in personal and professional spaces to realize worth and voice, compassion and courage, and value in our vulnerability. Consider listening to her podcast, Think Out Loud With Me.

Natalie believes in the power of #CONNECTION through learned experience as much as credentials. With a resume of unique roles and responsibilities, she has walked a life of many lessons, models, and mentors, and her diverse adventures are the very beauty she brings to the table. You'll find her experience and energy span the gamut of keywords and hot topics, industries, and insights. Capable across multiple disciplines, Natalie strives daily to educate and earn respect in the areas of Emotional Intelligence, Mental Health, Wellness/Illness Spectrum, Be-Do-Have Modeling, and more. Digital marketing is a space in which she is agile and valuable, and she does exceptional work on behalf of small businesses, start-ups, and non-profit endeavors.

Natalie believes in the power of #CURIOSITY, which allows her to connect with others in an authentic way through easy conversation, open-ended and thoughtful questions and reflections, and agreeable next steps. You'll find her honest, helpful, and downright dangerous as an accomplice in your life's mission, especially if it's one of achieving #CONGRUENCE.

Natalie believes in the power of #COMMUNITY. Above anything, she aims to support, make referrals, and noodle on ideas for the greater good. She resides in Northern Colorado with her partner and son, and she enjoys a full life of playing outside, writing, volunteering, reading, gardening, and more.

Find and follow Natalie online at https://www.bloomstruck.com, IG @bloom_struck or FB @bloomstruckcomm

CHAPTER 16

THE COURAGEOUS HEART

GRIEF AS A PATH TO RE-CREATION

Linda (Jyoti) Stuart

"Free from all old stories I've been told,
I walk through the valley of my own shadow"

~ Yaima

MY STORY

"Hey there! I'm headed to the Korean spa today, do you want to join me?"

"JT just told me he is taking a six-month hiatus from our relationship and moving away."

I had just finished a massage, my body melting into the cushy chair, my hands and feet supple. An easy smile arose from my relaxed jaw as I caught eyes with the therapist on her way out.

I glanced at my phone and noticed an email from my fiancé. It looked uncharacteristically long. This wasn't a "don't forget to pick up the bag of almonds" email. No, the text in front of me extended far beyond the usual scrolling.

As my eyes deciphered the words, my heart started pounding. I could feel my eyes beginning to dilate. I sat paralyzed; time halted. It occurred to me that I may have been sitting there much longer than I imagined. When my phone rang, it startled me out of my disoriented state. It was a call from my friend, Lori.

"What?!"

"I know, it's drastic."

"What happened?"

"I gave him an ultimatum a few weeks ago. I told him it was going to either be his drinking or me. I guess he chose to drink for now.

"Let me pick you up. This is crazy. We had so much fun with the two of you the other week!"

"I know, okay, but I just got a massage."

"Well, we are going to do a cold and hot plunge at the Korean spa; that'll feel good."

When her car pulled up, I jumped in, and although I had driven in LA for over a decade, I had no idea where we were or how long it took us to arrive. There was a sinking sensation in the pit of my stomach and a dazed expression across my face.

I walked into the women's locker room at the Korean spa, my legs shaking. I must have misplaced the key to the locker at least half a dozen times before leaving the locker room.

Sliding into the cold plunge drew my breath away. The water was so cold, but I forced myself to endure the iciness. When I retreated to the heated mugwort water, my stunned eyes drooped from sweat running down my forehead. My muscles turned to mush. The extreme temperature differentiation mirrored the extreme situation I found myself in.

JT and I had agreed to give it all up in LA and start a family together in Colorado. His email changed everything. All my plans of partnership, motherhood, and moving to Colorado vanished all together. We had barely a month left before our lease was up. I had let go of all my corporate wellness work and private clients just a few weeks prior. The career I spent over a decade cultivating was gone. My decision to leave my work and clients was irrevocable.

I went straight into victimhood. It was an unconscious, familiar, familial pattern that I indulged in under stress.

How could he? That bastard! But he promised!

As we left the spa, I slipped into the sludgy cesspool in my mind of victimhood. *Ah, better than a warm bath.* I didn't know what else to do except plunge into self-pity.

How could he do this?

When I returned home, the only thing I could think of doing was a road trip. I decided to go to the desert in the middle of summer. *Yeah, I know. Crazy!*

An image flashed in my mind of "The Tower" card from the Tarot. It depicts two people in mid-air that jumped off the top of a burning tower. *Yep, that turned out to be me and JT free-falling.* This violent image burned into my mind as I planned my escape.

On the road, heat waves rolled off the endless pavement. They added more ferocity to my internal inferno. My insides sizzled with the discomfort of moving into unknown territory. As I watched the miles of pavement underneath me, my stomach churned with anxiety. There was no breath awareness. I looked for an anchor, witnessing my mind doing mental gymnastics, trying to intellectually find stability.

Well, maybe I could go to this interesting place, or stop over here, and then maybe eat at this recommended restaurant.

But alas, nothing could take me away from the pain of the present moment's uncertainty.

What had happened?

Who was I?

My body felt like the inside of a snow globe—shaken up and ungrounded. There was nothing to hold onto except the steering wheel. On Highway 10, I was in control of the car and nothing else. Years of spiritual practice seemed swept away by the strong southwest winds whistling through the cracks of my Prius.

Why, why, why?

I found sitting upright in the driver's seat for so many miles gradually helped me feel my backbone. But I wasn't quite ready to face the truth yet. Hours elapsed on the open, heat-drenched roadway to. . .

Where was I going again?

The drone of monotonous hours lulled me into some kind of steadiness, finally opening space for grief. Tears flowed—rivers of tears.

What had happened?

Who was I?

I've read that grief changes your brain. This passing thought settled me for a few moments. Then random memories erupted.

Images came of my fiancé and me sitting at the dining room table, drinking cup after cup of yerba maté, talking about our processes on our spiritual journeys. This was one of the few places we truly connected. Unceasing tears flowed both for what could've been and for what maybe never was in the first place. Little niggling thoughts surfaced, reminding me of the many disappointing moments in our history—moments that revealed his inability to be with me.

What about my work, my career!?

I loved what I did and was good at it. Yet, there was a gnawing phrase that demanded attention. Golden handcuffs, golden handcuffs, repeated in my mind. I understood that although I was quite comfortable in my work, I was stagnating. The internal dialogue continued. But what the hell am I going to do? My mind flipped around like a dying fish on a fishing pier. I was caught between an inner knowing and a fear of the unknown.

You are too comfortable. How are you going to grow?

What the hell else am I going to do?

It'll come. Just wait.

I don't have the time or the resources to just wait!

Shit.

Shit.

Shit. I had it so good.

You were chained by golden handcuffs—the perfect work situation and compensation without the inner fulfillment. Let it go. Life wants to take you elsewhere.

Yet, how could he do this?

Seething on the inside, I felt pain in my chest. *Am I having a heart attack? How did I get here?*

While I felt some strength building through my rising anger, I couldn't quite muster the fortitude to fully answer the questions.

I kept driving and listened to a familiar ambient song through the car speakers. It reminded me of sweeter, softer times as it wove into my consciousness. I had this image of my fiancé and me lying down outside together, quiet and content. It pierced through my heart. One small tear trickled down my face. And then I remembered a teaching from an old spiritual friend. He called emotions that accompanied a memory "stack attacks." It's when we have a memory that gets triggered by a smell, sound, or a place. Anything we experience can trigger an emotional overtone if we allow it. As this teaching entered into my awareness, my sadness started to dissipate.

Wait a minute. Did that happen? Did we really have moments together, just being?

As the memories filtered in, I finally summoned the bravery to face the questions. The answer came: *No.*

The thought faded off into the horizon as I kept driving. More memories came through on these endless open roads. Rage, anger, sadness, pity, each given a voice. These long hours paved the way for self-honesty. More questions arose.

So what was real? What was the truth about the relationship and about what happened?

I stopped at a friend's home in Arizona. By the time I arrived, I was ready to open the door to my psyche and dig deeper into my situation. While there, I took the opportunity to work with mushroom plant medicine. I was excited yet apprehensive. During the experience, I saw that it wasn't my fiancé who betrayed me, it was myself. I saw how I betrayed myself by not following my intuition during the relationship despite seeing many red flags. Realizing this level of self-betrayal was heartbreaking and devastating.

JT may have been addicted to substances. But my addiction was not being honest with myself.

Ouch.

I decided to retreat to Colorado alone, where my meditation community resided. I allowed my heart to continue breaking, let myself cry, feel deeply, rage, and scream. Hiking through the Colorado mountains provided a sanctuary for getting real and healing. I evaluated the broken pieces and learned to be gentle with myself by halting the old tendency to beat myself up.

For the first time in twenty years of spiritual practice, I started listening to the stirrings in my heart instead of using my practices to bypass my feelings and 'fix myself.' Days were spent connecting to my body, heart, and soul through feeling my heart, yoga, meditating, playing and praying in nature, chanting, journaling, and devotional practices.

In contemplating how and why I betrayed myself, it was clear that I just wanted the relationship to work despite all its overwhelming challenges. I didn't want to let go of the dream of partnership and motherhood. Once I came to know this, my heart softened with compassion, and I was able to forgive myself and forgive him. I took full responsibility for my situation, and it was empowering.

Eventually, the emotional eruptions calmed. I gave my heart time to process, and a wiser part of me kicked in. I began to see patterns of self-limiting behaviors and beliefs clogging my experience of living. I realized that the root of these thoughts originated from beliefs adopted when I was young. Meditation practice and retreats enabled me to see that who I thought I was was a conglomeration of tendencies conditioned into me from my culture and family of origin. Working hard, making a lot of money, and having a family were all part of my programming. Yet, I yearned for a more authentic version of myself.

Over the next year, I practiced witnessing my thoughts and behaviors. At first, it was horrifying and shocking to notice the amount of image management, compensating behaviors, people-pleasing, and other nonsense I participated in. I aimed to observe myself but without judgment. I worked at not identifying with how I showed up. I noticed how sometimes I'd be unusually generous and that same day also stingy. I witnessed myself being kind, insensitive, tender, downright bitchy, and other character traits. But I was not any one of them. I was merely witnessing them.

The less I took any of it personally, the less I suffered.

It was very difficult at first, and just like any practice, it became easier over time. I also had it in the forefront of my mind that I was programmed from birth, and like so many people, was just trying to do the best I could in this world despite my wounds. I began to experience a kind of motherly care toward myself. There was a sweetness to this, and more self-acceptance came forth. I found myself engaged in a dual process of tenderly turning toward the wounded parts of myself coupled with reprogramming. I realized I was so hard on myself for so many years. This opened up space for self-compassion to grow.

The more I was aware, the less unconsciousness and patterned behavior controlled my life. After some months, I realized there was no need "to fix" myself. The natural unfolding of change organically happened from simply becoming more and more aware in this non-judgmental space. It was remarkable.

I started to notice I had more energy and enjoyed life more. Creativity and joy began to bloom as I created artwork, skipped, and danced. An inner yes to life emerged as I began to heal, appreciate, and trust myself and life. Miraculous opportunities presented themselves. Life felt like a smorgasbord, and I tasted a plethora of experiences and experimented with inspired ways to be of service. During this first year of my healing path, it felt like I was constantly throwing spaghetti at the wall. *Hmmm, I wonder what offering I throw out will stick?*

What initially seemed to be a never-ending cycle of grief, over time, metamorphosed into a chance to re-invent myself. And I did.

Seven years later, I experienced the dissolution of another significant relationship, and I grieved deeply. The pain this time was not of self-betrayal but of loss. It took me some time to see that the dissolving of the relationship was giving me what I always wanted—myself. What I've always wanted more than anything else was to intimately know the love in my own heart. To be filled with love from the inside out instead of constantly looking for it outside of myself.

As my heart softened from the grief, I felt a new kindheartedness toward myself. I appreciated my natural-born strengths and giggled at my flaws. I was more accepting of patterns of un-useful thoughts and behaviors.

Everything became seen through a gentler and kinder lens. Simultaneously, I was lovingly gazing at myself and neutrally aware of what I witnessed. I was beginning to experience the beloved in my own heart. It was the greatest gift—born out of pain and grief and well worth it. And I got to re-invent myself once again. Loving-hearted Linda 2.0.

The Courageous Heart is not personal. It's an energy, a grace that gives us the capacity to feel and accept what life asks us to experience. For healing and self-love to grow, we must welcome and witness everything and anything that comes up in our awareness. It includes victimhood and opening up to what is possible. It's all grist for the mill on the path to greater self-love and the strength to re-create ourselves into whomever we want to become.

THE SELF-LOVE PRACTICE

THE COURAGEOUS HEART SELF-LOVE PRACTICE

Lean in, let go, and open to possibilities

Leaning In

1. Allow the emotions to be fully felt once they arise. If you have difficulty accessing your emotions, start by simply being willing to feel. Be patient with yourself. Sit quietly, listen to music, or watch movies with strong emotional content. Put your hands on your heart and breathe into your heart. Give yourself space. It may take time to feel, cry, be angry, be resentful, full of regret, and everything else. Feel the grief. At some point, aim to adopt the attitude that things could not have gone differently. Embrace whatever you're experiencing to the best of your capacity. Honor yourself in this process.

2. Journal about everything you lost. Let it rip—hold back nothing.

3. Set aside 15 minutes a day to sit, feel, and notice what is arising from moment to moment, on or off a meditation cushion. The personal, wounded child needs tending to. Ask the inner child, what do you need? An old memory might resurface about when you went to a party and didn't feel welcome, or you are back on the playground when you were young and feeling left out. This is the perfect time to turn lovingly towards yourself.

Letting Go

1. Let go of identifying with what you're thinking and feeling or what is happening in your life. This means that whatever comes up, understand that it doesn't mean anything about your inherent value or worth. Realize that who you think you are is a conglomeration of cultural and familial conditioning. Do not take your situation, yourself, or your life personally.

2. Witness yourself as if you're observing someone else with fresh eyes. Let go of judgment of any neurosis, egoic behaviors, chaotic emotions, or thoughts that show up. You might notice something not particularly attractive about the way you operate in the world, maybe for the first time. As awareness grows, you may start to notice subtle patterns. Marvel at this human drama we're participating in.

3. Become aware of the inner dialogue. What are you telling yourself this morning? Maybe you aren't aware of a particular thought, but maybe you just feel a little grumpy. Become aware of insidiously negative thoughts. Is there a subtle yet potentially destructive attitude lurking in the recesses of your mind? Don't believe the thoughts.

Open to Possibilities

1. Disregard self-limiting beliefs, ideas, and identities with open-heartedness and discipline. Be willing to let them go once and for all. Write down each of these negative thoughts and replace them with an opposite statement. Feel the reality of each new statement. Eventually, be willing to let go of all thinking not related to the present moment and pay attention to the space between the thoughts. Our essence resides in that space, creating a doorway to infinite and pure potential.

2. Accept who you are and acknowledge who you want to become. Choose how you want to move forward. Make a list of qualities you want to cultivate within yourself. What can you do to emulate a few of those qualities each day?

3. Open your heart to yourself and recognize your SELF. This bigger self is that which every human being is. We are all of the same essence and we all have equal access to infinite possibilities in every moment of our lives. Be open to exploring your humanity. Become curious about yourself and enjoy the journey of re-creation.

Linda (Jyoti) Stuart is a healer with degrees in nutrition and dance and certifications in yoga, Thai yoga massage, reiki, and iRest yoga Nidra. She offers a unique, comprehensive, holistic approach to well-being, employing both ancient and modern modalities since 1997.

Linda guides people into their hearts and souls to become more of who they are, bringing decades of experience in yoga (many forms), breathing practices, non-dual teachings, shamanic practices and journeying, iRest yoga Nidra, meditation, and modalities that promote self-care, healing, transformation, and resting in one's True Self that needs no fixing.

She had a successful career in Los Angeles, leading seminars, managing wellness fairs and programs, teaching yoga and meditation in corporations such as Disney, AOL, The Wonderful Company, and Bloomberg, and taught several high-profile private clients.

Linda believes that holding a spacious container to witness people transform is an incredible honor and gift. She currently co-creates an enticing protocol of considerations, contemplations, and practices that support clients' processes. Clients are supported to experience whatever is needed to move through their journeys of transformation and awakening— structure and stability, alternative perceptions, motivation, inspiration, and accountability. Linda offers body, breath, and mindfulness, among other practices that attend to every aspect of our being.

After moving to Colorado, Linda was led to several training programs with elders of both non-traditional and traditional Shamanic practices with the Power Path School of Shamanism.

It's now one of her greatest joys to guide people through their times of challenge and transition and inquire into their inner wisdom and truth of who they are.

For more information:

https://www.luminousliving.net/services-4

https://www.linkedin.com/in/linda-jyoti-stuart-9833b7141/

CHAPTER 17

OPEN WATER SWIMMING
RELEASE PAIN, FIND FREEDOM, AND RECLAIM JOY

Lisa Swid

MY STORY

The moment my marriage came undone.

I can't believe this is happening. Will 20 diapers be enough? I can always buy more. Yeah, but with what money? We are already over-drafted. Fuck.

My thoughts are racing a million miles a minute.

Presentation at work tomorrow. Daycare fees are due Friday. Dinner for tonight. The gas tank needs to be filled. Clean underwear. Toothbrush. Phone charger.

My neighbor from a few blocks away is on the way. When he arrives, I will grab my phone and packed bag, and we will make a swift exit.

I can't be here anymore. We can't be here anymore.

I'm good at surviving. I inherited it from my refugee ancestors, and my body instinctively knows what to do. I look down at my hands and realize that life has been preparing me for this very moment. I can do this. I know what to do. I just need to jump.

I can't be here anymore. We can't be here anymore.

My neighbor arrives and we stick to the plan. We head to his house and he orders us a pizza but I'm not hungry. My stomach churns with nauseousness.

What am I going to do? Where am I going to go?

I call my best friend and tell her that Nikolas and I need a place to stay for the night. She was expecting the call and told me to come over. When we arrive, Nikolas wants to play with the Buddha statue. I distract him with some old Christmas decorations I found in the corner of the room. My breath catches in my chest, and I feel the urge to throw up. I tell Nikolas, "We're going to have a sleepover," so I can talk to my friend. He doesn't ask any questions; he just wants to play with the Buddha statue. My best friend makes a makeshift bed out of her couch for us—fresh, clean sheets and a soft pillow. After I read *Goodnight Moon* and tuck Nikolas under the covers, kiss his forehead, and turn off the lights, the tears start to come. They flood down my cheeks and onto the pillow like a faucet that won't turn off. I feel everything and nothing at the same time. I count my fingers, 1-2-3-4. . .

What am I going to do?

I stare into the darkness of the night.

The next morning, I wake early and look in the mirror. *I can't go to work like this.* My eyes are so puffy; no amount of makeup would cover up the pain. I can't remember the last time I ate food; my skin looks so pale. I feel translucent. I pull out my phone and look at Google Maps. Amazing luck. Nikolas' daycare is within walking distance, just a few blocks away.

When he wakes, I feed him a bagel and fruit that I found in the kitchen and tell him, "We get to walk to Cathy's house (his daycare) today, yippee!" I feign excitement at the newfound adventure we're on. I change his diaper, dress him in clean clothes, brush his teeth, and we walk to the home daycare. Cathy sees my face and asks, "What's wrong?" I disclosed everything to her in a few sentences. Like my best friend, she wasn't surprised. Another mom walked into the daycare just as I was sharing the details of what transpired the night before. The mom doesn't hesitate to offer her granny flat to us. She says, "Nobody is using it for the next two weeks, and you're welcome to stay there until then. It will be fun to have you both there."

Okay, that buys me some time to figure things out. I wonder if I should try to pay her for the room. With what money? I am so embarrassed. What am I going to do? I can't go back. We can't go back. What the fuck am I going to do? Fuck, fuck, fuck, fuck, fuck.

The texts from him haven't stopped—hurtful, drug-induced, nonsensical words. My friend tells me to ignore them. I can't. I keep reading. It feels like a dagger to my heart, and I want to defend myself. What he is saying is simply not true. *He wants me to apologize. How can I apologize for something I didn't do? Wouldn't that be lying? Wouldn't that make me just as awful as he is? I just need him to understand that I would never hurt him. I just wouldn't.*

I can't seem to stop the intrusive thoughts. *Am I a bad person? What did I do to deserve this?* I try to re-route them, deny them, or explain them away. But his language is so powerful, and I feel so small. His words land in my body and start to take up residence, making a home for themselves. *I am defective. I am sick. I am a bad person.*

What I didn't know at the time, but what I now know to be true, is that prolonged drug use can cause psychosis and vivid hallucinations so real that the user (and anyone around) loses touch with reality. The lines become so blurred because while you're still alive in the world, you're seeing and experiencing things that others aren't. My husband believed there were people dressed in camouflage, living in the canyon outside our house, watching our every move. He believed he was carrying around a very rare parasite from a trip he took when he was a teen that was killing him from the inside out. He believed there were bugs crawling under his skin. Incredulously, he even believed I was assaulting him.

If you engage with the user on their terms, you'll lose the battle—every time. The harder you try, the worse it becomes. So you're eventually left with a choice. Get pulled deeper into the chaos, or get out.

I got out. We got out. But I was left with scars, hurt, and pain that festered for years afterward. My psyche was scarred; my heart was broken. My sense of self whittled down to someone with no value or worth.

The day I called in sick to work, I went to a yoga studio. I collapsed into a child's pose, too weakened to lift my head up. Afraid to be seen in all my glorious weakness, there was a pool of tears on my mat, and I did my very best not to let an audible sob escape my mouth. *Keep it together, Lisa. You can't fall apart here. People will hear you. Not here.*

"Let's move into all fours and start moving through some gentle cat-cows," the teacher instructed. I tried; oh how I tried. But I felt so much shame. Looking around the room at the other practitioners, they all looked so prim and proper in their Lululemon activewear. No holes in their clothes, no dirty feet. Their hair looked freshly washed and trimmed; no split ends in sight.

How did I get to such a bad place? Where did I go wrong?

Eventually, I found the strength to move into all fours. And eventually, I even found the strength to do some sun salutations. Wobbly, weak, tear-stained, and heartbroken, I flowed. I moved. I placed both hands upon my heart and prayed for peace, for all beings everywhere to be happy and free. Namaste. My prayers continued.

Dear God, please help me, I begged in my head. *Please? I am so lost. I am so confused. Please, I will do whatever you tell me to do. Just please tell me where to go. Give me some sort of sign. I can't go back to our home anymore, and I don't have any money. Please help me find my way. I will do whatever you tell me to do; just show me where to go. Please?*

The days went on in this fashion. The days turned to weeks. Getting by, one day at a time, finding my way, our way, to a better place. Leaning on the goodwill of family, friends, and strangers, I asked for help when I needed it, which was daily. I prayed that one day, I'd be strong enough to offer help to others who needed it most. I didn't want to be in this needy position for long. I wanted out. I wanted freedom and liberation from my pain. I wanted a new life.

So, what does one do after the storm has passed? How do you reclaim your body, your sacred home? Your breath? Your self-worth? Your joy? As with everything in life, you start with one small step. A simple intention. A gaze set towards hopefulness.

I explored so many healing modalities in an effort to rebuild my life: various yoga teacher trainings (Hatha, Yin, Kundalini, Trauma-Informed), Reiki, 5 Rhythms Dance, art therapy, talk therapy, Al-Anon meetings, acupuncture, non-violent communication, and improv comedy. All played and continue to play a positive role in my journey. Eventually, my path led me to the healing balms of open water swimming. A place I had been before but had lost my connection to for too many years. Finding it was like a grand return home.

THE SELF-LOVE PRACTICE

To those who have experienced pain, grief, regret, confusion, shock, isolation, hopelessness, shame, anger, and fear because someone you love is struggling with substance use disorder, I want to share a self-love practice that has helped me to release pain, find freedom, and reclaim my joy. I promise that you're not alone and that there is hope. Happiness is your birthright. But it's up to you to claim it. It's a choice you must make every single day.

Before I share this practice with you, I invite you to place both hands over your heart. Inhale through your nose, filling all the way up. Pause at the top. Exhale all the air out. Pause at the bottom. *It is not your fault.* It's okay if you can't accept that right now, but it is not your fault. Inhale. Pause at the top. Exhale completely. Pause at the bottom. *It is not your fault.* You did everything you could to stay sane with the tools you had at the time. You did your best. *It is not your fault.*

Take a moment to recognize all that you're carrying in your body. Do an inventory of the beliefs you're holding on to. Ask yourself if you'd like to release any of it. And if your answer is yes, you're ready.

Find a natural body of water that is safe to swim in. The colder, the better. Dip your toes in the water and take note of how the chill affects your nervous system. Notice the pace of your breath. Did it speed up or slow down? Pause, simply noticing your surroundings. How does the air feel on your bare skin? Begin to enter the water, one step at a time, while staying fully conscious of your breath, body, and your judgment of the temperature. Is it too cold, too warm, or just right?

If the water is uncomfortably cold but bearable, you're in a good place.

Do not rush the entry process. Allow your body, which is made up of 60% water, time to acclimate. Stay in connection with your breath. It's okay if the pace of it increases or it becomes more shallow. The cold will have an effect. Just notice how your body responds. Do you want to scream? Scream! Do you want to laugh? Laugh! Do you want to cry? Cry! Allow yourself to feel all of the feelings. All of them. This is not the time or the place to hold back. You're free to be you in this place of home, this space of source. All of you is welcome and celebrated here simply because you had the courage to show up.

Ready to put your face in the water and start swimming?

As your body continues to acclimate to the temperature and you sync with the currents, find your flow. One stroke, then the next. Are your feet and arms working with each other or against each other? How is your breathing? It's okay to swim messy for now. The more you practice, the more comfortable you'll become. Transitioning from land to water, from walking to swimming takes time. Give yourself some grace to nurture your gills.

There's a high probability that most people around you do not practice open-water swimming. You're doing something special and out of the ordinary. Something brave and personal. Choosing to wake early and head to the water's edge while most everyone is still asleep, warm in their beds, is not easy. But you will be gifted with experiences most people won't ever have. Catching sunrises that take your breath away, cold water that evokes a response so primal, you can't help but feel alive and easing into a flow that solidifies your connection to something greater and more powerful than you will have a lasting effect on your nervous system and your psyche.

I have never had a bad day that started with an open water swim. No matter what may be happening in my life, I feel at home in the ocean. She shows me that turbulence and intensity are natural forces that will eventually pass. She shows me that every day can be different. The ocean shows me that tides and currents will shift and change, just like our emotions and moods. She shows me that showing up matters. That I matter. And that my joy matters.

During open water swims, you'll be blessed with the trifecta of solo time, meditation, and time in nature. In this space, you have the opportunity to ponder your life's big questions. What do you need in order to live a truly fulfilling life? So much of your baggage will inevitably be released through the repetitive motions of swimming. If you're not a swimmer yet, start small. You can start by walking along the shoreline and playing in the waves if it's safe. Find a pool to submerge your body in. Since time immemorial, cultures from all over the world have been using the medicinal and therapeutic qualities of water to heal, cleanse, and relax the physical body. Ancient Egyptians and those from the Old Testament practiced bathing rituals and soaked in mineral waters to heal their ailments. The Greeks and Romans built extravagant communal bathhouses. Jimjilbang (Korean bathhouse) has been used for medicinal purposes since the 15th century. There is no shortage of research that shows how being in water can improve emotional, physical, and mental health. When you connect with water, you'll discover and connect with the truth of who and what you really are. You are a vessel, a body, moving through time and space. You're already home, and you're worthy of love, attention, and joy simply because you exist.

My son's father has been sober for over a decade and is happily remarried with another child. I am so proud and grateful for the journey we shared because it led us both to the path of healing. Had it not been for the turbulence and chaos of substance use disorder, I may never have been challenged to find my peace. Had I not found my peace, I may never have found my way to the position I am in today—a place where I'm able to be in service to others because my cup is now full and overflowing. My sincere desire is that my story has helped you in some way to reconnect with yourself. And to recognize that you are not alone.

I am immensely grateful for the open-water swimming community that has shown me the ropes and has supported, encouraged, and celebrated my goals and my journey. People often think of swimming as a solo sport. But they're wrong. It's the opposite of solo. I challenge you to find swimmers in your local area to learn from and connect with to get started. Swimmers are a special kind of people. They're hearty and full of heart. So get out there and have some fun in the water!

Note to reader: Open-water swimming can be dangerous. Before attempting to swim in open water, always check local resources for tides, currents, temperature, and water quality. Speak with a lifeguard to confirm conditions. Never swim alone; swim with a partner. Be prepared with appropriate gear that matches your swim level, experience, and acclimation. If you're a beginner, it's best to start in a pool with swim lessons or a coach. Ask local experts about the best ways to find open-water swim groups and/ or a coach to get started.

Lisa Swid has decades of experience in the water and a love of teaching swimming. She is an Open Water Swimmer in San Diego, California, where she swims regularly at La Jolla Cove and La Jolla Shores. She has explored many healing modalities and has found open-water swimming to be the most effective way to release pain, find freedom, and reclaim her joy. She completed her first marathon swim in March 2023, swimming from Cancun to Isla Mujeres in the El Cruce crossing (10k), a Catalina relay swim with the iswim4 foundation in September 2023 (distance of approx 21 miles), and is scheduled to do a solo swim around Coronado Island in November 2023 (11.5 miles). She looks forward to doing more long-distance open-water swims in the future and pushing the limits of what she once thought impossible or out of her league.

Lisa has a Bachelor's degree in Global Studies from UC Santa Barbara, a Master's degree from Utrecht University in Conflict Studies & Human Rights, and a Master's degree from Tel Aviv University in Middle Eastern History. When Lisa is not in the water, you can find her soaking up the sun with a good book in hand, taking long walks through the charming neighborhoods in San Diego, planning her next backpacking adventure and dreaming of world peace.

Ways to Connect with Lisa:

Instagram: www.instagram.com/lisa_swid/

Linkedin: www.linkedin.com/in/lrswid/

CHAPTER 18

BEFRIENDING MY ANXIOUS PARTS

CULTIVATING PEACE FROM WITHIN

Sharon Siegler, MA, LMFT

MY STORY

I can hear the siren. My parents are ushering my two younger brothers and me to their bedroom, our shelter. My youngest brother is seven. My parents are helping him put his gas mask on. His is specially designed for little kids. I'm 16. I know how to put my gas mask on. I practiced it over and over again at school.

We sit on their bed. Luckily, their room has a bathroom attached, but I'm too scared to go. *What if the gas will go inside of me when I pee?*

The windows in their rooms have tape on them to prevent shattering in case a missile hits. After we put the masks on, my mother placed wet towels to block all airways from the rest of the apartment to seal our shelter, as instructed by the authorities.

It's silent. We wait. I breathe. Inhale. Exhale. Inhale. Exhale. I can hear my breath, just like in scuba diving. But this is not scuba diving, and it's not fun. It's scary. My parents are looking at us. They're trying to look calm, but it's not helping me. I'm panicking.

Will the gas and germs come from the bathroom window?
Will I have to watch my brothers die in front of me?
How will it feel inside of me when I breathe the gas in?
God, please protect my family and me.

Please let the rocket fall into the ocean.

My body starts shaking. I can't control it. My legs tremble. My heart is beating loud and fast. My breathing is shallow and gaspy, and the sound it's making through the gas mask just worsens the panic.

My dad notices me spiraling. He puts his hand on my shoulders. In a calm voice, he tells me to relax and massages my back, and it's helpful.

"It's going to be okay, Sharon."

I can talk with the mask on, but it sounds weird.

"What if the chemical weapon is already in your room?" I ask him.

"It's not," he says. "They are not going to throw chemical weapons on us."

I look at him. I look at my mom. She nods. Both my brothers look at us. Then, a second siren triggers. This time, it's the siren that signals that the attack is over. My father hugs me while we all take our masks off.

It's 1991, and the Gulf War just started. For months, I've been hearing the news anchors announce: "Sadam Hussein threatens to attack Israel with chemical and biological missiles."

I was sure we'd die a very painful and ugly death that night.

That first night of the war, no one died from the attack, and there were no chemical or biological weapons. Israel was never attacked with chemical or biological weapons during the Gulf War. Two people ended up dying in total from the missile attacks.

Living in a dangerous place was normal for me, so once the threat of biological and chemical weapons lifted, I returned to being a normal teen and even volunteered in shelters to support the injured in case of a massive attack.

As a born and raised Israeli, I grew up in a war zone. There wasn't always an active war, so I thought my life was *normal*. What was also normal was listening to the news with my parents and hearing:

"A father and his two daughters were stabbed to death by a terrorist while hiking."

And then seeing my parents' sad faces and feeling my heart sink. *That could be me and my dad yesterday when we went for a hike.*

"13 people died and 20 injured in a suicide bombing on a bus at the heart of Tel-Aviv. The bomber's house was destroyed by the Israeli military." Pictures of flowers and candles where the bombing took place. Picture of the bomber, usually a young man.

It feels like a punch in my stomach. *One of the people who died was 13. That's my age. She must have had dreams for her future like I do, but hers will never come true. Her parents must be so sad.*

I always have to watch out for myself. There is always someone out there to get me; I am not safe.

Three out of four of my grandparents were the sole survivors from their families after the Holocaust. At 16 years old, everyone they knew was murdered. After the war, with nothing in their possession and unsurmountable grief in their hearts, they came to Israel, a new country where they had to learn a new language, where they were surrounded by other grieving people, and where another war was starting.

My mother's parents lived nearby to my family. They were loving and caring. My grandmother told me more than once that I was her favorite. Yet, she never hugged me. Often, I'd come to have lunch at their house after school. I'd knock on their door and hear her and my grandfather behind it in Yiddish.

"Ella, who is this?" he'd yell.

"Look through the door hole, Srulik," my grandma answers.

I felt their suspiciousness through the door.

"Oh, it's Sharoni!"

They undid the locks, and my grandfather greeted me with a big smile. My grandmother had an almost-smile. I wrapped my hands around her, hugged her tight, and told her jokingly, "Hug me, Savta." Savta is Hebrew for Grandma. She tapped me on the back lovingly, but that's as good as it got.

Be nice to non-Jewish people, but never trust them. Deep in their heart, they want you dead. You are not lovable. If so many people worked so hard to exterminate our people just because we're Jewish, something must be wrong with us.

My grandparents never said it explicitly, but I heard it. I never believed it with my mind, but my body and cells did.

Not receiving hugs from my grandmother did not have a big impact on me, but it did on my mother. She also lost a brother when she was ten. My grandfather became depressed when Ze'ev, his son, died, and my grandmother stiffened even more. My mother's feelings of unlovability grew strong. It's not surprising to me that she chose to marry a person with whom she had a relationship, which affirmed that belief. Their relationship was one of conflict and hardship. Yelling and violence were no strangers to me.

Since I could not solve the problems Israel was having, I tried hard to solve the problems my parents were having. Selfishly, I wanted my mom to love herself so badly. *How could I love myself if my mother doesn't love herself?* Being the oldest and the only daughter, I had a job. I worked on making my mother happy and on standing up to my father to help him change his attitude and love my mother. I did not receive Employee of the Year. I failed.

It's all my fault my parents are fighting. I should try harder. I should be good. It's all my responsibility. If I take responsibility, I can fix it.

Though the people in my life loved, cared for, and provided for me, I was unintentionally taught to not love myself. My neuro-pathways are well-carved with this message and messages of fear, shame, doubt, and guilt.

That panic attack during the Gulf War was the first of many. Years later, I became a certified scuba diver and, after several dives, started to have panic attacks every time I dove. Panic attacks showed up more in my twenties as well.

Though I did not have a name for it then, anxiety was a daily experience for me. I thought that was how everyone was feeling. I didn't know any other way. Anxiety was my source of motivation, and it told me what to do. I was her bitch. If I didn't listen, she paralyzed me and made me feel very uncomfortable.

I did a good job masking it, even from myself. When I had panic attacks, I taught myself ways to calm down. I put on a well-practiced facial expression of indifference, and since I love a thrill, I managed to show everyone how courageous and fearless I am; that way, the stories I told myself were affirmed by everyone around me.

Ever since I can remember, I have loved and cared about my relationships. I love getting to know other people intimately, as well as myself. I'm a seeker of depth. I experience pleasure in being at the depth of my soul. During my twenties, I started going to therapy. The journey of depth-seeking had me shift my career from a Software Engineer to a therapist, where I get to spend hours of my day soul-diving.

"You worry a lot," one of my therapists told me.

I was shocked. *Me? Worry? I am a chill person; everyone says so. I let my kids ride their bikes everywhere on their own, rock climb, and I journey into my soul bravely. I am not a worrier; I am a warrior.*

But after that, a nagging voice kept saying: *Maybe she's right?*

I started paying attention and soon realized: *Oh my god, I worry all the time.* Not only that, but I was constantly expecting a disaster.

I had to come to terms with the fact that it was true that I was a warrior, but I also used it to lie to myself and everyone else that I didn't worry. The more I paid attention, the more I learned how anxiety ran my life. So, I started working on understanding my anxiety.

My anxiety, it turns out, is not all of me but rather anxious parts of me. They are versions of young me, freaking out, thinking the world will collapse because I'm about to be late for a dentist appointment. For the most part, they're like children having a tantrum, getting out of proportion. Even if there's a "good" reason to worry, like I can't get in touch with my teen, or having a deadline, how my body feels, and where my thoughts are taking me is blown out of proportion, and my ability to stay present and make good decisions is compromised.

The more I became aware of my anxious parts, the more I fell in love with them. As I got to know them and understood them, I listened to them and heard their pain. In a way, they're my children, and I know how to be a good mother to them. I can be there for them like no one was there for me when I was young.

I'm grateful for my therapist's intervention. I was ready to hear something I wasn't prepared to hear until then. I was ready to heal something I wasn't prepared to heal until then.

Just the other day, I had a doctor's appointment. I was meeting my new doctor. I always get nervous before a doctor's appointment—even a routine check. I waited for her to come in. My heart is beating fast, I hate being here; she's going to be mean to me.

A few minutes later, I became aware. I put my hand on my heart and breathed. Inhale. Exhale. Inhale. Exhale. *I am safe. I am beautiful. I chose to be here. I want to be here. I am a woman who loves herself and all her parts.*

I calmed down and had a great appointment. I love my new doctor. I love my life. I love me.

THE SELF-LOVE PRACTICE

It's possible to have self-love, joy, happiness, and fulfillment even if anxiety is a part of your life.

I believe the path is learning to live with anxiety rather than get rid of it.

As I accept my anxious parts, they're less anxious. As my anxious parts are less anxious, my nervous system can withstand and tolerate more, and I'm able to make good decisions even in stressful moments.

I have the power to regulate my nervous system when I'm anxious, and I haven't had panic attacks for many years.

Anxiety is common and widespread, yet still not out in the open enough. If you struggle with anxiety, my heart is with you. There's nothing wrong with you; this world is hard. Your anxious parts were or are trying to figure it out the best they could.

To change something means to change our relationship with that something.

The practice I'd like to offer you is about getting to know yourself.

You can do it at any point in your day; the more you do it, the more you'll know yourself. The more you know yourself, the more choices you'll have in moments of stress.

This practice is especially great if you're someone who struggles with daily practice. In this day and age, there's a strong message that you "should" have a daily practice. I agree that it's excellent to have one. It's also excellent if you know your limits and find your own way of healing.

The practice is simple. It's taking a moment to check in with yourself, bring awareness to the present moment and your experience, and examine your options and choices. I describe the steps below, but I invite you to download the guided meditation for a deeper experience. (See resources below).

1. Breath. Inhale. Exhale.

2. Again, taking more time to exhale.

3. Again, a bit more time to exhale.

4. Note sensations, feelings, breath, thoughts, and tension in your body. No judgment, just notice.

5. Now ask yourself: "What could be a loving action I can take right now that is within my capacity?"

6. Notice your response. Do you know the answer to this question? Perhaps it's stressing you out? Is your body expanding with relief? *Oh, washing my face with cold water right now would feel so good,* or *a cup of coffee, yes, please!* Or, *I'm going to go hug my beloved.* Or, is this bringing other thoughts up like: *I don't even know how to love myself, or great, just another thing to think about, my head is already hurting from thinking too much?* Whatever came up, just breathe through it.

7. Feel into this moment. Did you tap into having choices? Do you feel like you don't? If your anxious part is activated, she might tell you there are no choices—just notice. There is no right or wrong; it's about getting to know yourself.

8. Decide what you're going to do about this. If you're feeling stuck, it's okay; it's a sign that your nervous system is not regulated. Your action should be self-regulating (check the resources below for help with regulation). If you come up with an action, decide if you will be doing it or not and take note of it. The more you choose the loving action, the more you will feel empowered and that you have choices.

9. Give gratitude to yourself and all your parts for taking this moment to get to know yourself.

The more you do this practice throughout the day, the more you will get to know yourself and your choices. It's those little steps that we take that create the change in a big way. It's the time that passes that allows us to look back and see the little steps accumulate into that big change that we so desire.

All your parts are worth getting to know, even if some of them don't make you feel good. Knowing what's going on will open the door to more choices. Open that door now. It's never too late.

Sharon Siegler is a licensed Marriage and Family therapist living in Sebastopol, California. She lives with her partner, Daniel, and three teenage children.

Sharon has a thriving therapy practice where she helps her clients get to know themselves, recognize their strengths, accept their past, and explore how it impacts who they are today.

She loves seeing her clients move forward in life, manifest their full potential, and live a life filled with purpose, joy, connection, and any other goals her clients have for themselves.

Sharon's greatest resource is nature. Mother Earth, the sun, trees, animals, and flowers are all her teachers, lovers, and allies. You can find her lying naked on the ground, climbing rocks, schlepping her family on a backpacking trip, swimming in creeks and rivers, grieving with Mother Earth, and looking for new adventures.

Sharon loves to share her love of nature with her clients by offering them ecotherapy. Therapy in nature, with nature, and through nature. Many people naturally connect with nature as a healing source. Sharon offers a deepening of this experience by allowing nature to be the mirror, container, mother, father, or whatever is needed for her client to release their trauma, receive healing and resourcing, and get to know who they really are: a beautiful, wise, powerful, being, just like all elements of nature.

Connect with Sharon

Website: www.sharonsieglerpsychotherapy.com

Facebook: www.facebook.com/sharonsieglermft

Instagram: www.instagram.com/sharonsieglermft

Medium: www.medium.com/@mft.sharon.siegler

Email: mft.sharon.siegler@gmail.com

For the guided meditation of the self-love practice, resources about regulation, and more treats from me to you: www.sharonsieglerpsychotherapy.com/selflove

CHAPTER 19

NO MORE CRINGING IN THE MIRROR

WHAT SKIN CANCER TAUGHT ME ABOUT SELF-LOVE

Thais Harris, BCHN

MY STORY

I hold the little black mass, which I saved as if it were a precious gem, between my fingers. "What if I actually healed my skin, doc?" I show it to her.

"Oh, no, that's not possible," she replies with a dismissive tone. "It's not very conspicuous," she continues, looking through her dermatoscope, her face so close to mine I can smell berries and yogurt in her breath behind her mask, "but we have to remove a margin of error, as there could be more cancerous cells beneath it."

I breathe into my belly. My gut says no, but the fear of *what if* is strong. *I have to be responsible.* My body feels heavy in the surgical chair, my mind wanders off, thinking of how perfectly healed that spot looks, and I want to say: *Stop, just give me some time to think,* as I feel the blunted sensation of her scalpel digging into my cheek.

I wince as I hear the sound of being cut into, even though I feel no pain. After it's done, the swelling starts to close my right eye, and I approach the mirror with tentative curiosity. *What have I done?*

Walking to the surgeon's office, feeling the sunshine on my face and arms, I was in a deep state of gratitude, restricted only by the fear of what would happen. I was in Copenhagen, a place I imagined visiting for many years. It was like being in a vibrant dream: the shades of green in the arborized streets, the blue hues on the water's edge, and the bright red train that got me there. This appointment was my reality pinch.

After the procedure, I walked outside again, this time feeling a thumping sensation in my face with every step. I hold tears back as I try to reconnect with that gratitude from earlier. *Should I have waited? I didn't need to do anything I wasn't fully ready for. Maybe one is never ready for this kind of thing.* I can't help but feel violated.

What if my practices healed my cheek? And now we disturbed the skin that had just healed? I was fine, and now this wound, this swelling, this pain. I reach the fortress, where I'm meeting my husband and son. The irony is not lost on me. *I feel the opposite of a fortress right now.*

"Are you okay?" My husband's warm embrace opens the gate for the grief inside, and I cry in his arms, feeling both a sense of relief and loss. And so much doubt.

I heard someone say that when the grief train arrives, it brings all its cars. This moment felt like that. That small surgery and the cancer that made it necessary were only the top layer in the well of grief beneath it.

We sold everything: our house, our two cars, most of our furniture. We knew we wanted to explore the world, and 2019 was the right time to do it (and in retrospect, I'm so thankful we did it before Covid). We left for six months to figure out where we belonged. We were happily settled in Northern California until 2017, when our town was the site of one of the worst wildfires in the state's history.

After waking up at 3 a.m. with a knock on our door—our neighbor urging us to evacuate—I step outside to see a red glow over the town. *We have to get out of here!* My husband urges me to breathe a 4-3-7 breath. *I can't stop and breathe; I must act!* I resist at first.

Why am I choosing to panic? His embrace reminds me I can do this better if I'm calm and present. I inhale for a count of four, hold my breath for a count of three, and exhale for a count of seven. I breathe like this one more time and then sprint into action. I'm not calm, but I notice how even a quick pause improves my ability to be present.

My three-year-old son is sleeping peacefully, and I manage to pick him up from his crib and put him in his car seat without waking him. The air is heavy with smoke, and I lift my shirt's collar to my face, using it as a mask. Passports, clothes, computers—we pack all we can into our truck and drive away. I say goodbye to my house, not knowing if I'll ever return to it.

At that moment, I knew living in California was no longer viable for our family. We were one of the lucky ones; our house was still there to welcome us back. Even so, twenty months later, we began a process that culminated into moving to the Berkshires, Massachusetts, after considering a few countries in Europe.

The start of this new chapter was a dream come true. My husband and I spoke at a conference in Italy and events in Norway, Portugal, and Scotland, presenting the work we developed by merging my field of holistic nutrition with his of somatic psychotherapy. *Optimizing your D.I.E.T.: Your Daily Intake of EveryThing* was the theme we were teaching, and it was the perfect vehicle to travel and work while also considering a new home. Within the context of our work, we were acutely aware of what we were taking in—nourishment, activity, media, thoughts, and nature—at each place we considered.

At the end of the trip, we realized we wanted to be in the U.S., closer to family and friends, and more able to continue our work where we thought people would benefit the most. It felt too hard to be so far away from the community we loved: it would be hard enough being on the other coast; moving to another country lost its appeal.

Exciting as this new chapter was, I could no longer ignore the doubts surrounding leaving our home and our community. All my grief cars were pulling into the station.

Before leaving California, a mole on my cheek got scraped off and sent to pathology. "You're gonna get skin cancer!" My mother's words echoed in my head as the dermatologist called me the day before I boarded the plane to tell me it was cancerous.

"Squamous cell carcinoma," she says. "If you're going to have cancer, this is the best one to have."

Somehow, that was supposed to make me feel better.

"I am leaving town for six months," I reply.

To my surprise, she said, "Return to us immediately when you get back."

It mustn't be so bad. They are not asking me to cancel the trip. I wouldn't, anyway.

Since the mole had been scraped off, there was nothing visually reminding me of its importance, so I put the whole thing in one of those little boxes inside the attic of my mind, where the uncomfortable things are.

Ten days into the trip of a lifetime, a brown, then reddish, then black mole quickly grows on that same spot. It's undeniably cancerous – cells multiplying with no function or purpose, right in the middle of my face.

Every time I saw a mirror, I cringed. Whenever I saw a photo of myself, I felt a heaviness in my heart, and then my mind took over.

This looks so ugly. What could this mean? Are there more? Am I being punished for something? Maybe my life is too good right now. I should give my time and money to those in need, not enjoy a European trip! Who do I think I am? Is there a wicked power trying to show me some inner ugliness I have not yet acknowledged?

As a pale, blonde girl, growing up in Brazil was a challenge when it came to enjoying the beach. In my teens, I wanted so badly to have a golden tan like my friends. "Galega" or "Branquela" were names people called me for being so white. I was the fish out of water on that tiny-bikini-lined coastline. No matter what I put on my skin, or if I didn't put anything at all, I would not tan. I instead got red, and on too many occasions, was so sunburned I had blisters.

A couple of times, it got so bad I barely slept, keeping my arms and legs strategically propped up so they wouldn't rub against the bed. My mother understandably got worried-scared-mad and blurted out, "You have to protect yourself from the sun, or you're gonna get skin cancer!"

Thirty years later, she was right.

Some part of me, some of my cells, believed my mother. *What could happen if I turned that belief around? What if there was enough beauty, love, light, and power within me to help reverse and even heal this process?* Could I trust and practice all the holistic approaches I'd studied?

As a holistic nutritionist, my work is founded on the principle of including one's entire experience and transforming beliefs, thoughts, and habits to achieve wellbeing. I believed in my healing capacity, but I wasn't sure where to start. Changing my diet even more wasn't going to do it.

Losing my own dad to cancer six years prior to Squeamy (the loving name I gave the growth on my face) motivated me to learn everything I could about nutrition for cancer prevention. This led me to work with cancer patients at Ceres Community Project.

While there, I read an article about a pediatric oncologist who asked his patients to visualize a powerful bright light from within them, much like a lightsaber, beaming directly into the spot where the cancer was. He credited his high success rate to the children doing this work from the inside out.

One day, looking at the mirror with that familiar *ugh* expression of disgust toward my face, something inside asked me to step up, reminding me of that article.

Include this. Yes, the cancerous mole. You as you are in this moment. Love it all. Beam some light into it. Where is your inner lightsaber? Turn toward yourself.

This is what stepping up looked like to me: I spent a few minutes every day practicing a beam-of-light breath and sending it to my cheek. And I showed myself love and respect whenever my reflection greeted me in the mirror.

Old habits die hard, and showing love in the mirror took some getting used to. My habitual narrative of: *Your eyes look puffy. Your nose is huge. Oh no, that black thing is getting bigger and uglier,* had to be intentionally replaced with: *Good morning, love. I'm here for you. We can do this. You look lovely. Your skin is healing.*

When I caught my reflection with a look of disdain, I made myself return to the mirror with a loving look instead. It took diligence.

Ten days after committing to these two practices, Squeamy popped off into my fingers with the gentlest pull.

A month later, I had the margin-of-error surgery. Turns out I was right: the entire sample my Danish doctor removed was one hundred percent clear!

Squeamy might have been the manifestation of my grief. Holding it with kindness allowed me to transform the mindset of *this is happening to me* into *this is happening for me.*

I learned to take better care of my skin and made a healing pact with the sun, being smarter about when and how I enjoy its rays. I'm actively re-writing the beliefs my cells held for so long. *Your skin is healing every day. You take good care of yourself.*

I also learned from Squeamy that I could combine both a conventional medicine approach with my inner healing strength. I wasn't powerless, *and* help was welcome. I began to advocate for myself, taking steps that felt grounded both in science and within my body-mind-spirit.

Over the last two years, I had six other skin cancers surgically removed—basal cell carcinomas and one superficial melanoma. This was new territory; there were no moles to pop out. I went into these surgeries with a very different attitude. I felt more resolved and not so afraid. And I beamed my light at each spot before, during, and after the surgeries.

"You don't scar very well," my dermatologist tells me.

I imagine myself erasing his words as if he'd written them on a dry-erase board. I wish my cells hadn't heard that.

Neither good nor bad, these scars are part of my experience. I display on my shoulders, back, and chest the prominent reminder of my healing. And despite their pink, rugged appearance, I healed fast. I accompanied the process with awe for my body's ability to mend.

Between greeting myself with love when I see my reflection and focusing my breath into a beam of light towards areas that need healing, I found a way to feel empowered, confident, and engaged with my body and health in a more meaningful way.

It takes constant, active training. I'm trying on a new bathing suit and look at the flesh around the bra line on my back. *What kind of exercise are you going to do to get rid of that flabby skin?* Deep breath. *You are aging gracefully. I'm here for you, wise body of mine.* The new narrative comes a bit quicker. The micro-aggressions of the critic in the mirror have become less effective. Some days, she doesn't even try.

Body image has nothing to do with what we see in the mirror; it's how we feel inside. Working with women of all ages, shapes, and sizes, including models, has taught me that. My journey with skin cancer has made me painfully aware of it. Self-love is now an integral part of my daily intake of everything.

The fires in California kickstarted a chain of events that forced transformation in my life—leaving a beloved community, stepping into the unknown by traveling a new continent with my husband and five-year-old son, moving across the country, leaving a teaching position, starting my practice over again in a new town. This would've felt completely overwhelming had I not embraced the beautiful, vulnerable, perfectly imperfect woman in the mirror.

Being hostile with ourselves does not facilitate wellbeing, and it most certainly does not foster love and beauty. When we use our energy for beaming our light, rather than running the incessant mill of critical thoughts, we cultivate the kind of love we need to heal and overcome any challenge.

Are you ready to beam love at the mirror and within yourself?

THE SELF-LOVE PRACTICE

FINDING LOVE IN THE MIRROR

Notice the thoughts that pop into your head when you catch a glimpse of yourself in the mirror.

The habitual thoughts usually stem from your beliefs, yet you can upgrade your thoughts to reshape your deep beliefs.

Do you smile at your reflection? Do you feel warmth and contentment?

Or do you wince, cringe, or perform any of the not-so-subtle self-aggressions women have been taught? A quiet ugh of dissatisfaction, disgust, or shame.

Notice your response without judgment. Then, do a double-take. Return to the mirror with a compassionate message.

I love you. I'm here for you. You look lovely today. Those eyes shine. You are love.

Replace any inflammatory narrative with one of these sentences, or create your own love notes. If you need a reminder, put some post-it notes on your mirror at home to inspire a consistent practice. Consistency creates transformation.

It may feel inauthentic at first, but in time, this caring way of seeing yourself will transform your beliefs and clear the way for your energy to go into healing and living more fully.

And then, take this love a little further:

BEAM OF LIGHT

When a specific area of your body needs extra love, take a few minutes to sit quietly and focus on your healing intention.

Take deep breaths through your nostrils into your belly. Reaching the belly is key to connecting with your inner landscape and feeling more present.

As you breathe, become aware of all the life within you, all the cells in your body, all the microorganisms that protect you, and all the D.N.A. carrying wisdom from all your ancestors. Breathe into this awareness.

Next, become aware of the space around you, the air, the walls, the space outside your room, and the natural world around it.

Then give the air you breathe a color, a quality of light,

Increase this light's potency inside your belly with each inhale.

When you reach a brightness that feels sufficient, beam this light in one steady stream into the part of your body that needs it most.

See in your mind's eye this light washing over and cleansing that spot, freeing it from anything that ails it.

You can beam this light with your breath for as long as you wish.

When you feel complete, thank your cells, the life within you, the wisdom from your ancestors, and the intelligence in your soul for helping you heal.

Thais Harris is a board-certified holistic nutritionist who helps women love themselves into their ideal body, vibrant health, and an outstanding life.

She helps women prioritize their wellbeing while ensuring family and career needs are met. Cultivating deeper self-love as the guiding principle in making dietary and lifestyle improvements, her clients get crystal clear in their goals, understanding their unique needs with the help of current labs and D.N.A. reports. Together, Thais and her clients identify priorities and create a custom path forward to end self-loathing (and the sabotaging that comes with it) and rediscover vibrant health, transforming their relationship with body, mind, and food.

After working for five years with cancer patients at Ceres Community Project and a decade in private practice at Nourish Together, it is clear the biggest results come from a place of love and respect towards oneself rather than punishment, deprivation, shoulds, and don'ts.

Thais grew up in Brazil and moved to the U.S. in 1999 to pursue the life of her dreams. She graduated from C.I.I.S. (California Institute of Integral Studies) and completed a certificate in Holistic Nutrition from Bauman College, where she became faculty and taught therapeutic nutrition.

If you're ready to boost your self-love, transform your relationship with food, and empower your health, reach out for a consultation. Start by downloading my free guide below.

Guide: 3 Mindset Shifts to Love Yourself Into Better Health: www.self-love.nourishtogether.com

My website: www.nourishtogether.com

Instagram: www.instagram.com/nourish.together

Facebook: www.facebook.com/NourishTogether/

My children's Book, *Little Red: The Apple Who Wanted to Sparkle*: https://a.co/d/86XYRUj

CHAPTER 20

THE TEEN DIARIES
UNEARTHING THE PAST TO WRITE MY WAY TO HEALING

Jayne Jacova Feld

MY STORY

May 26, 1984

"There is this kid in the hallways that always harasses me. He pinches my ass, rubs his hand on my pants, stares at me all the time, and sometimes says stuff. A few of my friends know, and I finally told Mommy. They say I should either ignore him or tell my guidance counselor. I've been ignoring him, but he still persists. I'm scared."

Almost 40 years after writing that diary entry and rereading it today, a wave of nausea crashes over me. While the precise memory may be hazy, the tide of fear that formed those words hasn't receded. It feels as though danger still lurks in the surf, churning up insecurities and pent-up anger.

Once again, I'm questioning: *Was revisiting my written past really such a good idea?* I'm close to shutting this exercise in self-reflection down, slamming the cover shut, and shoving my teenage diary under my bed back into the darkness. Being 14 was confusing enough the first time around; why go through it again?

Yet it's this very passage that makes me realize I will read on. That teenage girl is crying out to be heard. And I can't abandon her. I can't be yet another person who fails to take that girl seriously.

Deep breath.

I envision my young self: big, teased hair in an unlikely shade of reddish-brown (thank you Sun-In); skin-tight red parachute pants, and a *Flashdance*-inspired off-the-shoulder sweatshirt. I don't judge her; she's tough enough on herself. Instead, I imagine taking her in my arms, assuring her she's not being a drama queen, or "acting like Sarah Bernhardt," as my father would say whenever I dared to voice my displeasure about anything.

It fucking sucks to have to walk to class with the fear of being groped, I tell her. It's not all in your head.

You're safe, sweet girl, and I'm on your side.

Lifting this decades-long burden is freeing. And now, a truth emerges: These journals I've stockpiled for years were kept for a reason. They hold more than memories. Each offers fragments of my evolving self, representing a past that's a part of me. It may hold the key to why, now that I'm grown, I'm falling short of living my soul's purpose.

Starting with this first diary—which sets the scene in that Orwellian year of 1984—I plan to read them all, cover to cover. It's hard work, emotionally. So it may take a while.

According to the version of me who wrote so earnestly in that inaugural journal, I'm living someone else's life.

REVISITING MY TEEN YEARS

Oct. 8, 1985

"I'm sooo psyched about being a writer. It's all I want. I have to start writing more. But I start stories and can never finish them."

This entry resonates so clearly. My younger self was set on leaving the New Jersey suburbs in search of herself and never looking back. She dreamed of writing genre-bending novels that would put her name on the top of *The New York Times* bestseller list. She'd find it surprising—scratch that, she'd be outraged—that 15 years post-high school graduation would find her returning from a vibrant life in New York City to her pedestrian hometown to start a family.

With the passage of time (I'm 54 now), I can truly say I have no regrets about coming home to my roots. It's the path I envisioned for my life as a storyteller where I feel I fell short. Yes, I became a writer, but not the way

I'd pictured. As a journalist, I weave tales, but rarely my own. The deepest stories of my heart are still buried inside.

July 10, 1985

"I feel like a fraud. How can I actually dream of being a writer? I can't even open up to myself."

In the present timeline, that long-expressed thought still gnaws at me. Accomplished authors I return to again and again advise the yet-to-get-started to "write what they know." I get it. It's a call to draw on genuine, lived experiences and truths. But memories, I find, can be tricky, heavy things. This deep dive into my journals is an attempt to navigate the murkiness. To break through, I will need to sit with these memories. Own them.

My writer's block, I've long suspected, traces back to a time before I started journaling. These diaries reinforce that intuition. As I read them, recurring themes emerge—reminders of when showing my true self felt dangerous, even if I couldn't articulate why or had any power to change that. In my family, fitting in demanded holding emotions in check. Vulnerability was seen as a flaw, and genuine affection often hid behind sarcasm. Praise, when given, carried with it a cautionary "*keinahora,*" a Yiddish invocation to ward off the evil eye, as if too much happiness might court misfortune.

Although love was a given in my upbringing, it's crucial for me to challenge and move beyond those formative teachings.

March 3, 1985

"I hope I'm giving an accurate view of my feelings so when I'm older I can tell if I'm crazy or not."

I ache to assure the 15-year-old version of me she's not crazy. Her feelings deserve validation, and it's not too late for me to provide that to her. Still, perusing these pages is like reliving a movie, a raunchy teen comedy from the 1980s. I see my younger self unknowingly stumble and falter time and again, but I can't change the script. The diary itself—with its cheerful cover featuring a grinning cat, fluffy clouds, and a fluttering butterfly—contrasts sharply with its angsty contents. Inside, it chronicles too many nights filled with aimlessness, substance abuse, and fleeting relationships borne out of self-doubt. Back then, my harshest critic clearly was me. And even now, in moments of gentler self-critique, the word "trainwreck" shoots through my mind. It's as though I believed I had to embody the storylines of movies like

Sixteen Candles and The Breakfast Club to fit in. It's exhausting just to read into the struggle and confusion guiding my pen.

The diary also reveals moments when I pushed genuine connections away and lashed out at my parents and others, unaware of the deeper triggers behind my reactions. A passage from sophomore year captures typical outbursts between my mother and me.

July 19, 1985

"I told her I'll show more respect and think B4 I speak, and we settled on 2 weeks with no sleepovers. It's not that I don't respect her; it's just that I don't respect anyone."

Ouch.

In the present day, now that I'm a parent, I see my choices with greater clarity. While I can't change the past, I can offer my younger self the compassion and understanding she yearned for. My story, after all, captured in its rawest essence in this diary, set the stage for my present life.

THE LIFE LESSON OF RAVI

Exploring these memories is more than just a path to healing old wounds and breaking through writer's block; an urgent necessity drives it.

On April 3, 2021, my son Ravi lost his life in a tragic car accident that the rest of us—my husband and Ravi's two younger brothers—escaped with only minor injuries.

I've turned to the power of words to wrestle with the unimaginable. Instead of seeking comfort in the Kaddish, the traditional Jewish mourning prayer, I chose an intentional grieving path more in tune with my bond with Ravi. For an entire year, I penned insights on paper about my forever 17-year-old. It felt like the truest way for me to honor his beloved spirit and to feel his presence.

The words spilled out for this gentle introvert who greeted life with curiosity and awe. Like me, Ravi found inspiration, understanding and joy through the written word. Unlike the dramas that play out in my teenage diaries, Ravi's short journey was marked by simplicity and intentionality. He favored genuine bonds with family and a small circle of friends over the fleeting fun (but clearly a lot of boredom and drama) of the teen party life and mind-numbing distractions.

Ravi was my greatest life lesson. From the day of his birth, his love dismantled the walls of protection I had built. Through him, I realized a profound truth that was unavailable to me before motherhood: that the essence of true connection is rooted in vulnerability. In his absence, a stark reality emerged: embracing such emotional openness and depth has unimaginable costs. Bearing the crushing weight of sorrow might have been insurmountable without my compulsion to write. The very act of transcribing my anguish—what I recount on paper of my son's life and all that we've lost—has served as an anchor and guiding light.

Then, months after Ravi's death, I discovered something incredible. He, too, kept a journal, if only for a precious short time. The black, cover-bound book was hidden in plain sight under his bed, waiting for me to discover it. Finding it felt like an invitation for a cherished exchange between two writers. I see it as a silent acknowledgment of what he knew; of all mementos in the material world, I would most prize hearing his voice. Reading into its pages magnifies the ache of his loss, yet it also brings great comfort.

While the journals of these two teenagers differ, reflecting their distinct worlds and experiences, they both resonate deeply with the person I am today. Together, the journals of mother and son guide my path through this journey of figuring out how to live on.

Considering today's social media-centric era, a 16-year-old boy penning a journal feels especially profound. In defying these modern norms, Ravi clearly wrote to understand himself. I slip on his voice as I immerse myself in his writings, feeling his presence in every carefully chosen word. His astute observations over intensifying social and political divides leave me in awe:

12/8/2019

"Even though I can't vote yet, I try to be as involved as I can in the pivotal, potent political climate that has seemed to grab America by its throat over the past three years of the Trump administration. Even after reading several articles and opinions on the subject, I still cannot explain how half of the population of the United States seems to be entrapped in his cult of personality."

In other entries, it's so clear how he loved simple moments: baking chocolate chip cookies for our family Shabbat dinners, listening to the "Hamilton" soundtrack with his brother while studying together, and the pride he felt after scoring a hat trick in his high school ice hockey. Yet, what truly touched me was his genuine excitement in landing the lead role in our synagogue musical despite his utter lack of stage experience. I knew what a stretch it was for him just to try out.

Ravi wrote honestly about his feelings. He devoted a lot of space to his inner turmoil over the question of confessing his feelings to the girl he loved. He wrestled with the potential fallout of telling: jeopardizing a cherished friendship, altering dynamics between our families, or facing the sting of rejection. Through his words, it's clear to me he was working out all the angles and building up the courage to act.

12/21/19

"This is what I absolutely know: future Ravi, maybe ten years later, will regret if I didn't muster enough testosterone to take a shot at something I really want."

TAKING MY SHOT, TOO

This sentiment captures Ravi's journey toward self-assuredness that I lacked at his age. His writing paints a vivid picture of a teenager daring to embrace challenges on his own terms. I was hoping for so much more. Sadly, the journal he started eagerly and early as a 2020 New Year resolution did not become a habit. He wrote in it solidly throughout December 2019, and then it petered off.

I could say I feel cheated that the writing did not go on for longer. I choose instead to deeply appreciate this precious treasure he left behind for me. Each page speaks volumes of Ravi's innate understanding and acceptance of himself, acting as a link between our two realms.

While Ravi didn't get the luxury of revisiting his thoughts with the maturity of years, I am now gifted that privilege. His unspoken directive, from son to mother, is clear: to find strength in our shared love. As a fellow writer, I feel him cheering me on in my journey to overcome writer's block. For the two teenage souls, Ravi and myself, I commit to facing the future with courage.

I've got a lot of writing and healing to do.

THE SELF-LOVE PRACTICE

When my parents put my childhood home up for sale, I was already a mother myself, raising two-year-old Ravi and his newborn sibling Lee. The sale meant I had to finally reckon with the old journals tucked away in my bedroom closet. But back then, I wasn't ready to revisit those penned memories. The idea that, perhaps someday, someone—maybe even my children—might read them and see my insecurities and missteps in blaring ink was unsettling. The diaries went straight into a trunk in my basement, pushed into the background for years.

Months after Ravi died, I published a personal essay called "Ravi's Story" on the theme of our shared love of the musical "Hamilton." I described how the song "My Shot," about making one's mark in life, resonated with us both. For me, I mused, wasting my shot would be to never give novel writing a serious chance. But after putting that intention out to the world, I didn't do it. I didn't so much as start a fictional story before abandoning it. I have carried the weight of that writer's block for the past two years, feeling I'm letting down my beloved heavenly son – and myself.

Transitioning from my role as a magazine editor to freelance writer earlier this year, I aimed to finally undertake the kind of writing I'd always envisioned of my grown-up self. And I felt a pull towards my journals, believing they held insights into my present hesitations and fears.

I began with the first diary, writing down observations about moments that seemed pivotal in my life. But it wasn't so simple. I started and stopped reading and annotating the pages three times before I hit upon the passage that convinced me I was on the right path. That girl who was groped needed advice and compassion that never came; she needed someone to take her seriously, and I realized the person she needed was me. If it felt a little strange at first to visualize myself at the time and offer her unconditional love, it got easier the more I've been making it a practice. Now, there's no going back, and I wouldn't want to. Engaging with my unfiltered memories not only lessens my internal burdens, it reignites my writing drive.

If you've held onto your old journals, there's likely a reason. Open them and start reading to reconnect with your younger self. You may find it hard to set aside judgment initially. But keep going if, and especially when, you feel tempted to slam the cover shut. Instead, take a breath and envision being back in their shoes – with the wisdom of today.

Here's a better breakdown: In a separate journal (I use Scrivener, an app for writers), copy out entries that tug at you – either because the thoughts ring true today or went against your nature. Describe what it is about your words that feels so haunting and how it connects (or disconnects) to the person you are today. The magic is in releasing the hold repressed, misremembered, or half memories had on you. Do it in short, consistent blasts because it is a lot to process. Bringing it up with trusted friends may also help with resolution.

When you feel your inner critic taking over, pause, reach through the ages, and offer that younger version of you kindness and compassion they deserved. This reconnection can serve as a grounding force, guiding you forward in your writing, healing, and self-love journey. You deserve it.

Jayne Jacova Feld, a seasoned storyteller, is never far from an old-school pen and cover-bound journal. Writing has always been her way of processing the world and making a living.

As a journalist and content writer, Jayne writes and manages projects on topics ranging from health to business to celebrity profiles. Her work has been featured in well-known publications, including the *New York Times*, *Philadelphia Inquirer,* and *The Journal News.* She has served as the executive editor of *SJ Magazine*, a monthly general interest publication with a focus on women's empowerment.

Recently, Jayne has turned to deeply personal essays, delving into the transformative power of turning grief into love. The loss of her son Ravi in 2021 prompted her drive to explore the past, seeking a clearer understanding of her core purpose and what has held her back. As the future unfolds, she trusts that embracing this mind shift will lead to paths more resonant with her authentic self. She is grateful that this memoir piece so clearly resonates with the theme of "The Life-Changing Power of Self-Love."

Jayne lives in Cherry Hill, New Jersey, with her husband Craig and teenage sons Lee and Cary. She holds a bachelor's degree in journalism from Syracuse University's S.I. Newhouse School of Public Communications and a Master of Art in Writing from Manhattanville College. She continues to write and edit projects about health, science, businesses, interesting people, and a smidgeon of everything else.

You can explore her work at jaynesays.info.

Here are other ways to engage with her:

www.linkedin.com/in/jayne-feld

www.facebook.com/jayne.feld

www.instagram.com/jayne_jacova/

CHAPTER 21

MEET ME IN THE MESS

THE ONLY WAY OUT IS THROUGH

Rev. Annie Mark CSC, CCM

"Those who undertake the full journey into their grief come back carrying medicine for the world."

~ Frances Weller

MY STORY

I was not quite dead like my husband Dean, who'd recently killed himself, but I felt dead all the same, physically, emotionally, spiritually, and mentally dead. Grief knocked me off the axis from which I lived my life. It was gone, no longer turning. The ground below me opened, and I plunged into a deep, dark well of a kind of hell.

I was the walking wounded. My guts and blood spilled out, exposed and raw, but nobody could tell by looking at me. On the outside, I looked normal and fine. My heart, my soul, my whole body was in deep pain, a throbbing, excruciating ache with no cure, no remedy.

I went through the motions of living. My three-year-old son needed me. Like a zombie, I fed him, clothed him, and even played with him. I witnessed the me doing those things, watching myself, but inside, I was falling apart, disassembled. Life as I knew it was over, and the Annie I had been was dead.

I felt so very different just a short time before my deep dive into grieving. Everything changed in a flash, turning my whole world upside down.

In the months leading up to my husband's death, I experienced an awakening. I was recently sober from alcohol and newly on a path of creative rebirth, writing songs, poems, and stories. Something in me came alive in a way I'd not experienced before. I felt like anything was possible. I was excited about life, and oh, I felt so in my body—sensual, sexual, vibrant, alive, and on fire!

For the last couple of years, I worked with the book *The Artists Way* by Julia Cameron. It changed my life. Writing what the author calls morning pages, I'd write three journal pages every morning, every day without fail. The daily writing led me to come alive creatively. It also led to facing my problem with alcohol and to the issues in my marriage I avoided and numbed myself to.

Our marriage certainly had its ups. We loved each other. We were buddies. We'd had lots of fun as drinking partners. We loved laughter, the beach, good food, family, friends, music, and especially of course, we loved our son. But ours was a virtually sexless marriage.

Although Dean was a dynamic, kind, generous, fun-loving, larger-than-life presence, loved by so many, he had almost no sex drive. I had an intuitive reading when we were first dating where the psychic told me: "There is a big problem with his sex drive, and this will become a big issue if not faced."

I ignored her warning. I was newly in love, and we were having a great time. She was not wrong. Our entire marriage was, except for a very few times, sexless. One of those few times led to conceiving our son. I am forever grateful for that.

It became the big elephant in the room.

I'd ruminate, why doesn't he want me? It's my fault, I'm a crappy wife, not a good housekeeper, I've gained weight, let myself go and on and on.

I vacillated between blaming and judging myself for his lack of interest and being so angry at him, at myself. We saw a marriage counselor who suggested perhaps I ought to be the initiator of sex.

I initiated, to no avail, leading to more feelings of being rejected rising in me. I so often had feelings of worthlessness and not being good enough. I wrote all about it in those pages, sometimes so hungover from the drunken night before, but still, I wrote and wrote and wrote. I realize today that showing up to write, no matter what, was itself a practice of self-love.

A couple of weeks before Dean's death, I attended and participated in an open mic for original music at a local club. In the bathroom at the venue, after singing a freshly written new song, I washed my hands. I looked in the mirror and smiled at my reflection and had the thought:

Who wouldn't want me?

I was falling in love with me, with myself. *I like me. I love me!*

For me, this feeling was both foreign and exhilarating. I'd recently discovered a quote by Anais Nin that shot straight to my heart: "And the day came when the risk to remain tight in a bud was more painful than the risk it took to blossom." I was beginning to risk and to blossom.

I asked for a separation after realizing I had strong feelings for another man. I was so hungry for touch, for attention, for tenderness. This man saw me, touched me, listened to me, and loved me. My husband moved into the apartment above our main house.

We began the process of settling into a new kind of normal as a separated couple. It was as if everything changed, but nothing changed. We continued eating dinner together as a family, took our son to the park, and celebrated Christmas. The fantasy in my head was once the dust settled, we could all be loving friends living in harmony together. I loved Dean, but I couldn't continue living half a life.

Dean did not want the separation. I had second thoughts about it too, but never voiced it aloud. I wrote about it all in my morning pages, sorting through so many feelings. *I still love Dean, and I also love this other man. Is that possible? I'm so mixed up and confused.* I realized and was beginning to face that I played a big part in our marriage problems too. We argued, but in between, life went on.

The night Dean died started like so many other nights. The three of us had dinner together. I planned to go out. Dean knew about the man I was seeing. He brought it up, saying, "I'm having crazy thoughts," and we argued to the point it escalated. I asked him to go upstairs to his apartment.

I didn't feel safe. Looking back, I realize now I was in some kind of hyper-aware mode. I locked the door from the main house to his apartment when I heard a loud, deafening crash. Dean busted down the wall and door and was back in the main house, threatening me.

This was out of character for him. I didn't know him to be a violent man. On the other hand, throughout our marriage, he'd always had a kind of simmering, fuming, pent-up anger that sometimes scared me. At those times, I'd find myself scurrying around trying to make things right in hopes of calming him.

But this night, he'd busted open the wall and door. I knew he was hurting and angry and not in his right mind. I felt deep in my gut an inner knowing. *I needed to get out of the house.* I felt an eerie calm come over me. I gently suggested we talk things through when we both cooled off. I started quietly getting ready to go, making no sudden moves.

My son looked at me, saying, "You're taking me with you, right Mommy?"

I nodded and dressed him while Dean pleaded with me to stay. I promised we'd talk when I got back, quietly carrying our son to the car and left. I drove and drove aimlessly, in what I realize now was a nervous state of shock. Hours later, I made our way back home. Police cars, flashing lights, and yellow police ribbon surrounded our house. My sister-in-law met me as I pulled up.

"Dean is dead, isn't he?"

She nodded yes.

My God, what has he done? My God, what have I done?

I went from being excited about living *(who wouldn't want me)* to being virtually gutted, cut open, and exposed with the rug ripped out from under me in two weeks. It was a time of full-on collapse. When I was alone in my car, I wailed like a wounded animal in excruciating pain, other times burying my head into my pillow, unable to stop crying.

The grief was so profound that brushing my hair seemed like a huge undertaking. I felt exhausted even attempting it. I was swimming in a sea of sorrow, guilt, shame, and regret.

'Dean is dead, Dean is dead, Dean is dead,' I wrote in my journal every day. I wrote and wrote and wrote, letting it all out. The missing, the regret, the remorse, the guilt, the shame, the anger, all of it, I poured onto the page day after day. Along with that, a kind of prayer emerged.

Dear God, help me to learn and grow from this. Walk with me. Carry me.

I showed up as best I could each day, for myself and my son, attending recovery meetings and finding a spiritual community that held me and supported me. I became a leader of the music ministry there, where sharing my music was a balm for my soul and spirit.

From there to my surprise, I found myself called to ministry, attending seminary in Manhattan and being ordained as an interfaith minister. I also became an associate minister at the congregation which was such a big part of my healing journey through my grief. I'm so grateful to *Gathering of Light Interspiritual Fellowship* and Rev. JoAnn Barrett for providing a spiritual home and safe haven through such a challenging time.

I have such deep, heartfelt gratitude and love for my sister Jennifer for being a second mother to my son, and for my cousin Debbie for showing up for him when I could not.

I look back on that time now and still cry about it. I miss Dean. I'll never get over what happened. The people we love and lose are unique and irreplaceable, and suicide adds a whole other multi-faceted gut-wrenching layer to grieving. Me, my son, our family, and our friends have been forever changed by his sudden, tragic, and unexpected death.

But I have gotten through it. That walking wounded woman I was is no longer so raw. The hole in my heart where Dean was remains, but now I feel a beautiful garden has grown around that hole, a wreath of love surrounding it.

Dean's death by suicide catapulted me onto a whole new path I had not planned on.

Broken open with a broken heart, diving deep into my grief, and being supported and carried along the way, I discovered more light shined on me and through me than ever before, not by avoiding my darkness, but by embracing it and by choosing not to abandon myself on the journey.

I have plenty of regrets and remorse for the choices and mistakes I've made. I know those choices and mistakes have had a profound impact on my loved ones, and I especially acknowledge the lasting impact those choices have had and still have on my son.

They also served as my greatest teachers and have shown me over and over my humanness. I cannot undo the past, but I do face it with humility and let it serve as the fertilizer for the me I am now and the me I'm still becoming. My heart has softened, and my capacity for love, compassion, and understanding for myself and others has grown.

These days, I laugh louder, cry harder, and love to dance with goofy abandon. I am able to experience both joy and sorrow as partners that don't have to cancel each other out. They live side by side within me and through me.

What I've learned through all of it is that life, birth, death, rebirth, love, loss, and everything in between, is messy. My life has not resolved and been wrapped up all nice and neat and tied into a pretty bow.

I've made a vow to stay with myself through it all. I show up no matter what. Being broken open by grief led me to a profound breakthrough that is ongoing today. I practice self-love. And I have most certainly found that it takes practice, practice, practice.

I remember and forget over and over, again and again. The deepest and most intimate relationship I've experienced is the one I've chosen to cultivate within myself. I show up with love for myself even when I don't feel like it, even when I feel like I don't deserve it.

I found it takes courage, kindness, compassion, and commitment to choose to really nourish and nurture and accept with love all the parts of myself, even those parts I've judged as unworthy or undeserving. I'm learning to become a devoted and dedicated disciple and student of my own individual inner and outer life in all its messy, miraculous, and mysterious incarnations.

I'm so grateful to be on this path and hope I can serve as an authentic, kind, and living example of continued resilience, rebirth, and resurrection.

Today, I no longer think: *Who wouldn't want me?* I want me; I choose me. All of me.

The truth for me is that I continue to discover that my relationship with myself has been and continues to be the juiciest journey there is!

When I lead and offer my Meet Me in the Mess series and sessions for groups and individuals, I listen, hold space, and support people right where they are. I walk with them as they birth new dreams, dive into their darkness, and grieve losses. I offer loving support, guidance, assistance, and helpful, practical tools to navigate their unique journey and struggles

through life. My experiences have shown me there is such power in facing, honoring, and acknowledging the messy in between where we are no longer who we've been but don't know yet who we are becoming.

So often there are messages in the mess and unforeseen gifts and treasures to be discovered there as we sift through it all with understanding, love, compassion, and curiosity. Meet me there.

My wish and prayer for you, the reader, is that you meet yourself where you are now and reach out to others for support when necessary. We are not meant to do this alone. I have needed and continue to need love and support from others along the way.

For example, when I said a reluctant yes to writing a chapter in this book, I immediately thought, *what the heck do I know about self-love?*

The fear came up, heart racing, the resistance, the doubt. My urge to keep those thoughts to myself was loud and strong, but instead of listening to that voice, I chose to risk being vulnerable and to share my thoughts and feelings with the other authors in this book during a Zoom meeting.

In doing so, I realized sharing my truth with them is my self-love superpower! I shared how mixed up, fearful, and messy I felt. They met me in my mess, and I could see them nodding in solidarity. I was not alone in how I was feeling. From there, I was able to write.

Being willing to call in all the help we need (spiritual, emotional, mental, and physical) is truly a self-love practice worthy of cultivating. May each phase and stage of your life serve as fertilizer to grow your deepest dreams and desires towards your life well lived and well-loved.

"So now I'm headed through the mystery, into the muddy seas, waiting for my eyes to clear and be seen. And this light that I have sought outside is burning bright within, until it chokes me in its struggle to be free."

(from the song, *"Whale Rider"* by Annie Mark)

THE SELF-LOVE PRACTICE

Start a Writing Practice.

Get a fresh notebook and or journal.

Set up a place in your home where you can write without interruption.

Make a commitment to yourself to stick with it even when you don't want to. I don't wanna is what I usually think every morning before I write. I write anyway. And when I miss a day or days, I start again and write.

The morning pages are one kind of writing practice where upon awakening, you write three pages. No editing or overthinking. Just write, write, write. Whatever comes up, write it down. Allow yourself the freedom to write your story, your truths, your trials, your triumphs. Let it all out onto the page. Three pages each day.

This has been and continues to be such a powerful self-loving, life-changing, and revealing practice for me all these years later.

Write a Self-Love Vow to Yourself.
A vow is a promise, a dedication.
Take some time to quiet your mind. Close your eyes. Place your hand on your heart. Go within. Give yourself some time and space to just be with yourself. In that quiet space, ask yourself, what is a vow I can make to myself? Write down what comes.

Keep it as simple as you can. I've found if I get too wordy and complicated, it has less effectiveness in my life.

These are examples of simple vows I've written for myself:
I vow to show up for myself, no matter what.
I vow to stay with myself when the going gets messy and rough.
I vow to ask for help when I need it.
When I forget to love myself, I vow to meet myself there and vow to return to love when I remember.
Post your vow in a place where you can regularly see it as a reminder.

Reach Out
When struggling, reach out and share with a friend, therapist, coach, minister, and or group. The shift that can happen when we are listened to and accepted right where we are can be so helpful and can create a ripple of self-love within us.

Rev. Annie Mark is a writer, an Interfaith and Shamanic Minister, Wedding Officiant and Ceremonialist, Certified Spiritual Counselor, Certified Contemplative Musician, Shamanic Breathwork Master Facilitator, Singer-Songwriter, Guitarist, Harpist, and a performing and recording artist.

She sings and plays harp prescriptively at the bedside of those who are sick and dying.

She is a contributing author to the Amazon bestseller *"Shaman Heart, 26 Tales of Turning Pain into Passion and Purpose"*.

She is the creator and facilitator of her Meet in the Mess series and sessions for groups and individuals.

She is the creator of Singing in the Sacred, an interactive experiential spiritual practice using singing, music, and silence to clear our minds, connect to spirit and tune into our truest and most authentic selves.

She is the creator of Build a Song, Build a Story experiential writing workshops.

She is the Co-Creator and Lead Teacher along with Rev. Stephanie Urbina Jones and Jeremy Pajer of Freedom Folk and Soul's Experiential Ministerial Training program.

She leads a variety of women's support groups, including empowerment and dream circles, and brings her heartfelt reverence and expertise to each ceremony, workshop, or offering, honoring as sacred all of life's many phases, stages, and passages.

If you are interested in working with me, I invite you to contact me for a free Meet Me in the Mess introductory session.

Connect with Annie:

www.revanniemark.com

www.anniemarkmusic.com

CHAPTER 22

SACRED HEART-WOMB MEDICINE

SURVIVING THE TRAUMA OF PURITY CULTURE

Dasha Allred Bond

"And the day came when the risk to remain tight in a bud was more painful than the risk it took to blossom."

~ Anais Nin

MY STORY

SAN SEBASTIAN - XOLALPA, MEXICO - FEBRUARY 2023

My words fell flat as I worked to form them between dry, heavy lips. "I think I'm dying." Life swirled around me at a half-time tempo. My senses stirred only slightly to the pulse of soft amber light twinkling about the room. The church bells from Iglesia de San Sebastian Martir echoed across the courtyard as the flutters and coos of mourning doves filled the room like ancient ghosts singing old Psalms.

A damp chill settled over my naked neck and shoulders. Ochre curtains billowed alongside the breeze, up and then down, trailing across my body like a veil. I fought to pull myself from fever-fed dreams. I tried to lift myself to sit up and failed. I sensed my roommate moving about the room. I tried again, with more urgency this time. "No, really. I think I'm dying."

Moments later, one of our retreat leaders, Jeremy, arrived with a make-shift first aid kit, the little plastic pregnancy-test-looking stick, and its corresponding nose swab. *This can't be happening! Not now! I worked in healthcare for the entire peak of COVID and never tested positive. I had been so careful leading up to this writer's retreat.*

Moments later, two lines appeared. I'd later find out I was positive for COVID and the flu. I was too sick to be angry, so I settled into a kind of bitterness. I felt defeated. I was laid off from work the year prior, so finances were tight. I only made the journey back to The Dreaming House and the ancient Sun and Moon pyramids because two dear friends insisted I pursue my writing dreams and loaned me the money to attend.

Our Lady of Guadalupe herself visited my night dreams and day visions, calling me back to her sacred lands. It was exactly a year prior that I first saw the pyramids and stood before the shrine of Guadalupe and felt her ignite my heart and soul and the deep-seated memory of a love like nothing I'd experienced.

Less than 24 hours into the retreat, a doctor stood at my bedside and explained in broken English that I'd have to be quarantined to the room for the entire trip, possibly even longer. The only person allowed to bring me meals was Jeremy, whom, at that point, I did not know very well. I was 3000 miles away from my family and the comforts of my own bed, pillows, bathroom, food, doctors, medicines, language, music, Netflix, bottled Cokes, oatmeal creme pies, and all the things that were within easy reach back home.

The next day, I awoke to horrible abdominal pains and a strange dampness beneath me. I was freezing, so I knew it wasn't sweat. I sat up and pulled back the blankets, and there, below my bottom, I found the sheet blood-soaked. *Nooooo! Not now!*

I checked the period tracker on my phone, and it was two weeks early. I wasn't prepared for this as I was always super regular. Then I remembered that the previous September, while on a three-week pilgrimage in another part of Mexico, I had also started my period two weeks early. *What is the deal with my uterus and Mexico? What medicine is the land trying to teach me with painful bleeding?*

I formed make-shift pads from wads of toilet paper until Jeremy arrived with my breakfast. He was my only contact with the outside world as I journeyed through new levels of vulnerability.

My face winced as I struggled to find the right words. "Jeremy, I know we have only just met. I am horrified having to ask this of you, but my period has started early. I don't have what I need. Can you please help and find pads? Tampons? Anything?"

Jeremy's eyes widened. "Oh, you poor woman. I am so sorry. Of course. Let me ask around."

Another day went by, and my symptoms were not improving. My cough and congestion were worsening. I was short of breath. I remembered the 80+ COVID-related deaths at the hospital where I worked prior. I remember meeting with their families and listening to the doctors explaining the progression of symptoms. The eventual move to intubation. And so on, until they died. Not only did it feel like COVID was attacking my lungs but also my womb. My ovaries felt like they were twisted in knots, and the bleeding was not letting up.

On the fourth day, Jeremy explained that the group would be gone all day. They'd visit the famous Blue House of Frida Kahlo and the Basilica in Mexico City to visit the shrine of Guadalupe. New pangs of devastation coursed through me. This was the excursion I was most looking forward to on the trip. *But no! I'm stuck in this room!*

Irrational thoughts flooded my mind as I watched the group's bus pull away. *Who's going to bring my lunch and dinner? Who's going to check on me? What if I run out of water? It's not safe to drink from the faucet! What if I stop breathing? What if I bleed to death?*

My body began to shake with panic. I pulled my pillow over my face and, holding it tight over my mouth, cried out. My fit led to uncontrollable coughing and gagging to the point of vomiting. I was a mess. Trapped and completely alone. Or so I thought.

At one point, I was lying on the cold tile floor of the bathroom, my head a few inches away from the toilet, when I heard a female's voice call my name. I waited and then heard it again. *Dasha?*

"One minute," I yelled back, thinking this must be someone else from the retreat center. I shuffled out into the bedroom and found no one there. The space felt different. There was a warmth to it. A smell and lightness to the air. It's like when you know someone has entered your room and plundered your things, but you can't prove it.

Standing in the middle of the room, It dawned on me that there were two beds in the room that were facing each other. I thought of Frida Kahlo and how she suffered in her physical body, yet she continued to paint through her pain. She had two beds—a day bed for painting and a night bed for sleeping. I decided to do the same. *If I can't go to the Blue House and Frida, I will experience her here.*

A little spark of energy coursed through me. Newfound hope and perspective worked their way into my heart as I reimagined different ways to navigate my situation. I created little altars near both beds. I picked pink Bougainvillea flowers from my balcony and placed them near a picture of Frida I brought from home. I also picked red roses and arranged them at the foot of a small statue of Guadalupe. I lit candles for both these guides and asked them to please stay with me, as I felt sick and alone.

As I waited for the shower water to warm, I stood staring at my naked body in the mirror. I didn't even recognize myself. My hands moved to my face first, then traveled over my rounded body. My lips were a pale blue, contrasting the dark circles that rimmed my eyes. My hair was a matted mess of black curls. I looked like a wild jungle creature. *I swear I have aged ten years. Everything hurts. My heart hurts. My womb hurts.*

I showered and wrapped myself up in a warm blanket. It was mid-day, but I found myself back in the night bed. My eyes blinked heavily. Closing them briefly, I heard the woman's voice calling my name again. "Dasha?"

In the liminal space between waking and dreaming, I saw her. It was Guadalupe. Framed with golden light and the blue veil of the universe itself. Bees encircled her, and the entire room smelled of roses and sun-warmed honey. I could feel the burn of tears streaming down my hot-fevered cheeks.

"Why did you bring me here? I'm stuck in this room, unable to participate with the other writers. Unable to visit any of the sacred places of this land."

"Child, you are here for a very specific kind of healing. The healing you seek is within your physical body. Trauma held deep within that needs to be released. Trust me to show you the way. Trust the energy of the land that surrounds you. Trust my people to care for you. I will not leave your side. You're not alone. You've never been alone."

I felt myself sinking into dark space, yet I could still feel the presence of Guadalupe just out of sight. My womb cramped intensely. I felt the warm gush of blood between my legs. My pulse quickened as my vision opened into memory—a nightmare of a memory that made my hands move down to cup my vulva.

I was nine years old and trying to get a glass from the upper kitchen cabinet. I was short and couldn't reach the shelf, so I was in the habit of climbing up, using the bottom cabinet door like a ladder. On this particular day, I forgot the bottom door was still open and jumped down, straddling it full force. The edge of the door split me in two down there.

I was in shock but managed to find my mother and tell her what happened. I was a modest child. No one had seen my private parts since I was a baby, not even my mother, so when she pulled down my pants to look, I felt exposed and humiliated. We went to the ER, where a male resident examined my cut. I still remember the feel of his fingers forcing me open so hard that I tore even more. He instructed my mother to take me home and follow up with my pediatrician if the bleeding worsened.

We got home, and my mom changed my pad and put me in her bed to rest. It felt like hours passed. I felt weak and lifeless, like I wasn't even inside my body anymore. *It's taking too long for someone to check on me. I'm so thirsty.*

Eventually, I fell asleep, and after a while, my parents came to rouse me. When they pulled back the blankets, I was hemorrhaging blood.

They rushed me to the pediatrician, who also brought a gynecologist to evaluate my wound. *More strange males looking at my private parts. Touching me there.*

I tried to look away as the shame of exposure was flooding my nervous system; however, what I then saw with my turned head was police officers interrogating my father. *How could they think he did this? He's embarrassed. He's ashamed of me.*

I was abruptly whisked back to the ER. My feet and legs were positioned into stir-ups made from towels, as I was too tiny for the adult metal pair attached to the bed. So many strangers were walking by. *They can all see my privates! They can all see the blood dripping out of me!*

The nurse reached for a syringe on a tray near my head—a large needle they'd use down there. I panicked and tried to get away.

My mind flashed back to *the shot.*

The summer before the accident, my cousin and I stayed at an in-home daycare whose owner was a retired nurse. She threatened us with this large epidural needle to get the kids to listen to her and lay down for naps. We were terrified of getting *the shot*.

I screamed for my parents to help me. For God to help me. It took four adults to restrain me as the doctor poked the needle into my bottom and then stitched me up.

When we finally returned home that evening, I thought the nightmare had ended. My mom helped me into a warm bath. Then, we both watched in horror as the clear water turned dark red. Somehow, the stitches had broken. Back to the ER, we went.

The medical team finally agreed I needed to be put to sleep and managed surgically. As I was waking up from the anesthesia, I overheard an older relative asking my mother questions about my virginity.

"Is she even still a virgin? Is she going to be able to get married now? You know how funny some men can be."

I was nine years old and had no idea about virginity, or hymens, or even sex. Yet this line of questioning. This accident would haunt me for the rest of my entire adolescence and teenage years as I struggled with shame and body dysmorphia from this trauma. I thought my vulva was flawed and impaired. I believed I was ruined because I was no longer a virgin. I even thought I was damned to Hell because I had somehow sinned, and this sin was marked on my body.

It wasn't until I saw images of nude women and finally found the courage to look at myself down there with a mirror that I realized my body was fine. I had all the same parts in the same places. Psychologically, though, even into adulthood, I struggled with the imprinted beliefs of super-conservative Christians around purity culture.

My encounter with Guadalupe, the remembering, allowed me to hold space for that little girl part of myself who dissociated from this trauma. I found myself mothering her. I often travel back to her in the dreamtime, offering comfort instead of judgment. *You are beautiful. You are worthy. You are loved. You are not separate from the Divine. You are Holy and whole. Together, we will rewrite this story.*

I heard Our Lady's words again, "Trust the energy of the land around you. Trust my people to take care of you."

I realized so many gifts surrounded me. I saw the mystery teachings of the Divine at play. I understood the transformative power of the vision quest I experienced and that, even though I was confined to my room, I was on a pilgrimage back to a lost soul part of myself. I understood what it meant to be initiated into Spirit.

I also witnessed the gift that was Jeremy. I was placed in that room with only a male to provide for me because I needed to learn how to trust again. Guadalupe helped me to see how so many of my poor choices over the years were based on unconscious fears that were corded to this trauma. I now choose to honor my womb space and my cycles of bleeding consciously. I'm grateful for the miracle of my body and the wisdom it holds to help me continue to heal my whole being.

THE SELF-LOVE PRACTICE

In my meditations with the bees and Guadalupe, I learned much about the connection between the energy centers of our hearts and wombs. In Chinese medicine, the uterine vessel connecting these organs is known as Bao Mai. Our wombs hold the traumas too heavy for our hearts, impacting our creativity and abilities to birth and manifest our dreams and the healing visions we hold for ourselves, our families and communities, and even our planet. For the last couple of years, I've practiced a mindful ceremony that honors and clears an energetic pathway into the heart-womb connection.

Once a week, I place fresh flowers on an altar I have set up in my bedroom that honors Guadalupe, the bees, and my heart-womb space. I light a candle and spend time alone, exploring my body. I call in the energy of honey from the bees, imagining it being poured all over my body, anointing me from head to toe.

I go very slowly. Listening and feeling into what hurts, what feels good, what still carries shame, or what feels like it needs more time to open. I imagine my vulva opening up like a flower, allowing my fingers to softly caress my many petals. Instead of chasing it, I wait for the orgasm to come to me. Then, I ride the waves into the dreamtime, asking my dreams to help me release old patterns or beliefs within my womb that no longer serve me.

Another mindful practice that has been a lot of fun and has helped to create more balance and alignment with the shadow aspects of myself has been the creation of a pen name I use to write out sexual scenes. This practice allows a deeper part of me to feel less exposed while also honoring wild desires that show up and want to be expressed.

I chose the pen name Natalia because it comes from natalis, which means "pertaining to divine birth." I create stories depicting the beautiful unions between my divine feminine and masculine aspects of self and then use the energy to expand into more significant healing and manifestation potential.

I have also created a line of herbal teas and body products that help women connect with their heart-womb space more intentionally through the dreamtime. You can find my product line at https://www.penelopeponders.com

To access my website's free Heart-Womb Connection Meditation, use the password - Natalia's Naughty Knickers.

Dasha Allred Bond is a bestselling author, certified Dream Coach, and Shamanic Healer who has studied with Laura Hileman, Freedom Folk & Soul, Gaia Sisterhood, Robert Moss, Sandra Ingerman, Dana Micucci, Ariella Daly, and the late Will Sharon. With her beloved husband, Kenny, and two children, Lilli and Avery, she has pilgrimaged across Southern France and England as well as sacred parts of Mexico and North America, attuning to the energetic leylines of our lands and the stories carried by the rocks, the rivers, the trees, and the bees. She feels a deep connection to the language of nature and the divine feminine and masculine aspects of herself revealed to her through the dream archetypes found in classic myths and personal stories.

In 2021, she began dreaming with the bees and Our Lady of Guadalupe. Answering their calls, she visited Our Lady's Shrine in Mexico City and the Pyramids of Teotihuacan. This journey catalyzed the rebirth of her true story and more profound work into the mysteries of consciousness, the multi-verse, and the many ways trauma shows up in our minds, bodies, and energy fields.

Dasha is a certified End of Life Doula. Much of her focus is on helping dreamers move through their seasons of grief. Early this year, Dasha was among 25 bestselling authors who released the book Shaman Heart: Sacred Rebel. She will end this year leading another book project titled Dreaming with Bees: Sacred Medicine from Beyond the Veil of Loss and Grief. The anticipated book release date is World Bee Day, May 2024. She is also completing a memoir, Wild Life Whispers: Book of Remembering, and a novel, A Nun's Tale. You can find more details about her Dreaming with Bees circles, healing sessions, written works, and other intuitive offerings at the website below.

www.penelopeponders.com

CHAPTER 23

MAMA YOUR TRAUMA
A RUNWAY TO REBIRTH—MOTHERING AS A JOURNEY TO SELF-LOVE

Rev. Stephanie Urbina Jones

MY STORY

"Mama?" I could hear my daughter's voice trembling.

It was rare because she was so strong and, in some ways, trained by me to hold it all. But she let me in, into her crushing heart.

"Do you remember Michael Stone? Mama, he died. He took his life last night."

I couldn't breathe. "Oh, honey, I am so, so sorry. What happened? Are you okay?"

I started trying to fix it, to make it okay for her, but I felt her pull away and shut down. She had to go. I was grateful she called me and let me hold her broken heart for a moment, broken by what she shared. How could it be?

I didn't know this boy well but knew of him. He was the best friend of a boy who accidentally overdosed and died nine months before. Both boys went to the private school with my girl and had beautiful lives and bright futures. My heart was heavy for her, their parents, their generation, and me.

It began a tsunami of grief that opened up decades of pain over the next month and swept through every cell of my body—memories I had dissociated from and brilliantly packed away with socially acceptable and necessary ways, from working to drinking to eating to screaming, to controlling and blowing up things and relationships I loved.

It was almost 15 years since I had been depressed, but without any warning and on the precipice of my daughter spreading her wings and me spreading mine, I was plunged into an empty nest of unrelenting grief and untreated trauma.

I tried not to feel it, but with the suicide of this young man, I regressed deep into the darkness of my teen years two weeks before we were to take my girl to college. It couldn't have come at a worse time.

Or did it? Only time would tell.

It was the day before our ministerial training, leading and teaching how to be sacred witnesses in life and minister to the moment and the necessity of creating and holding sacred rites of passage. One week after facing my fear, I wrote, stood, and delivered my first sermon in a church where I shared my vulnerable crisis of faith that led me down this path.

Two and half weeks before, we were teaching our Toltec Medicine Wheel of Transformation initiations of death and rebirth in Dallas. One month earlier, I sang one last song to my dear friend Christina "Angel Heart" Aguilar, the day she took her last breath and transitioned from this world to the next.

And it was one month before the release of my long-awaited, ten-years-in-the-making album, *Manuel's Destiny.* It was the culmination of the most intense, bittersweet, beautiful, and pain-filled month, all while being committed to writing this chapter on the amazing power of "self-love."

The last thing I felt was any self-love. I was physically and emotionally exhausted. I tried to take most of the month off to be home with my girl before she headed to college. I kept waiting for her to need me to help her get ready to go, but she and her stepmom had it covered.

Ouch! That hurt.

As I watched her pack, I thought about how reluctant I was to have a child 19 years ago. I was so scared. I didn't feel like I had what she would need because my mother was often cruel, didn't want me, and had rejected me growing up.

I didn't feel like I knew how to nurture and keep a plant alive, much less a human. I remember praying and asking God for a sign. I was so grateful to see my daughter in a vision before I conceived her. I saw her dark hair and felt her strong spirit. She was my answered prayer. I took the leap of faith, inviting her spirit to come to me. I believed I could and would continue to live my dream and become her mother.

Within six months, I was pregnant. I loved being pregnant and feeling her come alive in me. I'll never forget the moment I first felt her, like a minnow in a pond flipping around in my womb as I sang, "I feel a party coming on" in the studio. I toured through seven months of my pregnancy and came home excited about this new adventure.

Her nana and I painted her room yellow with a safari theme filled with giraffes, elephants, and the wild kingdom. On September 10th, while the cable guy was fixing the TV, I felt something warm run down my legs.

I froze and blurted, "I think my water just broke."

He looked up in terror and said, "Is your husband home, ma'am?"

I called my husband, and he rushed home to take me to the hospital. I wish I could tell you I was excited then. I wasn't. I was terrified on the ride to the hospital and kept saying, "I don't want to do this. I don't want to do this."

I'm ashamed to admit I was relieved when my doctor said, "I'm sorry, Stephanie, she is breech. For her safety and yours, we need to do a C-section."

If I knew then what I know now, I would've insisted they try to turn her, but I wasn't who I am. I was emotionally young, scared, and wanted to run.

As I lay in the hospital bed, they placed this perfect baby burrito in my arms. My heart melted. It was a love like I had never known.

A few days later, I held our baby as my husband left for work, rocking her and staring across the river behind our house. I knew in that moment my life had changed. He went back to work, and I went into postpartum depression.

I winced as I realized I'd never have the freedom I had before or ever be the same. I was tethered to this being, to care for and protect for at least the next 18 years. It felt like forever. I loved her more than anything I had ever loved, but the truth is, a part of me died the day she was born.

Of course, it did. It does for all mothers. We naturally, gratefully give up a part of ourselves, our lives, and our dreams to become the keepers and mamas of their lives and dreams.

As my Tio, Rudy, told me the day she was born, "Mija, it's the hardest job you'll ever love to do."

He was right. I never slept a whole night again. Even now, I check the weather, worry, and try to control from wherever in the world I am and pray for her safety.

When she was six weeks old, we hit the road with my guitar, a breast pump, and my dream in tow. I wasn't giving up everything, but everything changed. Since I had not felt nurtured or wanted by my mother, it was a destined but hard road.

Some days and nights, my body didn't know how to hold or rock her. I felt that old rejection, and I ached to be more present and loving. I didn't know how, and it was painful. I didn't want to pass that on to her.

While it was glorious at moments, it was torturous in others. It was a journey that took me back to and through my sacred aches and traumas. To mother her, I had to re-mother myself. I learned early on to bring myself home, time and time again.

Whatever age or stage she was going through was a mirror and often a trigger for my pain and trauma. Thankfully, I was committed to taking my sacred ache to task relentlessly. I transformed the pain into compassion and self-love. It was a hard journey. Often, I couldn't will myself past my wounds and old stories of shame and unworthiness.

There were many moments I'd like to forget when I couldn't show up and hold her like she needed. There were times when the rage I was raised in came through me and scared her. I'm not proud of that, and I've beaten myself up over and over again.

What I do know is I did my best. I got busy healing as fast as I could and got better. By the time my daughter graduated, I didn't rage anymore and could be fully present for her wherever she was, even if she was raging at me.

Did my pain hurt her? Probably so, but I did my work and found a way to forgive myself. I didn't want to burden her with my pain and history. It wasn't what I wanted for "herstory."

She was my inspiration and motivation. I had to learn to live. I knew my life would inform and guide hers more than anyone else in her world. What I did, first for her, became for me. She saved me. In raising her, I was consciously reparenting myself.

Many have questioned the time and money I spent healing myself, calling me selfish. In truth, it was and is the most centered-in-self gift I could give my daughter, myself, and all those I touch and serve.

There have been a lot of "what ifs," especially after I went through a divorce. I prayed and figured out how to best support my child financially and teach her how to follow her heart. I was willing to try and use my college degree for a more traditional job, but my destiny called me in obvious ways to keep following the dream God put on my heart to sing and be a messenger of love.

Sharing her with her father and having her go back and forth between our hearts and homes was hard for her and for us. It had its challenges and blessings. Eventually, I met my husband, spiritual partner, and the man who led me to the healing ways that helped me transform generations of pain and pathology into powerful love and medicine we share with others through our nonprofit Freedom Folk and Soul.

Jeremy is a great parenting partner, and we've had many adventures, which we shared with her. He taught her about the connection to the Earth, a love of the great outdoors, camping, community, prayer, ceremony, dancing, joy, and how to walk through tremendous grief and trauma.

Jeremy is a father to her and a man of great faith and recovery. She witnessed his relapse and how he came back to life to live in a powerful way, talking about his journey and inspiring many. She also witnessed people we love die from addiction.

She saw and felt deep grief and how we moved through it with prayer and vulnerability. Since the age of five, she's had a love for community and sacred ceremonies like sweat lodges. At 15, after watching countless fire walks, she turned to me out of the blue and said, "Mama, I am ready to walk."

I grabbed my baby girl's hand and walked with her across the fire in the mountains of North Carolina. I felt something change in her as she stepped more fully into her love and personal freedom.

We taught her the power of initiation. At 12, she had her first coming-of-age ceremony in the Smokey Mountains during the solar eclipse. Then, at 15, honoring her heritage, we created a quinceanera like no other. We held it under a giant tree with family and friends surrounding, witnessing and celebrating her stepping into her womanhood.

The day before she graduated, we danced in our yard in the spring of 2023. She was surrounded by her tribe of four parents, six grandparents, godparents, family, and friends. We did our best.

As her time to leave drew nearer, I felt lost. I didn't know how to move forward and create my life after 19 years of my every day being centered around what she needed. I keep reaching back as I try to move forward. One month after this month of life has lived me, I can't stop crying.

This bittersweet grief is my self-love. It's the bookmark to mark the life we've lived. I'm still in it, but I'm also able to hear children playing in the street and feel the sunshine on my skin. My heart is calling me forward. I'm getting grieved up so I can be present in every moment to live and dream on.

Who will I be? I can feel her—the new me—emerging, just like I saw my daughter before she was born so many years before. I'm excited to know the new me. I'm writing, singing, and calling her forward. I'm finding moments of surrender to cry and making dinner plans with fabulous friends. I'm amazed that just as my daughter is being given her wings, I'm being given mine.

As fate would have it, in January 2023, I bought a set of wings on the Avenue of the Dead in the Pyramids of Teotihuacan, where it is said that man becomes God (or Goddess) on a journey of death and rebirth. It was an author's journey to write our book *Shaman Heart - Sacred Rebel.*

It was there that I recovered, reclaimed, and rewrote the story of my lost teen years, bringing that powerful, beautiful dreamer back to life. As we say in our work, intent is working all the time. By May, the book was released and became a bestseller, and at the same time, my daughter graduated high school.

Within the same week, I filmed not one but four videos with my new passion and purpose while getting ready to launch my new album, *Manuel's Destiny.* As old parts of me died, the Avenue of the Dead in Teotihuacan became my runway for rebirth.

I wore those wings from Teo when I sang the song that inspires us to never give up on our dreams, *Rhinestone Cowgirl,* a duet with the incredible Wendy Moten. Looking back, I honor my journey as a mother, daughter, and a woman. I've been relentless in healing and bringing myself home.

Like a Russian doll, I've rescued, stacked, and gathered all the parts and ages of me into wholeness. From the little dreamer to the sacred rebel teen, maiden, mother, and now sage, I'm ready for this new stage and to sing my song.

I traveled the medicine wheel of my life and transformed my pain into passion and purpose. I forgave my mother, my lineage, and, most importantly, myself. In doing so, I've set my daughter free. It's finally time to live the joy of those dreams I've held since I was four, knowing it's never too late to let old stories die, to be reborn, and to live the amazing power of my own self-love.

After all, we are the ones we've been waiting for.

THE SELF-LOVE PRACTICE

MOTHERING THE MOMENT

We all come to crossroads moments in our lives. Our sacred aches need our attention. With tenderness, self-love, and compassion, we can begin to hold and heal the heart of our hurts and find more wholeness.

Find a quiet time to honor yourself, light a candle, and sit in loving prayer and reverence as you travel through the first of seven initiations as a sacred witness and mother for you. I encourage you to deeply honor each turn of the wheel in your life.

THE WEST—INITIATION ONE

This is the place of water, emotion, and introspection.

It's time to surrender to the bittersweet story calling your heart to heal. Take a deep breath and put your hand on your heart. Find the fully empowered great mother within you and call her forward. Once she is firmly in place, imagine yourself at that younger time when you felt pain or shame.

Dream into the moment and allow your younger self to remember it. Let her feel and express it all while you hold sacred space and witness lovingly mothering the moment. Listen with your heart and encourage the younger you to write, paint, and cry it out.

Honor whatever the feeling is and send the message that you will not abandon your younger self. Offer your younger self unconditional love; imagine taking them into your arms and holding them tightly until they surrender and feel safe with you.

Find a sacred witness, friend, or counselor to honor and integrate this experience as you repeat the initiation. With this self-love practice, you will transform the charge or pain and bring honor to who you were. Honor the choices you made, reminding yourself that you did your best.

Be honest with yourself, and if the charge or pain continues, commit to do whatever it takes to bring the self-love practices and healing to your hurt until you've found your freedom and self-love.

There are seven initiations on our Toltec Medicine Wheel of Transformation. Each is vital to learning how to mother yourself in each moment and granting yourself forgiveness.

Through this process, you will support and make peace with your past and ultimately rebirth a new you and vision for life. To experience the last six initiations and get a taste of your lasting freedom, follow this link and sign up to receive the gifts of this full wheel of your life transformation.

www.freedomfolkandsoul.org/self-love

Singer, teacher, writer, sister, friend, mother, wife, and lover of life; **Stephanie Urbina Jones** brings her passion and experience of living a life of creative freedom to people all over the world.

This rockstar shamama has a passion for transformation and is a living example of not only dreaming but bringing those dreams to life. Whether she is writing a song, performing, or leading sacred journeys of transformation as co-founder of Freedom Folk and Soul, Stephanie is following her heart and chiseling out her soul.

She sees herself as a kind of midwife, guiding folks on their journey of self-discovery, healing, and transformation, empowering those who seek to live a life of passion, and purpose.

Stephanie has spent over 25 years in pursuit of her personal freedom. She has studied, prayed, walked, talked, worked, and turned over stones in the road and in her heart to heal and create a life of humility, passion, and purpose.

A true "walker between the worlds," SUJ shares inspiration in music from her albums including, "Shaman Heart," a transformational journey in song with audiences and fellow journeyers everywhere.

SUJ is a Bestselling Author of Shaman Heart: Turning Pain into Passion and Purpose and Shaman Heart: Sacred Rebel. She is a #1 Billboard Country Music Songwriter traveling with her Honky Tonk Mariachis, sharing joy, and her history-making "Country Music with Chili Peppers" all over the world.

To learn more about Stephanie Urbina Jones and her work in the world:

Websites:
www.freedomfolkandsoul.org
www.stephanieurbinajones.com

Facebook:
www.facebook.com/Freedomfolkandsoul.org
www.facebook.com/StephanieUrbinaJonesandTheHonkyTonkMariachi

CLOSING CHAPTER

SELF-LOVE
IS THE ANSWER

How can I be happy and thrive when my partner is depressed? If I ever figure it out, I will write a book about it.

I originally had the fleeting idea to write a book ten years ago when I was depressed and in a profoundly codependent relationship with my husband, who suffered from chronic depression and addiction.

I searched for the book, article, or blog post that would provide an answer. I couldn't find anything other than "Leave the marriage; it will never change."

I felt alone.

The spirits were listening because years later, after I exposed the roots of my shame, released it from my body, and entered into co-dependency recovery through multiple 12-step programs, coaching, and counseling, I recognized self-love was the answer.

I needed to focus on myself and ensure I met my needs instead of obsessively focusing on my husband's needs. I needed to put myself first rather than constantly abandoning myself to support everyone else. I needed to let go of my perfectionism.

When I was ready to write the book, I discovered many people had written about this topic in the past ten years, and self-love was often at the top of their list.

I pivoted to write *The Life-Changing Power of Self-Love* as a collaborative book that included 22 true stories of overcoming through self-love, hoping there would be something for everyone.

Self-love is the answer to most of what ails our culture today. It's also the most effective form of resistance to oppression.

When a person truly loves themself, everything changes, and anything becomes possible.

They no longer:

- Abandon or reject themselves
- Strive to meet everyone's needs at their own expense
- Judge themselves or others
- Cringe when they see a photo of themselves
- Believe the lie that they are not good enough
- Believe whatever lie their oppressor is telling them
- Stay in toxic relationships
- Act against their own best interest
- Blame others for their circumstances
- Deny the truth

Self-love is a practice.

Like most relationships, your relationship with yourself must be nurtured and tended to for your entire life. There is no finish line.

There is a reason you've chosen to read this book. Your sacred longing is calling out for attention.

What is it that you're longing for?

What do you need?

What does your 18-year-old, 15-year-old, 12-year-old, 8-year-old, and 3-year-old, in-utero self need?

You have a unique life journey, and every interaction has brought you to this moment of awareness. Only you can take ownership of your life. Only you can determine what is supportive for you and what is not.

What do you want to release from your life that no longer serves you?

What do you want to shift in your life?

This book holds strategies, mindset practices, and wisdom to empower you to illuminate the hidden truth, move the energy, and deepen your healing. Are you ready to upgrade your operating system?

The 22 co-authors of this book are leaders and healers in their field. I invite you to step out of your comfort zone, where the magic happens, and step into one of their offerings to receive vital support to become aware of, honor, and release your barriers to fully loving yourself so you can rewrite your story and return to your authentic self.

I hope this book is an ongoing resource for finding your unique self-love path. I hope the inspiring, vulnerable stories in this anthology resonated with you and helped you understand that you, too, can love and accept yourself as is.

You can take a stand for yourself, change your operating system, and create a foundation of self-love.

WITH DEEP GRATITUDE

To the spirit world, profound gratitude: The great mystery, my ancestors, guides, and especially the divine mother, my holiest of spirits, who infused me with the unconditional love, nurturing, and guidance. I longed for and needed your love to walk through my healing journey to self-love. I love you.

Deep gratitude, love, and respect for my husband of 17 years, Jason Green, who invited me to walk with him on the powerful healing path from which he has deeply benefited. On that path, I broke through my shame, co-dependency, and al-anon ways and learned to love myself. I indeed married my medicine. Our formidable journey is ongoing, and our friendship and family remain intact against the odds. I celebrate that! I love you.

To my daughters, Grace and Sierra, you inspire, motivate, and teach me every day. I cultivate, write about, and teach self-love as much for you as for myself. You both bring me so much joy. Grace, you are a brave, intelligent, talented, and beautiful actress, singer, and human. Sierra, your strategic, focused, and passionate pursuit of your dreams is magnificent to witness and support. You're a talented, committed, brave, and beautiful violinist. I am excited to see how you both lead in the world. I love you.

To my friends and teachers, Jeremy Pajer and Stephanie Urbina Jones, co-founders of Freedom Folk and Soul, profound gratitude. You infused me with your wisdom and passion. You held a loving, safe container for me to break open, speak about things I've never spoken out loud, and be witnessed. You empowered (and sometimes challenged) me to be vulnerable, take on my fears, expose the roots of my shame, own my part, rediscover my spirituality, and ultimately love myself. You invited me to become an author and teacher and hired me to help you reach more people. This book would not have happened without you illuminating my path, loving me, and walking beside me. I love you both.

To the 21 brave co-authors of this book. Thank you for trusting me and stepping into this portal of self-love with an open heart and a desire to heal the world. I love and respect each of you. Your courage, talent, passion, and inspiring stories of self-love blow me away! I am humbled and proud to walk with each of you to bring the vital message of self-love forward.

To my Freedom Folk and Soul community: We have witnessed each other walk through our pain with grace, compassion, and forgiveness while we released shame, addiction, co-dependency, lies, and old agreements that no longer served us. I celebrate the freedom, sovereignty, leadership, and joy we have gained from continually walking this path together. You are all sacred to me, and I feel immense gratitude and an unbreakable bond with you. I love you.

To Ruth Souther, our loving writing wrangler and my dear friend. I have so much reverence and respect for you. Thank you for supporting and guiding the entire author cast with your wisdom, expertise, endless energy, and humor. I am humbled to collaborate with you. I love you.

To my soul sister, Jayne Feld. Thank you for editing my writing and for seeing the missing pieces of the story that needed to be written or clarified. Your feedback has made me a better writer. Most of all, thank you for loving me, truly seeing me, and being on this journey with me. We have lived a lot of life together, and I'm thrilled to be walking into this next stage with you. I have so much respect for you as a mother, writer, and leader. I love you.

To Laura Di Franco, my publisher, teacher, and friend. Thank you for inspiring, motivating, trusting, and teaching me. You bring so much healing, wisdom, and magic to the world. I am so grateful to have written in four Brave Healer Productions books. Each experience has empowered me, upleveled my writing and business, and has been part of my healing journey. Thank you also to the entire team at Brave Healer Productions for your excellence, talent, and commitment.

To my dear friends whose unique flavor of wisdom, love, talent, example, support, and guidance have been instrumental in helping me bring forward my message of self-love through this book: Natalie Petersen, Annie Mark, Mick Weiland, Cami Roberts, Sage Cohen, Jennifer Sedna, Ahriana Platten, Sharon Siegler, Kim Eden, and Sherrie Phillips. I love you all.

To my teachers and mentors throughout my journey through adulthood, deep gratitude. Your wisdom and counsel have been invaluable in guiding me through the different ages and stages of my journey: Dave Ellis, Ruby Falconer, Joanne Bangs, Charles Hallac, Lynne Twist, Bill Rentz, Marcella Friel, Alberto Hernandez, Mary Sheila Gonnella, and Kashi Ananda. I love you all.

To my current, future, and former clients, your bravery and desire to become your best self and reach your full potential inspires me daily. I hope you find inspiration from the stories in this book to continue in the practice of cultivating self-love. I love you.

To my parents, I love you. Thank you for your patience and love while I expose my roots to the world. I know you did your best in raising me. No human gets out of childhood unscathed, and no one is the perfect parent. I write to break the silence because silence begets shame. I write for my healing. I write to inspire others and know they are not alone. For all the challenges I write about, many fun and supportive moments also built my foundation as an independent woman who had success in multiple careers and many areas of my life. Everything happened exactly as it was supposed to for me to be the person I am at this moment, the leader who is creating this anthology and bringing inspiration and empowerment to all those striving for self-love. Thank you. I love you.

Thank you to everyone who has read my writing in blogs or books and felt compelled to provide me feedback. Your support and encouragement have fueled me to continue sharing my musings, wisdom, and teaching. I love you.

MORE ABOUT TINA GREEN

Tina Green's life has taken many unique twists and turns through many careers, degrees, certifications, life circumstances, and locations.

Her closest friends often call her a master of intent and manifestation.

At age 23, in 1992, Tina relocated from Pennsylvania, the only place she ever called home, to New York City. She had no job, a credit card, and a modest savings account. She considers this one of the best decisions she ever made.

Being in New York City was fun and exciting, and it opened Tina's mind and heart to diversity in race, ethnicity, LBGQT community, culture, religion, and food. She created lifelong friendships there, attended college at Pace University, and landed a job at a boutique investment firm, BlackRock.

Tina's career at BlackRock took an impressive and rare trajectory from Administrative Assistant to Managing Director in ten years. She shapeshifted through many roles and responsibilities, traveled the world, and became the Manager of Western U.S. Client Relationships for BlackRock Solutions. She relocated to the San Francisco Bay Area to open a West Coast office, where she managed relationships with the largest foundation in the world, the largest corporate treasury in the world, the largest investment management firm in the world, and the largest public pension fund in the USA.

Tina loved her life in the Bay Area; the natural coastal beauty, wildlife, healthy lifestyle, culture, and hiking opportunities were a dream come true. She decided she made enough money at BlackRock and was ready to direct her energy to causes more rewarding than investment management. So, after thirteen years, she unlocked the golden handcuffs, took a leap of faith, and left BlackRock.

A lifelong learner, Tina was always taking a class in something new and interesting. In her final year at BlackRock, Tina trained as a Life Coach with Dave Ellis and practiced as a staff coach with the Brande Foundation, providing coaching to non-profit leaders. Tina has always been passionate about living her best life and helping others create the life of their dreams.

Shortly after that, she trained as a massage therapist to lean into her fears around intimacy, and this is where she met her husband Jason; within two years, they married and birthed two beautiful daughters and relocated to breathtaking Sonoma County, California.

Becoming a mother was not in the plans, but it was the most beautiful, joyful, rewarding, intimate, painful, frustrating, and challenging time of her life. Marriage and motherhood is no joke! These three humans have been her teachers, and Tina has had to surrender many times. They held up a sacred mirror and served up the exact medicine she needed to become the author, healer, and teacher she is today. Her daughters are her greatest joy; she loves nurturing and supporting them in their education and performing arts pursuits.

Tina was a stay-at-home mom for eight years. When her children reached elementary school, she went to culinary school and became a holistic chef. She taught cooking classes to parents and went to work at a local non-profit, Ceres Community Project, providing healing meals to community members with cancer and mentoring and teaching teens how to cook.

Tina again shapeshifted through many roles and responsibilities over her seven years at Ceres, ending as the Program Director and member of the leadership team.

It was in her final years at Ceres, during the Covid-19 pandemic, that Tina stepped onto a very powerful healing path with Freedom Folk and Soul. She broke through her shame, leaned into her fears, entered co-dependency recovery, and learned to love herself.

She felt so much freedom and joy that she became passionate about bringing this medicine to others. Everything changed for Tina. All her life experience and training came together to fuel her passion for creating her coaching practice to assist women in cultivating self-love as their foundation. In 2022, Tina joined Freedom Folk & Soul as their Director of Operations and Communications,

Tina continually learns, grows, and adds wisdom and tools to her toolbox. Tina has completed ministerial training and is a non-denominational ordained minister, ceremonialist, and certified Celebrant.

She has also master apprenticed with Jeremy Pajer and Stephanie Urbina Jones of Freedom Folk and Soul, and she will begin co-facilitating *The Toltec Medicine Wheel of Transformation* in 2024. This year-long program served as the container in which Tina and hundreds of others have been able to transform their life and gain self-love.

Tina's lived experience is a big part of her wisdom and service. She brings her grounded, loving mother energy to everyone she works with.

Tina blogs about Self-love on Medium, and she has contributed chapters about self-love in three other #1 best-selling Brave Healer Productions books:

- *Shaman Heart: Turning Pain Into Passion and Purpose* By Stephanie Urbina Jones
  o Tina's chapter: *Exposing The Roots of Body Shame - Carving a Path to Self-love, Acceptance, and Freedom*

- *Rites & Rituals: Harnessing The Power of Sacred Ceremony* by Ahriana Platten
  o Tina's Chapter: *I Married Myself: A Ceremony of Self-Love, Commitment & Integration*

- *Shaman Heart: Sacred Rebel* By Stephanie Urbina Jones & Jeremy Pajer
  o Tina's Chapter: *Taking a Stand For Me: Transforming Codependence Into Self-Love*

Tina still lives in Sonoma County, California, where she enjoys morning walks on the beach, hiking in the redwoods, and attending live music and theatre; her daughters are now teenagers.

Join The Women's Self Love Community on Facebook for inspiration and access to free offerings: https://www.facebook.com/groups/theselflovecommunity

Connect with Tina:

Website for Self-Love offerings: https://www.ExposingTheRoots.com

Website for Celebrant offerings:
https://www.morethancakeandpresents.com

Website for book: https://www.LifeChangingPowerOfSelfLove.com

Self-Love blog: https://exposingtheroots.medium.com/

Facebook: https://www.facebook.com/ExposingTheRoots

Instagram: https://www.Instagram.com/ExposingTheRoots

Freedom Folk and Soul: FreedomFolkandSoul.org

Email: Tina@ExposingTheRoots.com

TINA GREEN
EXPOSING THE ROOTS

EXPOSINGTHEROOTS.COM

Tina partners with women to create a foundation of self-love.

She empowers women to rewrite their stories and honor and release old stories or beliefs that no longer serve their lives.

When working with Tina, you can expect to have an experience that will assist you in increasing self-awareness, discovering your stories and beliefs, honoring them, releasing them, and rewriting them.

Current and former clients report feeling more self-aware, joyful, and free. They are clearer about relationships, boundaries, and what no longer serves them.

We all need a scared witness, someone to listen fully, brainstorm, be a mirror, and hold us accountable. Tina is honored to hold this space for women of all ages.

In addition to private coaching, Tina regularly offers breathwork, women's circles, workshops, retreats, ceremonies, and initiations.

Both in-person and via Zoom

For an updated calendar of events:
https://www.ExposingTheRoots.com/Events

Join her Women's Self-Love Community on Facebook
for access to inspiration and free offerings:
https://www.facebook.com/groups/theselflovecommunity

Freedom Folk and Soul

The Adventure is On

Tina's work with Freedom Folk and Soul

Tina co-facilitates The Toltec Medicine Wheel of Transformation both in-person and via Zoom

Toltec Medicine Wheel of Transformation

A Shamanic Journey of Personal Freedom

A journey of empowerment through the ages and stages of your life using the ancient symbol of the medicine wheel. If you are at a crossroads in your life, this safe, loving container is waiting for you to step in.

In this powerful program, you can expect to:

- Connect with a heart-centered tribe
- Gain self-awareness around your biggest obstacles and the belief system you have created
- Discover where you gave away your sovereignty
- Explore your family of origin and ancestral lineage
- Discover the story you tell about yourself and the parts of it that no longer serve you
- Be witnessed
- Uncover parts of your story that you have denied or hidden.
- Face your fears, release your shame, discover your own love
- Commit to yourself
- Rewrite your story and reclaim your personal power
- Dream the life you've always wanted.
- Celebrate your freedom

Through Toltec and Native American wisdom, sacred initiations, ceremonies, and breathwork, we will recover and bring home those pieces of our soul we had to leave behind.

From the foundation of self-love, we will hear the calling of our heart's desire and step into our soul purpose.

Learn more about Freedom Folk & Soul at https://www.FreedomFolkandSoul.org

MORE THAN CAKE AND PRESENTS!

Celebrate life's milestones with intention and meaning

Tina loves to celebrate and wants us to celebrate more.

Celebrating life's important milestones and moments helps us move through the ages and stages of our lives with confidence, clarity, and joy.

Tina is a certified celebrant, ordained minister (non-denominational), and a ceremonialist located in Northern California.

She brings her love of meaningful, sacred ceremony and a heart-centered and grounded approach to the following offerings:

- Weddings/Renewal of Vows - Tina can help you craft the ceremony of your dreams, whether religious, non-religious, or nature-based. She can guide you through the process of creating a beautiful, sacred, meaningful ceremony and bring her reverent, grounded, joyful energy to officiate your wedding.

- Milestone birthdays and anniversaries

- Retirement

- Divorce celebrations / Uncoupling ceremonies

- Rites of passage / Coming of age ceremony

- Baby blessings

- Home blessings

- Elemental Initiations

For more information, visit
https://www.MoreThanCakeAndPresents.com

ADDITIONAL RESOURCES FOR CULTIVATING SELF-LOVE

Books:

- *The Four Agreements* By Don Miguel Ruiz
- *Mastery of Love* By Don Miguel Ruiz
- *Facing Codependence: What It Is. Where It Comes From. How It Sabotages Our Lives* By Pia Mellody, Andrea Wells Miller, J. Keith Miller
- *Codependent No More* By Melody Beattie
- *Beyond Codependency: And Getting Better All the Time* By Melody Beattie

Organizations:

- Freedom Folk and Soul http://www.FreedomFolkandSoul.org (Toltec Medicine Wheel of Transformation)
- Al-Anon https://al-anon.org/
- Adult Children of Alcoholics & Dysfunctional Families (ACA) https://adultchildren.org/
- Codependents Anonymous (CODA) https://coda.org/
- The Pachamama Alliance https://pachamama.org/
- The Body Image Movement https://bodyimagemovement.com/
- Women Food and Forgiveness Academy https://www.womenfoodandforgiveness.com/

Films:

Embrace- Documentary film by Taryn Brumfit

DEAR DEBBIE

By Sage Cohen

Dear Debbie,
When I left you at age 23
for a name of my own
I didn't know you needed
me still. I didn't know how
to love you any better
than we were
loved. I never told you
you are welcome
just as you are
that your beauty
is as unquantifiable
as the cosmos that
the ugly girl
name they gave you
could not contain
your glittering tides
your salt-sprayed light.
Just look at you, Debbie.
Poems beating your broken heart.
Tears blessing your cheerful cheeks.
I am here with you now.
I see you.
Let us belong
to each other.
Let us stitch stars
into the veil of night
that has held us
all along.

Sage Cohen is the author of *Writing the Life Poetic, Fierce on the Page,* and three other books. An instructor and coach, she helps people write more, write better, and come alive. Learn more at sagecohen.com. Join her in community-powered writing at wewrite.circle.so.

Made in the USA
Monee, IL
06 November 2023

45862070R00144